SIN IN
SOFT FOCUS

Sin in Soft Focus
Pre-Code Hollywood

MARK A. VIEIRA

HARRY N. ABRAMS, INC., PUBLISHERS

To my mother and father

—Mark Alan Vieira

EDITOR: Elisa Urbanelli
DESIGNER: Raymond P. Hooper

Library of Congress Cataloging-in-Publication Data

Vieira, Mark.
Sin in soft focus : pre-code Hollywood / by Mark A. Vieira.
p.   cm.
Filmography: p.
Includes bibliographical references and index.
ISBN 0–8109–4475–8
1. Motion pictures—Censorship—United States—History.   2. Sex in
motion pictures.   3. Sensationalism in motion pictures.   I. Title.
PN1995.62.V54   1999
363.31'0973'09043—dc21   99–13834

Printed and bound in Hong Kong

Harry N. Abrams, Inc.
100 Fifth Avenue
New York, N.Y. 10011
www.abramsbooks.com

CONTENTS

PREFACE

Every decade has its cultural rediscoveries. The 1990s have rediscovered "pre-Code" movies. As Joan Crawford and Norma Shearer flaunt their forbidden charms, ever-growing audiences enjoy the pre-Code period and decry the censorship that ended it. Revival theaters, cable TV, and videotapes celebrate restored pre-Code titles. Scholarly books recount the coming of the Legion of Decency. Audiences discover a beguiling blend of the cynical and the sentimental, then want to see more and know more.

Interest in pre-Code movies has caused a reappraisal of performers such as John Gilbert, Warren William, and Norma Shearer. Says Elliot Lavine, programmer for San Francisco's Roxie Theatre: "During our Norma Shearer festival, people would come up to the box office and ask: 'Are these *pre-Code* movies?'" According to the *San Francisco Chronicle*: "Scores of patrons were turned away from sold-out screenings of *The Divorcee* . . . making the Shearer series the most successful Roxie retrospective ever." Indeed, the availability of her pre-Code titles in repertory and in MGM-UA's "Forbidden Hollywood" videotape series has begun to melt the popular and critical indifference to Shearer.

The term "pre-Code" is slightly misleading. Films of the 1920s abound with risqué elements, and studio self-regulation began in 1927, but for the purposes of this book, "pre-Code" will describe films made between March 1930, when the Production Code was adopted, and July 1934, when it was amended and enforced. The Code forbade profanity, excessive violence, illegal drugs, "white slavery," miscegenation, "sex perversion," suggestive dancing, lustful kissing, and just about everything else that makes the world go 'round. Unfortunately, the Code arrived at the same moment as the Great Depression. Hollywood faced ruinous losses and, for nearly five years, flouted the Code. Mick LaSalle of the *San Francisco Chronicle* writes: "Before the censors clamped down in 1934, Hollywood made movies for adults who didn't want to be lied to about human nature . . . [it was] a complex, diverse, socially responsive American cinema."

Hollywood threw out the Code in 1968. Our culture has recovered from thirty-four years of censorship, but some pre-Code films have been less fortunate. Before 1934, state censor boards cut only release prints. After that, studios cut the master negatives of films such as *Animal Crackers, A Farewell to Arms,* and *Mata Hari* to qualify them for rerelease. The cut sequences were never restored. When audiences see these classics, they wonder why there are gaps in continuity. The most controversial films, however, were not rereleased, and therefore not cut. One film was completely destroyed. Only in long-buried censorship files did I discover what the cut classics were missing. *Sin in Soft Focus* looks at the original versions of these films, using unpublished documents, scripts, and still photographs.

My purpose in writing *Sin in Soft Focus* is threefold. First, I present available pre-Code films as a complete body of work, in chronological order, giving a sense of how they look and sound. Second, I tell the history of the Code, how it made these films and, in many cases, unmade them. Third, I provide the first reference book on this increasingly popular genre. Film historian Karl Thiede has prepared an appendix of 100 selected titles, providing data such as negative cost, profit and loss, and current availability. With a few conspicuous exceptions, I discuss only films that can be screened; it would be unfair to rave about titles that the reader can never view. Happily, most of these films do exist in complete versions. Whenever possible, I use plates and captions to tell what to look for, which version is available, and where. The appendix lists the owners of the films, and if they make them available. The copyright holders of these films are aware of this book and of the interest in their pre-Code holdings. I encourage the reader to contact them.

With the help of these companies, and with the assistance of New York's preeminent photo agency, Photofest, I have seen more than 300 films and found 275 images from them. As much as anyone leaving a pre-Code festival, I have wanted to know more and to find more. I hope that what I have found will be glamorous transports, taking the reader to pre-Code provinces—the sands of Morocco, the penthouses of New York, the dives of Pago Pago—and to the most exotic locales of all, the soundstages where Hollywood artists labored and created. It was they who made the art of pre-Code Hollywood.

The story of *Sin in Soft Focus* begins in 1922, when the motion-picture industry, only twenty-eight years old but America's sixth largest, was under attack. Every week the industry brought adventure and romance to 40 million people. Its critics, a consortium of clubwomen and churchmen, cried that it brought immorality. Provocative films such as *Male and Female, The Four Horsemen of the Apocalypse,* and *The Sheik* found resonance in three Hollywood scandals: the "Fatty" Arbuckle sex trial, the drug addiction of matinee idol Wallace Reid, and the unsolved murder of director William Desmond Taylor. Yet the motion-picture industry had more to fear than the censure of self-appointed moralists. There was the government.

Beginning with Adolph Zukor's Paramount Pictures, each company took the form of a vertically structured monopoly, borrowing money from financiers, such as Attilo Henry Giannini and Halsey, Stuart and Company, to manufacture feature films, which it then "block-booked"* into independent and second-run theaters. Antitrust legislation was a threat. Federal censorship was imminent, and the studios had no protection against it. In 1915, the Supreme Court ruled that moving pictures were merchandise, not protected by the First Amendment. *Mutual Film* vs. *Ohio* upheld the right of prior censorship, and local censor boards opened all over the country. The real problem were the seven state censor boards, which influenced entire regions. In January 1922, Massachusetts voted in the eighth. A referendum was scheduled to approve federally mandated censorship at that board. Editorials and letters flew from coast to coast. One by one, thirty-seven states introduced bills to establish censor boards. If the Massachusetts referendum passed, every state could have a board, and the federal government could use each board to tell Hollywood what to do. The film companies had to act.

On March 10, 1922, the film industry incorporated a trade protection organization, the Motion Picture Producers and Distributors Association (MPPDA). As director, it appointed Will H. Hays, a Presbyterian elder and former postmaster general. His conservative affiliations and sterling public image spoke well of the industry's intentions. What better individual to be czar of the movies? To earn his $100,000 salary, Hays began a forceful campaign against the Massachusetts referendum. He repeated the strategy he had used to elect Warren Harding—propaganda films and bribery. Massachusetts rejected the referendum, and though its own board remained, no more state boards opened. For the time being, federal censorship was held at bay.

Reasoning that no one would bother Hollywood if Hollywood could keep her skirts clean, Will Hays began a program of self-regulation. He instituted the Department of Public Relations, which recruited members from the very organizations that had criticized the industry. These included the Boy Scouts, the General Federation of Women's Clubs, and the International Federation of Catholic Alumnae (IFCA). He made little headway with the Protestant churches, because they were not centralized, but soon established a rapport with the National Catholic Welfare Council. He saw to it that Rita McGoldrick of the IFCA used her weekly radio broadcast to rate films and laud his improvement of them. One improvement was his 1924 "Formula," which discouraged the adaptation of disreputable plays and novels. As the industry moved

Will H. Hays, president of the Motion Picture Producers and Distributors Association (MPPDA). Portrait by Underwood and Underwood. Courtesy Bison Archives.

through the prosperous twenties, the silent cinema told its flickering tales with increased subtlety, style, and sophistication, using provocative scenes and off-color intertitles. For all his improvements, Hays could not hold off the state censor boards.

There were eight boards: Florida, Kansas, Maryland, Massachusetts, New York, Ohio, Pennsylvania, and Virginia. Their effect was pervasive, influencing as many as ninety local boards. Many state censors were civil servants who had happened onto a good thing. For $200 a month, they could watch movies all day and then cut them, reedit them, and even write new intertitles, without regard for continuity or aesthetics. Film companies subsidized this "service" at a rate of $3 per thousand feet and $5 for each rewritten intertitle. In 1928, the Virginia board proudly reported receipts of $27,624.75, gloating: "Never before in the history of censorship has the volume of business been so great." Inexplicably, the film companies kept it that way.

Metro-Goldwyn-Mayer's *Ben-Hur* had nude scenes, and its male star posed nude for publicity portraits. Film Booking Office's *Human Wreckage* featured graphic scenes of drug use, albeit in an antidrug context. Scenes of drunkenness and debauchery occurred with increasing regularity, as in Goldwyn Pictures' *Three Weeks*. An orgy scene in Paramount's *The Wedding March* hinted at "advanced sex practices" with a brief flash of one man kissing another, but same-sex attraction usually got by in comic camouflage. M-G-M's *The Callahans and the Murphys* had a scene in which an Irish-American matriarch and her sewer-digger son determine the race of an abandoned infant. "Maybe it's a Jew baby," suggests her son. Mrs. Callahan looks under the baby's diaper, then declares, "It ain't a Jew baby!"

Universal Pictures' vice president R. H. Cochrane wrote to Will Hays, complaining about the production heads at the two biggest studios: "Unless . . . Paramount can curb the natural lasciv-

iousness of Bennie Schulberg and unless . . . Metro can tone down Irving Thalberg (who, though fine in other respects, has a leaning toward the suggestive because of his showmanship) there is going to be a lot of dirty pictures during the coming season." Will Hays saw the handwriting on the wall, and the splices on the screen.

In January 1927, he moved his public relations department to an office at 5504 Hollywood Boulevard, where it could keep a closer eye on film producers (then called "supervisors"), consult with them on scenarios, and eliminate censorable elements before they could be filmed. This department was headed by Colonel Jason S. Joy, a former American Red Cross executive. It inspected fifteen scenarios a month and submitted recommendations. Most supervisors ignored it.

In May, Will Hays called for the formation of a committee of studio executives to address the problem of censorship. Irving G. Thalberg, vice president in charge of production at M-G-M, joined Sol Wurtzel of the Fox Film Corporation and E. H. Allen of Paramount. The three executives formulated a set of guidelines called the "Don'ts and Be Carefuls." The MPPDA adopted them in September, and Hays created a "Studio Relations Committee" (SRC) to implement them. Jason Joy now had an exact method for reviewing both scenarios and finished films, and the film industry could boast of self-regulation. In October, the Federal Trade Commission approved the "Don'ts and Be Carefuls."

Then, on October 6, 1927, Warner Bros., one of the smaller companies, opened a film called *The Jazz Singer*. Al Jolson spoke dialogue on the screen, and talking pictures had arrived. Before Jason Joy could say "don't" or even "be careful," movies went "from bad to voice."

The complete text of the "Don'ts and Be Carefuls" may be found in Appendix I, on page 214.

5504 Hollywood Boulevard, the home of the Studio Relations Committee (SRC). Courtesy Bison Archives.

Mrs. Wallace Reid and Bessie Love in a scene from the lost 1923 film Human Wreckage.

TOP:
*John Sainpolis and players
in a scene from the lost 1924 film*
Three Weeks.

CENTER:
*Chorus girls in a scene from the lost
1925 film* Bright Lights.

BOTTOM:
*Quintus Arrius (Frank Currier,
at left) enters the galley in the 1925
M-G-M epic* Ben-Hur.

OPPOSITE:
*This 1924 portrait of Ramon Novarro
as Judah Ben-Hur was made in
Rome by Bragaglia.*

PICTURES THAT TALK (RUDELY)

Colonel Jason S. Joy came from Montana. He was even-tempered, deliberate, even thoughtful. He was not apt to attack a film because it dealt with adult issues. He was more likely to look for a way to express its complex morality without shocking anyone. According to censor Jack Vizzard, who worked with him years later, Joy was "a big, good-looking man, but bland . . . almost a milquetoast. But he must have had a core of steel. He tried to maintain the integrity of the Code, and at the same time, he could be almost obsequious, trying to please everyone." The "talkies" made it hard to please anyone. The Studio Relations Committee—Joy and a diligent staff of four—met with six film supervisors a week, suggesting ways to avoid censorship and viewing finished films. Yet the nine major film companies were not cooperating with the SRC. They only submitted 203 scenarios of the 489 films they made in 1929. The SRC managed to see 323 finished films, but too late to stop the censor boards from attacking.

Kansas was a "dry" state, so it cut scenes of drinking. Maryland targeted "disrespect of the law and condonation of crime by officers of the law . . . and antagonistic relations between labour and capital." The Ohio board cut anything that might harm impressionable minds. In *The Magnificent Flirt*, an old man tells his nephew to look out the window; the old man sees a girl exercising in her underwear, but the boy is distracted by a biplane's stunts. The old man says: "I show you a beautiful young woman and you look at an airplane—you pervert!" The Ohio censor, John Leroy Clifton, rewrote and refilmed the intertitle in order to delete the last

Colonel Jason S. Joy, director of the Studio Relations Committee.

word. After viewing D. W. Griffith's *Drums of Love*, he issued this order: "Cut scenes showing hero in tight trousers bowing and standing at top of stairway." The censors went after good films and bad, mutilating the last of the silent masterworks and the first of the innovative talkies—titles such as *The Crowd*, *Our Dancing Daughters*, *The Patriot*, *Sunrise*, *The Lights of New York*, and *The Cockeyed World*.

The Cockeyed World was the Fox Film Corporation's talking sequel to *What Price Glory?*, which had made folk heroes of rambunctious Marines, Flagg (Victor McLaglen) and Quirt (Edmund Lowe). Having disposed of World War I in the silent film, director-writer Raoul Walsh now had these rough-and-tumble characters ransack the rest of the world in search of cheap female companionship. *The Cockeyed World* had something to offend everyone: dirty songs, racist remarks and caricatures (bestial Russians, dopey Swedes, nervous Jews, effeminate Central Americans), horizontal love scenes, a heroine wearing no underwear, and lines that came straight out of a locker room.*

"Her old lady came home—I had to *get it* on the run."

"I'm bringing you the *lay* of the land."

"Son of a *bitch!*" was clearly mouthed by Quirt in one scene.

The film's references to social diseases were unprecedented. Flagg: "I bet you twenty bucks I can make her!" Quirt: "That's a bet. I been itching seven years to get your dough." Flagg: "You been *itching* for seven years, but don't blame it on me!" Quirt: "Why, the minute she saw me, [Charmaine] gave you the gate." Flagg: "And what she gave *you* was *plenty!!!*"

12

The film did offend everyone, even Warner Bros., now one of the largest film companies. Harry Warner wrote to Will Hays: "Anyone employed by our Company, who would ever send a picture like that into our office, with the slang, vulgarity, and insinuations, would never work for us another day—even if it was my own Brother." *The Cockeyed World* brought Fox Film a staggering gross of $2.6 million. It also set a precedent: the most profitable films were usually the most protested, too.

The Cockeyed World demonstrated that talking pictures could be offensive in ways that silent films could not have been. Dialogue now gave films a literal, immediate quality. In *Sunny Side Up*, Marjorie White asks Janet Gaynor: "Then what the hell are you cryin' about?" In *Not So Dumb*, William Holden declares: "You know I don't give a damn about pictures!" In *Voice of the City*, detective (and director) Willard Mack barks at a suspect whom he calls a "snowbird" (a cocaine addict): "Shoot *that* in your arm, hop . . . *either* arm." A Catholic educator wrote: "Silent smut had been bad. Vocal smut cried to the censors for vengeance." Most film companies were using

Edmund Lowe, Jeanette Dagna, and Victor McLaglen in The Cockeyed World. *The Fox Film Corporation was the first to offend both reformers and other studios.*

Vitaphone's sound-on-disc technology. Since there was no way to cut a piece out of a sixteen-inch acetate disc, dialogue could not easily be censored. When Movietone's sound-on-film supplanted this awkward setup, censors had to find squiggles on the edge of the film a foot ahead of the picture. They found them. Some of these offending lines came as a surprise to Jason Joy, who then realized that actors were ad-libbing lines that were not in scenarios he had approved.

Under the auspices of what was by 1929 known as "the Hays Office," Joy had no authority to make supervisors change scenarios or even screen finished films for him. The "Don'ts and Be Carefuls" only said what to keep out of a film, and they were rather vague about that. The SRC was a good idea, but not a perfect one; only 20 percent of the film

studios acknowledged it. The rest bypassed it and endured the consequences. In 1928, the New York State Board of Censors cut 4,000 scenes from 600 films. The Chicago board cut 6,000 scenes. Censor boards were costing the film companies $3.5 million a year in review fees, salaries, and the waste of expensively mounted scenes. Even with the increased profits of sound films, companies could not afford a ruined product, nor could they afford the ill will that spawned the 1928 Brookhart Bill, which could deprive them of block-booking. Will Hays defeated it but could not still new voices of disapproval.

One resounding voice was that of Catholic layperson Martin Quigley, who published the *Exhibitor's Herald,* an industry trade paper. According to Geoffrey Shurlock, who was Paramount's liaison with the SRC, Quigley was "an institution around here, because of his magazine—and because he made himself an institution." He was also "a worrier about morals and decency." In 1929, the Chicago publisher took the industry to task for not solving the problem at its source, the studio. He warned that if films were not made uniformly acceptable to the public and to the government, the industry would lose block-booking and gain censorship. Chicago's population was at this time 50 percent Roman Catholic. Its censor board had become so troublesome that Hays dispatched his chief legal counsel, Charles P. Pettijohn, to reason with its censors, one of whom was Father FitzGeorge Dinneen. In so doing, Hays unknowingly caused the birth of the Production Code.

Pettijohn's 1929 visits led Father Dinneen to speak with Martin Quigley. The censor and the publisher were of one mind, agreeing that the industry needed a formula, or a "code," to order the manufacture of "decent" moving pictures. In October, they invited Father Daniel Lord, S. J., editor of the Catholic youth magazine *The Queen's*

In Paramount's Applause, *burlesque queen Kitty Darling (Helen Morgan) sends her daughter to a convent "so she can grow up to be a lady, not a little tart."*

Work, to join them in a series of discussions. They also had the counsel of one Joseph Ignatius Breen, a militantly devout public relations man. Martin Quigley and Daniel Lord made notes, and Lord began to draft a document.

On October 29, 1929, the stock market crashed. Hollywood shrugged off predictions of disaster. The major film companies were raking in profits, M-G-M with $12 million, Warners with $14 million, and Paramount with $25 million. Only the Fox Film Corporation was troubled; William Fox had overextended his credit, first to build the largest studio complex in Hollywood and then to buy up Loew's Inc., M-G-M's parent company. The stock market crash and an antitrust suit kept him away from M-G-M, but his company still managed a $12 million profit. Universal, one of the smaller studios, asked Hays if it could film John Colton's sensational stage play *The Shanghai Gesture*. ("Uncle" Carl Laemmle had told his vice president, Robert Cochrane, that "the public now knows that we stand for clean pictures and that invariably they are too damn clean and they stay away on account of

it.") *The Shanghai Gesture*, a story of miscegenation, opium addiction, and genocide, had been proscribed by the Formula. Hays said no to Universal and then allowed a dozen films of lesser pedigree and greater tawdriness, all the while placating the advocates of censorship. He was given to pious dictums: "This industry must have toward that sacred thing, the mind of a child, toward that clean virgin thing, the same care about the impressions made upon it that the best clergyman or the most inspired teacher of youth would have." Anticensorship authors Morris L. Ernst and Pare Lorentz expressed their dislike of Hays in their 1930 book *Censored: The Private Life of the Movies*.

A man used to the ways of political subterfuge, with no especial literary or scientific background, Will Hays particularly epitomizes the class-conscious, fearful yet aggressive spirit that has made the American movie an industry, and little else. Search hard and find a man more fitted to handle petty politicians, middleaged meddling prudes, and aggressive financiers. The controllers, the movie barons,

The SRC thought that Marie Dressler's drunkenness in M-G-M's Anna Christie *might signify the "degradation of a woman," but the public loved it.*

14

SRC reviewer W. F. Willis did not like Eugene O'Neill or Greta Garbo: "It is just too bad, but she is no more Anna Christie than Sally O'Neil would be." A photograph of Sally O'Neil appears on page 57.

are satisfied with his work. The dividends are coming in. We can expect no fight for freedom, taste, or mature thought in this product so long as the Bishop of Hollywood chants his platitudes and swings his pot of purity.

Ironically, several of the problem films of early 1930 were both mature and tasteful. *The Love Parade* was the legendary Ernst Lubitsch's first sound film, the first to team Jeanette MacDonald and Maurice Chevalier, and the first talkie to integrate musical numbers into the plot. SRC staffer James B. M. Fisher screened the film and wrote, "There is a bathtub scene—very discreetly handled. There is also an early scene which shows Jeanette MacDonald in a very décolleté gown. There are a few lines with a rather explosively sophisticated meaning. None of these things should cause any adverse comment, however, because the picture is entirely free from vulgarity." The New York State censor board passed *The Love Parade* without cuts, but letters poured into the SRC. Palo Alto attorney Egerton D. Lakin wrote: "'The Love Parade' is a silly, indecent, and disreputable production. I could hardly blame the [Stanford] University students for 'razzing' the show as they do." Yet *The Love Parade* was a hit, making stars of MacDonald and Chevalier.

In reviewing the script of Rouben Mamoulian's *Applause,* Jason Joy advised its supervisor not to clarify the relationship between an aging burlesque queen and her young common-law husband. Joy wrote supervisor Walter Wanger: "[The] dialogue between Helen Morgan and Fuller Mellish, Jr., in which she urges him to marry her because of the return of her daughter, might well be eliminated, allowing anyone to assume that they either have or have not been married, depending on the desire of the person who looks at the picture." Joy believed that he could address the range of sophistication in the American audience only with a strategic vagueness. To his mind, children would not know (or care) whether the marriage was common law, but adults would read between the lines and understand the screenwriter's true intent. Joy carried this vagueness to the point of duplicity. "The assumption that they are married is clinched further on in the picture, when she speaks of him as her husband." This is how he adapted to the demands of spoken dialogue. When he could not approve a thorny plot point, he suggested a contradictory line, thus forcing the audience into two groups— duped or clued-in. In the years ahead, this deliberate ambiguity served him well and often. It did not stop censors from cutting one narrow-minded line in *Applause*. When asked his name, Henry Wadsworth shyly answers, "'Tony.' I never liked it. It sounds like a Wop bootblack."

For Greta Garbo's long-delayed first talkie, Irving Thalberg chose Eugene O'Neill's play *Anna Christie*. It was an unlikely vehicle for the star who had almost coined the words "exotic" and "mysterious." In tough, slangy dialogue, it told the story of a Swedish-American girl driven to prostitution by her father's neglect. Could it be filmed? Jason Joy thought so, writing to Thalberg's assistant, Albert Lewin, "if Anna's past life is indicated and not actually picturized." There was also Anna's dialogue: "I was in a house. Yes, *that* kind of a house! The kind that you and Matt go to. And all men, God damn them!" Joy suggested changing it to "something like 'I was the kind of girl sailors liked to play 'round with in port.'" SRC staff member W. F. Willis viewed the finished film in December 1929:

> Then in reel nine is Anna's great effort, in which she inveighs against "all men, God damn 'em!" I have been told authoritatively that this line was the high point of the spoken play, but I cannot believe it. Much as I do not like Eugene O'Neill, and firmly convinced as I am that he is not the modern Shakespeare, but a dramatic charlatan whose vogue will soon pass, I could not accuse him of not writing anything else so good in this play as this line. But of course these comments are superfluous. I will be prudent and withdraw them, and refer, instead (how I wish I could contrive a whisper on the typewriter), to the very first commandment of the famous endecalogue of June 8, 1927. Do you answer that here the "God damn" is used "reverently, in connection with proper religious ceremonies"?

When New York audiences braved the February 1930 chill to hear Garbo's voice, they didn't notice the "bup"—the sound of a splice on the sound track—where three words had been cut and replaced with "I hate them! I hate them!" In Hollywood, meanwhile, *Anna Christie*'s supervisor had been doing some writing of his own. Working with a committee of supervisors, Irving Thalberg had drafted the "General Principles to Govern the Preparation of a Revised Code of Ethics for Talking Pictures." Hollywood was giving birth to the Production Code.

THE PRODUCTION CODE

The Code had no one author, Irving Thalberg's influence notwithstanding. Like a motion picture, it was made by a committee to serve the needs of many. Will Hays needed to appease the Midwest Catholics and the increasingly unified Protestants, who had mounted a campaign against him in the liberal Episcopalian journal *The Churchman*. The moguls needed to restrain the censor boards. The bankers needed to protect their investments from boycotts, such as the one that pulled *The Callahans and the Murphys* from distribution. Clubwomen and churchmen needed films as edifying as the few to which the supervisors defensively pointed: *The Ten Commandments, Ben-Hur,* and *The Big Parade.* The Catholics needed much more than the absence of objectionable material; they needed to impose moral order. To this end, Father Daniel Lord drafted a document that would make the new code unassailable. He called it "The Reasons Supporting the Code."

Martin Quigley took it to Will Hays, who later recounted: "My eyes nearly popped out when I read it. This was the very thing I had been looking for!" While Hays sought support from the New York executives of the MPPDA, Quigley persuaded Cardinal George W. Mundelein of Chicago to bring in Halsey, Stuart and Company. By January 1930, Irving Thalberg, and then Jason Joy, had written "The General Principles." On February 10, Hays, Joy, Quigley, and Lord met with the MPPDA's West

Irving Grant Thalberg, M-G-M production chief, and coauthor of the 1930 Production Code.

Coast branch, the Association of Motion Picture Producers (AMPP). Its board of directors included M-G-M's Thalberg, Paramount's B. P. Schulberg and Jesse Lasky, Warner Bros.' Jack Warner, and Fox Film Corp.'s Sol Wurtzel. These executives immediately saw that Father Lord was seeking to arbitrate the "morality of entertainment."

"We do not create the types of entertainment; we merely present them," Thalberg countered. "The motion picture does not present the audience with tastes and manners and views and morals; it reflects those they already have." Lasky agreed: "We are really in the hands of men and women writing the current fiction, the literature of the day. They are our reporters; and they are the ones that set the standards for the present type of entertainment." Thalberg's document said it best: "The motion picture is literally bound to the mental and moral level of its vast audience."

Lord disagreed: "You set standards; you inculcate an idea of customs; you create fashions in dress, and you even go so far as to create fashions in automobiles." He saw the American audience as malleable adolescents who "sit there passively—ACCEPT and RECEIVE; with the result that they go out from that entertainment either very much improved or very much deteriorated; and that depends almost entirely on the character of the entertainment which is presented," especially when otherwise moral films placed their emphasis on the "immoral pleasures of individual episodes rather than on the moral conclusion." The latest draft of the "General Principles" had a convenient loophole that allowed restricted material if "a special effort shall be made to include compensating moral values." When Thalberg and Lord reached an impasse over this issue, Will Hays called time out, sending Quigley and Lord to rewrite the entire document in "three lively and sleepless sessions." The two authors returned on St. Valentine's Day, having married the "Reasons" to the "Principles." Hays immediately annulled the marriage, hiding the Catholic "Reasons" from the MPPDA board, who might not want the press to know that a Jewish-American industry was being influenced by an Irish-American constituency.

On February 17, the board unanimously adopted the "Code to Govern the Making of Talking, Synchronized and Silent Motion Pictures," thereafter, the Code. Although Quigley saw the wisdom of not publishing the "Reasons," he assumed his *Exhibitor's Herald* would be the first to publish the Code. On February 19, *Variety* scooped him with the article "Warming Up Film Cinderellas," which printed the "General Principles" in toto. Quigley, assuming that Hays had leaked the text, wrote to Daniel Lord: "Hays is a worm."

Quigley still wanted the Catholic editors' cooperation, and he dispatched the aggressive Breen to secure it. He also wanted sole credit for the Code, which he was able to take when he caught Father Lord accepting a $500 stipend from Will Hays. In the midst of all this intrigue, Father Dinneen cautioned Cardinal Mundelein against publicly endorsing the Code. When Quigley began to take credit for the Code, Mundelein, Lord, and Dinneen wondered who had done the double-crossing. It may not have been Hays who leaked the Code to *Variety*. Any of the executives could have done it, but the Midwest Catholics chose to blame Hays. They left Hollywood in March, slightly less unified and much less idealistic.

On March 31, Will Hays got the New York board of the MPPDA—the actual center of power—to endorse the Code. He trumpeted his achievement in an April Fool's Day press release: "Sound, which revolutionized the art of the screen, has brought about the formulation of a new Code by the motion picture industry." Cardinal Mundelein, who felt that he—not Quigley, Lord, or Hays—was responsible for the Code, refused to endorse it for six months. The secular press was mostly unimpressed.

"How can a movie which satisfies a child of twelve be made morally safe for a man of 35?" asked *The Nation*. "Thus far the censors have spent all their time protecting children against adult movies; they might better protect adults against childlike movies." The *New York World* predicted: "That the code will actually be applied in any sincere and thorough way, we have not the slightest belief." The Catholic press reflected Quigley and Lord's resentment. *Commonweal* thought Hays had made a "nom-

inal alliance with the church to camouflage an actual alliance with the devil."

Whether for haloes or horns, Hays had to make the Code work. He gave Jason Joy, who had reviewed seventy-one scripts since January, a larger staff. Lamar Trotti and James B. M. Fisher would assist him with reviews. Florence Sell and Betty Seely would read scripts. John V. Wilson would watch for elements offensive to foreign countries. Alice Ames Winter would represent the General Federation of Women's Clubs. In May, Fred W. Beetson, executive vice president of the AMPP, visited the SRC and reported to Hays that the "entire office has developed into a beehive." It appeared that the studios were abiding by the Code, or at least willing to submit material. However, one of the films released that month was not a product of the Code. Irving Thalberg's *The Divorcee* was the first film released in the context of the "General Principles," and would be the first to test the hidden part of the Code. For the next four years, the absence of the "Reasons" and the presence of "compensating moral values" would make for some lively movies. And the Catholics were watching.

The complete texts of the published "Code to Govern the Making of Talking, Synchronized and Silent Motion Pictures" and the unpublished "Reasons Supporting the Code" may be found in Appendix II, on page 214.

A CYCLE OF SOPHISTICATION

At thirty, Irving Grant Thalberg was a figure of unparalleled brilliance and untrammeled confidence. Louis B. Mayer's management had made M-G-M the most powerful film studio in the world, but Thalberg's taste kept it the most respected. According to supervisor Lawrence Weingarten, Thalberg "had a sixth sense about a manuscript. He was a film doctor. You could go out [to a preview] with a film, and if there was something that didn't quite come off, he could put his finger on it. Some of the great films that came out of Metro were *re*made at his suggestion. He had that uncanny ability." With the Production Code in place, Thalberg looked to his audience.

Ninety million Americans were attending the movies each week. The industry needed films to feed this appetite. For source material, it turned to successful books and plays. Irving Thalberg bypassed the Formula and bought Ursula Parrott's scandalous novel *Ex-Wife*. How could the coauthor of the Code buy such a property? He explained to the other members of AMPP that the book "presents divorce in the light of the growing evil it is looked upon to be, but . . . with less suspicion than it was looked upon before." In deference to the Formula, he changed the title to *The Divorcee* and promised that advertising for the film would never mention its source.

Casting *The Divorcee* was Thalberg's next hurdle. According to Weingarten, Thalberg believed that the film should be a "showcase for an actress. That's how we built the female stars, the Garbos and the Crawfords." Joan Crawford, whose films were hugely profitable, wanted the part. Thalberg's wife, Norma Shearer, was as popular, but she was known for virtuous, clearheaded roles. When Thalberg began to look outside M-G-M, Shearer campaigned for the part. Thalberg later said: "She had to fight all the studio heads—including myself—to put her idea over." She got *The Divorcee*. Such unlikely casting made the project look subversive. The SRC fretted, but the preview was a relief. W. F. Willis wrote: "It is a great picture."

It was a thought-provoking picture. In it, Norma Shearer portrays Jerry, a commercial artist, whose husband, Ted (Chester Morris), justifies a casual

In Paramount's Animal Crackers, *Groucho Marx tells Louis Sorin and Margaret Dumont: "We took some pictures of the native girls, but they weren't developed. We're going back in a few weeks."*

Lew Ayres decides to go to Yola D'Avril's room in Universal's All Quiet on the Western Front. *This scene was cut for a 1938 reissue, but restored by the Library of Congress in 1998.*

affair with the phrase, "It doesn't mean a thing." Jerry is so stunned that she finds herself testing the limits of 1930 convention: she sleeps with Ted's best friend, Don (Robert Montgomery), then tells Ted: "I've balanced our accounts." When Ted explodes with self-righteousness, Jerry delivers an electrifying fade-out line: "And from now on, *you're* the only man in the world my door is closed to!"

Joan Crawford, furious at losing *The Divorcee* to the invidious Shearer, had a sexy success with *Our Blushing Brides,* then got lucky when Shearer went on maternity leave. Crawford got *Paid,* the story of a falsely imprisoned girl who wreaks vengeance on the rich folk who sent her to prison. Sam Wood shot a five-minute fight scene in the women's shower, then had to shoot a ten-second replacement when the graphic scene was cut, not by the SRC, but by the studio.

Exposure of a different gender took place in *All Quiet on the Western Front,* Lewis Milestone's film of Erich Maria Remarque's antiwar novel. One censor board dictated: "Where men are bathing in river, cut out all scenes of them turning somersaults, or otherwise unduly exposing themselves." James

The SRC noted Jeanette MacDonald's tendency "to expose her body to the audience" in Paramount's Monte Carlo.

Constance Bennett was riding the crest of newfound notoriety when she made Sin Takes a Holiday *with Basil Rathbone and Kenneth MacKenna. Pathé Pictures photograph by Emmett Schoenbaum.*

In First National's A Notorious Affair, *Paul Gherardi (Basil Rathbone) courts the Countess Balakireff (Kay Francis), but she prefers her stable groom.*

Christine Maple was one of the showgirls personally chosen by Florenz Ziegfeld for Samuel Goldwyn's Whoopee!

Norma Shearer flouted the Code as a sleekly defiant Divorcee.

In M-G-M's The Sea Bat, *the "cloth" does not stop escaped convict Charles Bickford from sampling the succulence of Mazatlan—or Raquel Torres. Photograph by Bert Lynch.*

Gavin Gordon was another passionate prelate in M-G-M's Romance. *The object of his ardor was Greta Garbo, directed by Clarence Brown and photographed by William H. Daniels. Photograph by Milton Brown. Courtesy the Kobal Collection.*

B. M. Fisher reviewed the film at the Carthay Circle Theatre, since the SRC had no screening room:

> The line in which Kat tells the recruit, who loses complete control of himself during a bombardment, to go back and change his drawers, seemed to pass over the heads of the audience almost unnoticed. Only a few men in the audience caught the significance of the remark and laughed.
>
> On the whole the picture held the audience very well. . . . There was no applause at the end of the film but the line spoken by Kat when he says that at the next war all the statesmen should be put in a field and given clubs so that they can fight it out among themselves received a great deal.

One of the many affecting sequences in *All Quiet on the Western Front* has three young German soldiers spend the night in a farmhouse with three French girls. It concludes with silhouettes on the bedroom wall and the voice of the hero, Paul (Lew Ayres), telling a French girl, Suzanne (Yola D'Avril): "I'll never see you again. I know that—and I wouldn't know you if I did, and yet I'll remember you—always. *Toujours.* Oh, if only you could know how different this is from the women we soldiers meet." According to Fisher, "audience reaction here was good; there was no snickering or laughing as there would have been had they considered the scene at all off color." The Ohio board thought otherwise, and cut the entire sequence.

Equally powerful and more controversial was Howard Hughes's *Hell's Angels*. While Irving Thalberg worked around the Code, Hughes ignored it, released the film, and then had to seek help from SRC reviewer Lamar Trotti, who wrote to Will Hays: "The difficulty, as you know, lies in the fact that the story

Robert Montgomery harasses Joan Crawford in Our Blushing Brides: *"Who wouldn't take advantage of the opportunity of seeing a lovely lady's lingerie—before the bridegroom sees it?" Courtesy the Kobal Collection.*

In M-G-M's Paid, *Joan Crawford plays an unjustly imprisoned shopgirl.*

of 'Hell's Angels' is stupid, rotten, sordid, and cheap." He noted that scenes between British soldiers and French bar girls showed open-mouth kissing. "When the couples kiss each other, for instance, they invariably open their mouths and try to swallow each other; the men kiss the girls on the ears and the girls squeal." The film was attacked by both critics and Hays's allies, including James E. West, chief scout executive of the Boy Scouts of America, who wrote: "I didn't relish the idea of exposing my children to the unnecessary disgusting evidence of passion and lust, the worst I have seen on the screen." For its climactic aerial battle, *Hell's Angels* had enough swearing, screaming, vomiting, and dying for three movies. Because of its outsized production and publicity costs, the film was not profitable, but it established Hughes as an independent producer and made a star of nineteen-year-old Jean Harlow, she of the platinum hair and quotable exit line: "Would you be shocked if I put on something more comfortable?"

As one mogul appeared, another disappeared. William Fox was ousted from the company he had founded by an avaricious triumvirate: the American Telephone Company, Halsey, Stuart and Company, and would-be president Harley Clarke. The Fox Film Corporation lacked star power, so head of production Winfield Sheehan pushed projects that were fantastic, extravagant, and racy.

One of the first was a "science-fiction musical," *Just Imagine.* In it, 1980 Manhattan is an unpleasant place, its denizens known only by numbers and not allowed to procreate naturally. Three young men escape to Mars, where they encounter the Martian Queen, Looloo (Joyzelle Joyner), and her brutish bodyguard, Loko (Ivan Linow). Loko approaches earthling Single 0 (El Brendel) and caresses his face. Single 0 exclaims to his comrades,

This brutal scene was cut from Paid *before its release. One of the inmates snarls: "Say, sister, howdja like to kiss my—"*

M-G-M's Madam Satan *has Trixie (Lillian Roth) parachuting from a zeppelin and into a locker room.*

In Madam Satan, *Angela (Kay Johnson) finds Trixie in bed with her husband's best friend, Jimmy (Roland Young), but we know that Trixie is really after Angela's husband.*

Kay Johnson goes to a masquerade ball on a zeppelin to find her husband (Reginald Denny, left). Dressed as the eponymous devil lady, she asks the crowd: "Who wants to go to hell with Madam Satan?"

pointing first to Looloo, then to Loko: "*She's not the queen! He is!*" This Broadway humor was not lost on the SRC's John V. Wilson: "Some of the censors may want to eliminate from Loko's actions that which seem to make it appear that he is 'queer.' "

Each victory emboldened other studios. In August, Lamar Trotti found M-G-M contentious. Cecil B. DeMille would not rework his sex-and-Deco musical *Madam Satan*, and Thalberg would not cut Marie Prevost's lines in *War Nurse*: "[What do you wear to clean the latrine?] Your dark brown taffeta, dear." Trotti wrote: "Not the usual Thalberg reaction. Their attitude at the moment is, why should any small group of people decide what the rest of the world should see?" One of Joy's colleagues wrote him: "After reading the suggestions you made on 'Madam Satan,' you have my entire sympathy. The marvel is that you are getting away with as much as you do."

Paramount, envious of M-G-M's success with Garbo, imported Marlene Dietrich, whom the autocratic Josef von Sternberg had directed to stardom in Germany's first sound film, *The Blue Angel*. For her American debut he transformed a California desert into hypnotic *Morocco*. His equally hypnotic (and hypnotized) discovery was again playing a lady with a past. Dietrich's biggest censorship news occurred at the Colorado Theatre in Pasadena, where an audience expecting *The Blue Angel* instead got a chopped-up condensation; the response was "a terrific razzing." Censors were increasingly vigilant, and with good reason.

"We are struggling mightily with the cycle of sophistication which the success of 'Divorcee' induced," wrote Jason Joy. By year's end, the cycle had yet to run out, as evidenced by this editorial in the *New York Telegraph*.

By the way, whatever became of that Hays code? It seems that all the producers got together when Hays issued his proclamation of picture cleanliness and they all nodded their heads sagely and agreed to follow the code. Then along came Metro with "Divorcee," the picture version of "Ex-Wife," and knocked the code for a

Affecting a French accent, Madam Satan tells her husband: "You are een *love* weez *love!" When the film ran into trouble, Jason Joy interceded for Cecil B. DeMille, who wired him: "Hurrah for you and the Ohio censors! Let Joy be unconfined!"*

row of big figures. Now every picture concern is trying for something sensational and startling.

There was reason to try. In ten months, weekly movie attendance had dropped from 90 million to 60 million. On December 11, 1930, the secretary of Guaranty Savings and Loan announced that he had lost $7,630,000 in the stock market, and closed his doors. A raft of businesses followed, and the motion-picture industry finally believed that the Depression was real. Maybe the "sensational and startling" would retrieve 30 million customers.

Paramount's Morocco *made Marlene Dietrich an American star and Gary Cooper a star in his own right.*

In Morocco, *cinematographer Lee Garmes created a new face for Dietrich, and director Josef von Sternberg created a new image of woman.*

BULLETS AND BOX OFFICE

Darryl F. Zanuck was Warner Bros.' production head at twenty-eight, having risen through the ranks by dint of hard work and an infallible story sense. When an old friend and mentor died in a bootleg dispute, Zanuck decided to produce a crime film. According to screenwriter John Bright, Zanuck was "a man of considerable talent, a man of many abilities . . . he was good at editing a script and very creative; for that I gave him a great deal of respect. But his personality was imperious. He was Hollywood's Napoleon." What better hero for his crime film than a conqueror?

In 1929, Chicago newspaperman W. R. Burnett visited the scene of the St. Valentine's Day Massacre and saw seven well-dressed corpses reflected in pools of blood. The result was a novel, *Little Caesar.* Zanuck paid $15,000 for it, assigned it to Mervyn LeRoy, and let LeRoy cast it. Edward G. Robinson's face had some secret allure. Three thousand people showed up for the opening. The pressure of their bodies broke the glass doors of the Strand Theatre at Broadway and 47th Street. Of equal impact was the report that "children applaud the gang leader as a hero." The gang leader was based, of course, on Chicago's Al Capone, the person responsible for the St. Valentine's Day Massacre. New York congressman Fiorello LaGuardia threatened to sponsor federal censorship legislation if Hollywood continued to exalt murderers. He was further angered by Robinson's portrayal of Little Caesar as unmistakably Italian. Will Hays's executive assistant Maurice McKenzie wrote Jason Joy that "[LaGuardia] is going to publicly denounce Mr. Hays as a hypocrite . . . [because] Mr. Hays would not dare to produce the picture with a Jew as that character—he would lose his job if he did. My guess is that LaGuardia is sore because Little Caesar looks like him."

In January 1931, Dr. James Wingate was the head of the Motion Picture Division of the State of New York Education Department. His censorship decisions affected not only his state but also much of America. The hero worship accorded *Little Caesar* angered him: "Children . . . see a gangster riding around in a Rolls-Royce and living in luxury, and even though some other gangster gets him in the end, the child unconsciously forms the idea that he will be smarter and will get away with it." Meanwhile, Joy was writing to McKenzie: "I saw 'Little Caesar' with an audience last night and how they ate it up. How anybody, including LaGuardia, Wingate, and the British Columbia censors, can object to that or to any part of it is beyond me." Then, atypically colloquial, he wrote: "Everything else seems to be OK except the New York Censor Board. They are riding hell out of us. One of us is awfully wrong and my guess is it ain't me."

Wingate demanded extensive cuts. Joy argued against them, saying that "the more ghastly, the more ruthless, the criminal acts, the stronger will be the audience reaction against men of this kind and organized crime in general." In an earnestly written letter, Joy tried to convince Wingate:

> Always drama has been permitted to paint the unconventional, the unlawful, the immoral side of life in order to bring out in immediate contrast the happiness and benefits derived from wholesome, clean and law-abiding conduct and thus, without actually preaching a sermon, giving audiences the opportunity of inevitably forming the conclusion that the breaking of human or divine laws brings punishment of some kind. . . .
>
> [I]t was never intended that censorship should be destructive, picking at details, but rather that its duty should be a constructive one of influencing the quality of the final impression left on the minds of audiences by the whole, irrespective of details, possibly objectionable in themselves.

Wingate was unconvinced. He cut *Little Caesar* to shreds, and the Pennsylvania censors followed suit.

Edward G. Robinson began the troublesome gangster cycle in Warner Bros.' Little Caesar.

Spencer Tracy was an ambitious gangster and Sally Eilers his moll in Fox Film's Quick Millions.

Thelma Todd made a voluptuous Iva Archer in Warner Bros.' The Maltese Falcon.
Photograph by Mac Julian.

The combined scents of smoke and money were irresistible to other film companies. Fox Film released *Transatlantic* and *Quick Millions,* followed by M-G-M's *The Secret Six,* and Paramount's *City Streets,* but the most charismatic gangster was at Warner Bros. He was created when Chicago producer Rufus LeMaire came to Darryl Zanuck, peddling an unpublished novel by two former druggists. LeMaire thought that *Beer and Blood* would be his ticket to a supervisor's job. Zanuck sidetracked him into the casting department, then hired John Bright and Kubec Glasmon to scenarize their manuscript. Acting out all the parts in story conferences with staff writer Harvey Thew, Zanuck had them build up one character, Tom Powers, and call him the *Public Enemy.* "Our character was a swashbuckling, hard-fisted guy," said Bright, "a hoodlum who had come up from the Irish ghetto to the top. He had an income of ten thousand dollars a week or more. Notches on his gun. Been shot at many times."

Zanuck submitted the script to Jason Joy with this pitch: "In PUBLIC ENEMY, we also have a very strong moral theme, to-wit: If there is PLEASURE and PROFIT in CRIME, or the violation of the Eighteenth Amendment, then THAT pleasure and THAT profit can only be momentary, as the basic foundation of law violation, ultimately ends in disaster to the participants." When Joy approved the script, Zanuck took an active role in the production, casting, recasting, and then exhorting director William Wellman: "People are going to say the characters are immoral, but they're not because they don't *have* any morals. They steal, they kill, they lie, they hump each other because that's the way they're made, and if you allow a decent feeling or a pang of conscience to come into their makeup, you've lost 'em and changed the kind of movie we're making." *Public Enemy* was shot in twenty-one days, at a cost of $151,000, and Zanuck invited Irving Thalberg to its preview. Thalberg was stunned. "That's not a motion picture," he said to Zanuck. "It's beyond a motion picture."

Public Enemy opened on April 6, 1931. Will Hays chose this inopportune moment to say: "The greatest of all censors—the American public—is beginning to vote thumbs down on the 'hard-boiled' realism in literature and on the stage which marked the post-war period." Hays looked pretty foolish when *Public Enemy* outstripped *Little Caesar's* box-

office take. This time, James Wingate admitted that it was "a story that ought to be told," but lamented the weak role played by the police in the film. The SRC's Lamar Trotti agreed that "it is another picture in which the gangsters fight it out among themselves without police interference." While admitting that "the picture probably is defensible as a piece of realism of current conditions," Trotti had reservations about a scene "showing Tommy buying a new suit of clothes. The tailor is unmistakably a 'fairy,' with hands on hips, Nice-Nellie talk, etc." The tailor was the only sex object in the film whom Tommy Powers did not manhandle.

Most state censors cut pistols, machine guns, and "pineapples" (hand grenades) from the film, but it was a grapefruit that separated *Public Enemy* from the pack. The film showed James Cagney, in pajamas, eating a grapefruit breakfast with Mae Clarke while, in the next room, Edward Woods chewed Joan Blondell's earlobe—in bed. Few moviegoers saw (or heard) what followed. "At the end of the scene between the two boys and two girls in the apartment, cut sound track where action ceases and dialogue implies intimacy." Only Ohio and Maryland cut the scene in which Cagney shoved the grapefruit into Clarke's face, but every state slashed this unsettling sequence: "*Reel 8*—Eliminate view of woman turning out light and going back to bed, when Tommy lies in drunken stupor and accompanying spoken words: 'I'll take your shoes off, too. I want to do things for you, Tommy. You don't think I'm old, do you, Tommy?' [And Tommy's lines:] 'Aw, in your hat. Aw, go away from me.'" The censors also cut the lines from the morning-after scene: "Do you mean—? Why, you—" Tommy, realizing that the woman has crawled into bed with him, slaps her. *Time* reported that one audience, "long trained by the Press to glorify thugs, last week laughed loudly at such comedy and sat spellbound through the serious parts."

While *Public Enemy* made news, Will Hays received letters of complaint from the Daughters of the American Revolution, the Veterans of Foreign Wars, the United Presbyterian Church, the Catholic Knights of Columbus, the National Federation of Men's Bible Classes, and the Milwaukee Film Board of Trade, who requested that "every effort be made to eliminate the gangster type of picture and avoid the adverse criticism of the industry if possible." Even Al Capone had a comment: "Well,

ABOVE:
Five months after Jean Harlow completed M-G-M's
The Secret Six, *she was a sensation in Warner Bros.'*
Public Enemy. *On April 1, 1931, she came back to M-G-M for*
a special session with photographer Clarence Sinclair Bull.
Courtesy the Kobal Collection.

OPPOSITE:
Edmund Lowe was a suave crook in Fox Film's
Transatlantic. *Photograph by Frank Tanner of a Gordon Wiles*
set, with lighting by James Wong Howe.

BELOW:
James Cagney and Jean Harlow in Public Enemy.

TOP:
James Cagney punctuates Mae Clarke's sentence. According to Darryl F. Zanuck: "It was my idea, the grapefruit." Numerous censor boards cut this scene.

CENTER:
This set-reference still shows the aftermath of Cagney's attack.

BOTTOM:
Joan Blondell began this scene by bringing Eddie Woods breakfast in bed. Zanuck boasted: "When I made Public Enemy, *I was way ahead in thinking. No love story, but loaded with sex and violence."*

OPPOSITE:
"At least you might get a shave!" Blondell protests to Woods. This scene was cut from the Public Enemy *negative in August 1953.*

these gang pictures are making a lot of kids want to be tough guys, and they don't serve any useful purpose." At Warner Bros., Darryl Zanuck was so happy with John Bright's work that he invited him to a stag party that, according to Bright, "involved everything, including a lesbian show by two prostitutes. I remember commenting to myself that here were the leading creators of the nation's entertainment, including children's pictures, and they were behaving so obscenely."

Three thousand miles away, James Wingate regretfully remarked to Lamar Trotti that "there is a general break-down in respect for all laws, and . . . prohibition is probably responsible for this condition." The unpopular law made for popular films, as Hollywood showed "bootleg hooch," its purveyors, and its purchasers.

IGNOBLE EXPERIMENTS

The Volstead Act became law on October 28, 1919. Herbert Hoover called it "The Noble Experiment." It prohibited the sale of alcoholic beverages. It could not prohibit their consumption, or films about their consumption. Jason Joy admonished the industry that drinking scenes should be included only if "absolutely necessary to the plot development."

Some drinking scenes were indeed plot points. In Raoul Walsh's *The Yellow Ticket,* a Jewish schoolteacher, Marya Kalish (Elissa Landi), struggles against Tsarist oppression: "Every Jew not serving in the Army is to be closely confined within the Pales of Settlement." To reach her imprisoned father, she must obtain a "yellow ticket," the passport available only to prostitutes. One of the demimondaine directs her to a brothel. Cinematographer James Wong Howe uses a kaleidoscopic filter to suggest its besotted depravity—a spinning blur of piano

Warner Bros.' The Last Flight *was the only pre-Code film about the Lost Generation; its original title was* Spent Bullets. *Left to right: Richard Barthelmess, David Manners, Johnny Mack Brown, Walter Byron, Helen Chandler, and Elliott Nugent. Photograph by Elmer Fryer.*

keys, vodka bottles, female legs and underarms.

More often, films used drinking scenes to comic effect. How else could RKO-Radio Pictures' *Millie* show two women getting drunk on Christmas? Good-time girl Millie (Helen Twelvetrees) is sad because her boyfriend has not called. Her pal Helen (Lilyan Tashman) says, "Ah, don't cry, Millie. Y'know what *you* need. A good *drink*." The scene dissolves to the two friends, swaying and slurring: "Men are all tramps. Aw-ful tr-ramps. *Sköl*." American women were not amused by this spectacle, said Alice Ames Winter, who described *Millie* as "a sordid melodrama with frequent lapses from good taste," and singled out its "excessive drinking." She also criticized Tod Browning's *The Iron Man* for its "unnecessary drinking and [the] costumes of Jean Harlow."

Flying High was an M-G-M comedy that Lamar Trotti described as the funniest he had ever seen. Written by the team of DeSylva, Henderson, and Brown, the authors of *Just Imagine,* it has a doctor asking an aviator, Rusty Krouse (Bert Lahr): "Have you ever used narcotics?" After much dodging, Rusty finally answers: "Yes! Ex-Lax!" Behind the doctor's back, he pours liquor into the bottle given to him for a urine specimen. The SRC told M-G-M to remove the scene. The studio at first refused, but when various censor boards raised a stink, it cut the scene from all prints.

The Last Flight was a sad, quirky film, described by director William Dieterle as the story of "an ex-flier [Richard Barthelmess], who, with four roughneck buddies and a girl—whom the five adopt—is scouring Paris to find excitement to equal that of war days." *The Last Flight* was more depressing than daring, with its coterie of Lost Generation characters, each trying to heal a psychic war wound with alcohol or drugs. Of concern to Jason Joy were alcohol's side effects: "The replies when each one of the men leaves the table and Nikki asks where he is

Jean Harlow is a two-timing boxer's wife in Universal's The Iron Man.

TOP:

Impresario John Barrymore refuses ballet master Luis Alberni drugs in Warner Bros.' The Mad Genius.

CENTER:

Charles Farrell, an unidentified player, and an opium pipe in Fox Film's The Man Who Came Back.

BOTTOM:

The Man Who Came Back, *Charles Farrell, finds his girlfriend, Janet Gaynor, in an opium den. She describes it: "Everybody has his own way here. That's the beauty of living in this 'celestial palace.' A few little smokes, and you dream life as you want it to be, not as it is. It'd be beautiful if it were always like that— with no awakenings."*

OPPOSITE:

One of the saddest images onscreen in 1931 was John Gilbert in M-G-M's West of Broadway. *Gilbert's career was failing because the press had reported that his voice was high-pitched. According to film editor Chester W. Schaeffer: "It was because Louis B. Mayer had told the sound department to equalize his voice to make it sound high-pitched." The proud star refused to capitulate and began drinking heavily.*

going—'To shave a horse,' 'To take a Chinese singing lesson,' etc.—contain a vulgar inference in that they convey the idea that the person in question has gone, or is going, to the toilet. We believe that this inference is likely to cause offense to many people." Dieterle answered: "The taste for treacle has passed."

CENSORING HORROR

On August 28, 1929, Carl Laemmle, Jr., turned twenty-one. In a gesture as grand as it was nepotistic, Carl Laemmle, Sr., made him production head of Universal Pictures. The studio with the largest acreage made small but profitable movies such as *The Cat and the Canary*, a haunted-house mystery that in its last reel revealed its "monster" to be a mere madman. With more profits in mind, five Universal readers reviewed Bram Stoker's 1897 novel *Dracula*. Two said it was too gruesome. A third said it would make the viewer want to "seek a 'convenient railing.'" A fourth said "Absolutely no!!!" A fifth was prescient: "It will be a difficult task and one will run up against the censor continually, but I think it can be done." By the summer of 1930, the play version of *Dracula* by Hamilton Deane and John Balderston had become a multimillion-dollar hit by presenting as fact the vampirism so vividly enacted by its star, Bela Lugosi.

Novelist Louis Bromfield and screenwriter Dudley Murphy submitted a first-draft script of *Dracula* to "Junior" Laemmle on September 8, 1930. When he read that Count Dracula was attacking a hapless real estate agent, he wrote in the margin: "Dracula should go only for women and not men." He also wanted to drop Dracula's lines: "To die, to be really dead. That must be glorious. There are far worse things awaiting man than death." When director Tod Browning and writer Garrett Fort polished the script, they ignored most of Junior's suggestions. Shirley Ulmer, then related to Junior by marriage, remembered: "As a producer, he may not have been creative within himself, but he knew how to put a package together." Universal was already feeling the economic slump, so the studio offered forty-eight-year-old Bela Lugosi a paltry $3,500 for the role he had made famous on Broadway. Lugosi, whose identification with Count Dracula was

already legendary, accepted. Economy was Universal's watchword, and Browning, who had made eight lavish horror films at M-G-M with the recently deceased Lon Chaney, found it frustrating. "Everything that Tod Browning wanted to do was queried. Couldn't it be done cheaper? Wouldn't it be just as effective if—? That sort of thing. It was most dispiriting," recalled Lugosi. According to the film's romantic lead, David Manners, Lugosi insulated himself from studio politics by "parading up and down the stage, posing in front of a full-length mirror, throwing his cape over his shoulder, and shouting, 'I AM DRACULA!'"

The Transylvanian count who "prolongs his unnatural life by draining the blood of the living" did not frighten Jason Joy. He viewed *Dracula* a week after its final retakes and pronounced it "quite satisfactory from the standpoint of the Code." There was still the "foreign angle." Would the Rumanian government take umbrage at this loathsome characterization? James B. M. Fisher thought not: "Dracula is not really a human being so he cannot conceivably cause any trouble." *Dracula* opened at the Roxy Theatre in New York on February 12, 1931. Within 48 hours, it had sold 50,000 tickets. When he heard about movie patrons fainting, Joy had second thoughts: "Is this the beginning of a cycle which ought to be retarded or killed?"

Junior Laemmle presented Mary Shelley's *Frankenstein* to his new star. Lugosi refused it: "I was a star in my country and I will not be a scarecrow over here!" Tod Browning had retreated to M-G-M, so Junior Laemmle offered the project to James Whale, a British director who had just made a success of *Waterloo Bridge*. Said Whale: "I chose *Frankenstein* out of about thirty available stories because it was the strongest meat and gave me a chance to dabble in the macabre."

Frankenstein was the parable of a headstrong man who assembled a creature from the parts of various corpses. In a parallel process, Whale, Balderston, and makeup artist Jack Pierce used disparate literary and visual elements to transform an unknown British actor named Boris Karloff into a cinematic monster. Karloff later said: "This was a pathetic creature who, like all of us, had neither wish nor say in his creation and certainly did not wish upon itself the hideous image which automatically terrified humans whom it tried to befriend."

With a flair both theatrical and sadistic, James Whale took his man-made monster to a man-made lake* for the scene in which he meets one human who does not shun him. Whale coached eight-year-old Marilyn Harris: "Here is Mr. Karloff in a funny costume who's just being friendly. You just look up at him and say, 'I am Maria.' " The child liked working with Karloff: "He had such warmth and gentleness about him." As Karloff understood the scene, the monster would mistake the little girl for the daisies they were tossing into the water. Thinking that she, too, would float, he would gently place her in the water—and be horrified when she sank. Karloff recalled: "Well, Jimmy made me pick her up and do THAT [motioning violently] over my head, which became a brutal and deliberate act."

Actress Mae Clarke agreed that the scene should not be violent or end in death: "This was the nearest the monster came to having a soul, without having one." But Whale answered, "The death has to take place." When Karloff continued to protest, Whale "fumbled for his words as he tried to convey 'why' to us, because in a strange way, we were all very hostile about it. He couldn't just bully us into acceptance. Then he said, 'You see, it's all part of the *ritual.*' " The shooting of the scene was as harrowing as its content. In the first take, Karloff's costume limited his throw, and the child landed too close to shore. Her mother yelled: "Throw her in again! Farther!" Whale agreed, and two technicians replaced Karloff. They were too forceful; the little girl landed in lakeside weeds and had trouble surfacing. Whale rewarded her pluckiness with two dozen boiled eggs.

The first preview took place on October 29, at the Granada Theatre in Santa Barbara, California. According to Paramount producer David Lewis, who accompanied Whale: "As it progressed, people got up, walked out, came back in, walked out again." Junior Laemmle was frightened: "Jesus, God, we've got to do something! This thing's a disaster!" Lewis's boss at Paramount, Eddie Montagne, phoned Junior: "You're insane. If we had a picture like that, we'd clean up." For the next preview of *Frankenstein,* Junior Laemmle included an unlikely reviewer: Martin Quigley's newly incorporated trade paper, *The Motion Picture Herald.* After foolishly voicing his misgivings to Quigley, Laemmle had to read this: "I don't know what it might do to children, but I know I wouldn't want my kids to see it. And I won't forgive Junior Laemmle or James Whale for permitting the Monster to drown a little girl before my very eyes." Laemmle opened the film in New York at the Mayfair Theatre on December 4. It grossed a startling $53,000 in one week, but the state boards were less enthusiastic.

Massachusetts, Pennsylvania, and New York cut the drowning scene and Henry Frankenstein's speech: "In the name of God! Now I know what it feels like to *be* God!" Kansas refused to pass the film without dozens of cuts. Universal wrote to Jason Joy: "Junior urgently requests you to do anything you can to have these cuts re-considered." Joy sent the forceful Joe Breen to Kansas, and he managed a compromise. In most of the country, though, the film was seen intact.

Before Universal could release another horror film, Paramount got to "clean up," too. Its vehicle was Rouben Mamoulian's *Dr. Jekyll and Mr. Hyde,* starring Fredric March. This version of Robert Louis Stevenson's 1886 novel was as much a study of sexual frustration as a horror film. Mamoulian later said: "I didn't want Hyde to be a monster. Hyde is not evil. He is the primitive, the animal in us, whereas Jekyll is a cultured man, representing the intellect." To effect the transformation from Jekyll to Hyde, Mamoulian worked with the gifted cinematographer Karl Struss, who used colored lights, filters, and Wally Westmore's makeup to transform March's face from good to evil. Struss rejected Mamoulian's atavistic concept: "The change from Jekyll should have been largely a psychological one, with subtle changes only in the make-up. But they foolishly changed the hair and put false teeth in and made him look like a monkey." Mamoulian insisted: "Hyde is the Neanderthal man, and March's makeup was designed as such." Hyde's scenes with Ivy (Miriam Hopkins) smacked of bestiality, and Joy wrote Schulberg that an undressing scene looked as if it had been "dragged in simply to titillate the audience." The film received critical plaudits and made a respectable profit.

Joy wrote to Will Hays:

Frankenstein is staying for four weeks and taking in big money at theatres which were about on the rocks . . . resentment is surely being built up. How could it be otherwise if children

Edmund Lowe starred in Fox Film's The Spider. *Adapted from a play by
Fulton Oursler and Lowell Brentano, it was typical of early horror films, explaining its
weird occurrences in natural terms.*

Paramount's Murder by the Clock *has a black widow at its center. Lilyan Tashman,
by turns menacing and facetious, lures men to their doom. Irving Pichel plays her crazed cousin.
Photograph by Frank Bjerring.*

In Universal's Dracula, *Bela Lugosi (here with Frances Dade) created a screen character who was literally immortal. "Ah, what letters women wrote me!" Lugosi recalled. "Letters of a horrible hunger. Asking if I cared only for maiden's blood."*

Carl Laemmle, Jr., did not like the implications of Dracula's relationship with Renfield (Dwight Frye).

Dracula's wives were wordlessly portrayed by Dorothy Tree, Geraldine Dvorak, and Cornelia Thaw (a.k.a. Mildred Peirce).

A Jack Freulich portrait of Boris Karloff as the monster in Universal's Frankenstein.

Frankenstein used sylvan settings to good effect. Here, Colin Clive and Mae Clarke relax in Busch Gardens, a popular film location in Pasadena. Photograph by Sherman Clark.

This much-censored scene in Frankenstein included a mackerel tabby kitten who abruptly disappeared between shots, but not as abruptly as Marilyn Harris's drowning sequence. The end of the scene was cut from the negative in 1937 but restored by MCA-Universal in 1986. Photograph by Sherman Clark.

This on-the-set portrait by Gordon Head captures the brooding brilliance of Fredric March's Henry Jekyll in Paramount's Dr. Jekyll and Mr. Hyde.

Scenes between Mr. Hyde (Fredric March) and Ivy Pierson (Miriam Hopkins) were randomly cut by local censors. The film's negative lost fourteen minutes for a June 1935 reissue, but Turner Entertainment Corporation restored it for release by MGM-UA Home Video in 1989.

go to these pictures and have the jitters, followed by nightmares? I, for one, would hate to have my children see FRANKENSTEIN, JEKYLL, or the others and you probably feel the same way about Bill [Will Hays, Jr.]. Not only is there a future economic consideration, but maybe there is a real moral responsibility involved to which I wonder if we as individuals ought to lend our support.

Will Hays had no comment. He was fighting another cycle.

TROPICAL TRAMPS

The "kept woman" cycle wheeled into Hollywood with a proscribed 1909 play, *The Easiest Way*. Jason Joy had dissuaded First National, Paramount, United Artists, Universal, Fox Film, and Columbia from producing it. Irving Thalberg ignored the Formula, bought it, and assigned it to supervisor Hunt Stromberg, who was known for sexy films. Constance Bennett played Laura Murdock, a slum girl whose modeling job leads to a liaison with Brockton (Adolphe Menjou), owner of an ad agency. Joy prevailed upon Stromberg to show Laura punished for her immorality. Stromberg shot additional scenes showing Laura ostracized by her priggish brother-in-law (Clark Gable).

After previewing the film, Joy wrote Thalberg: "We were rather disappointed in our expectation that it would more thoroughly bring out contrasting moral values to balance the evident attractions and benefits of the life of a 'kept woman.'" Before Joy could gauge public response, another film with a similar theme opened, Clarence Brown's *Inspiration*. Without seeing the films, James Wingate lit into Joy, who responded with a telegram: "While the kept woman idea is evident it is by inference and not treated explicitly." Wingate's reaction was: "Have you people changed your standards?" Wingate did not know that Joy had improved both films, especially *Inspiration*. Its first script, by Jacques Deval, had this sequence:

> YVONNE: I like your eyes. Do you mind?
> ANDRE: (embarrassed) Why, I—
> YVONNE: (closer to him) Who are you?
> From the orchestra—savage music: the

scene between them becomes more and more charged with sex.

> ANDRE: My name is Andre . . .
> YVONNE: (gently) How old are you?
> ANDRE: (hesitant, embarrassed) Twenty-one.
> YVONNE: (with all her allure) Will you take me home?

The second script, by Gene Markey, made Andre (Robert Montgomery) twenty-four, but he still took Yvonne (Greta Garbo) home. *Inspiration* and *The Easiest Way* opened a week apart. Before long, letters rolled in.

Father Daniel Lord wrote: "'The Easiest Way' made immorality alluring to young people before it reached its final lesson." Alice Ames Winter reviewed it: "Moral values swamped by attractive life portrayed." Wingate wrote Joy that it showed "alluring evils of life," and that both films were "too explicit in details." Harry Cohn, head of Columbia Pictures, wanted to know why M-G-M got the film Columbia had been denied. A local censor wrote Joy: "Yesterday we ran a picture called *The Easiest Way* that had been cut so badly to make it decent before it reached us that we had to stop in the middle of it because we thought we were looking at the wrong reels." Lamar Trotti summed it up: "We have a hell of a time, don't we?"

If the cycle had detractors, it had fans, too, and Constance Bennett did well by it. Within a year, she was "the queen of confession films." With *Born to Love, The Common Law*, and *Bought*, the sagacious Miss Bennett hopped from studio to studio, each of which added elements of her success to upcoming productions. M-G-M's *This Modern Age* has Joan Crawford learn that her mother, Pauline Frederick, is a kept woman. In Warner Bros.' *Five Star Final*, tabloid editor Edward G. Robinson dredges up a sex scandal and ruins four lives. In RKO's *Kept Husbands*, a rapacious rich girl (Dorothy Mackaill) marries a lanky laborer (Joel McCrea), and stops him from working. In Fox Film Corp.'s *The Brat*, an urchin played by Sally O'Neil declines a ride to a Long Island estate: "That's where they have them orgies an' seduction scenes!" In *Dance, Fools, Dance*, Joan Crawford has just such a party. With this film and *A Free Soul*, M-G-M added sex to gangster films and sealed their fate.

A Free Soul was Adela Rogers St. John's autobiographical story of a lawyer's daughter who has a tor-

In her first movie, the First Lady of Broadway was a tropical tramp: Helen Hayes in M-G-M's The Sin of Madelon Claudet. *Photograph by Charles Pollock.*

rid affair with her father's client, a gangster. When the film opened, it was hard to tell what was more eyebrow-raising, the plot or Norma Shearer's costumes. *Photoplay* said: "Her clothes are breathtaking in their daring. But you couldn't get away with them in your drawing room."

Jason Joy told M-G-M to cut a scene between Jan Ashe (Shearer) and Ace Wilfong (Clark Gable) "at the moment she extends her arms to him and lies back on the divan and Ace comes down beside her." Metro cut neither the scene nor her suggestive line: "C'mon. Put 'em around me." Wingate went wild, as evidenced by a telegram from M-G-M supervisor Bernard Hyman: "Eliminations they want would make continuity unclear. . . . If you can help us in this situation you will have the heartfelt gratitude of the Lion and me." Joy intervened, but the film popularized another gangster, so Will Hays appealed to the AMPP, and it imposed a moratorium on crime films.

The runaway success of M-G-M's *Trader Horn* added a new element to 1931 cycles. In it, an African expedition finds a half-naked "White Goddess" (Edwina Booth). As her wild deportment captured America's imagination, the studios turned vast backlots into exotic locales, and willing starlets into tropical tramps. Fox Film Corp.'s *Goldie* was the first in which a woman (Jean Harlow) was called a tramp, but it was not the first to exploit a shady lady in an alien clime. *Strangers May Kiss* had that distinction.

In Paramount's Dishonored, *Josef von Sternberg once again cast Marlene Dietrich as a lady of the streets.*

This project threatened to eclipse even *The Divorcee*. Jason Joy spent a Sunday in Santa Monica containing it: "Mr. Irving Thalberg telephoned and invited me to come to his house for the purpose of discussing with him, the director, and several writers, the story STRANGERS MAY KISS by Ursula Parrott." Joy purged the script of its heroine's most sensational speech: "This world wasn't made for moralists, Steve. You take what you want—if you can get it. You take it from people who have scruples and no brains."

Lisbeth (Norma Shearer) believes that a woman, like a man, "can love, and ride on." She tests her philosophy when Alan (Neil Hamilton), a fickle journalist, leaves her brokenhearted and unmarried in Mexico, then later castigates her for her "promiscuous" behavior. Jason Joy approved the film and counseled Thalberg to "vigorously oppose any major cuts, not only for the protection of this particular picture, but for the subsequent effect which such an attitude will have." The first attack came from within the SRC; Alice Ames Winter wrote: "I saw STRANGERS MAY KISS during the weekend and it would be difficult for me to exaggerate my revulsion at this picture and my sense of horror that our present set-up is permitting a product of this type to go through. This picture is a reflection of the initiatory stages of the degeneration of a people." Oddly, the only permanent cuts in *Strangers May Kiss* were occasioned by the Mexican consul, who protested that scenes of torpid natives were "derogatory to the customs of the Mexican nation."

A Central American dive was the most exotic setting in *Susan Lenox: Her Fall and Rise*, a Greta Garbo vehicle. Thanks to Jason Joy, this kept-woman film spent as much on retakes as it did on footage seen in theaters. Garbo blamed the studio for its inability to write a coherent story, and the studio blamed the Code. Thalberg learned his lesson. When director Edgar Selwyn sold his play *Mirage* to M-G-M, the studio changed its title to *Possessed* and ignored Jason Joy, who had not seen two-thirds of the scenarios filmed that year anyway. On October 8, 1931, Will Hays got the MPPDA to pass a resolution that made script submission compulsory, but *Possessed* got by.

George Fitzmaurice's *Mata Hari* also got under the wire and became M-G-M's biggest hit of the year, with a profit of nearly a million dollars. It was thick with exotic glamour—Garbo makes her entrance dancing in a Javanese costume before a statue of Shiva—and heavy with eroticism—two

The "kept-woman" cycle began with Constance Bennett and Adolphe Menjou in M-G-M's The Easiest Way.

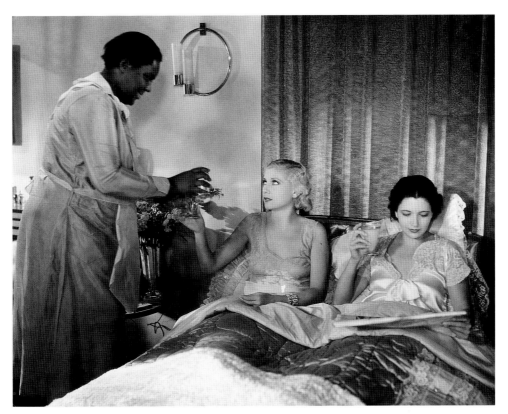

In Paramount's Girls About Town, *"escorts" Lilyan Tashman and Kay Francis are served breakfast by Louise Beavers at the scandalous hour of five P.M. Tashman's droll theatricality enlivened many pre-Code films. Photograph by Frank Bjerring.*

In Europe, American women who danced the tango (Norma Shearer, Strangers May Kiss) . . .

. . . were talked about by regular folks (Will Rogers, Ambassador Bill) . . .

. . . who were shocked by "sophistication" (Joan Crawford and Monroe Owsley, This Modern Age).

bedroom scenes with Ramon Novarro. In the first, she seduces him by coming from behind satin curtains, dressed in a diaphanous peignoir. Cinematographer William Daniels described the second: "She is seducing him and it's very romantic. I wanted to illuminate the whole scene with just the glow from his cigarette. . . . I had a dummy cigarette made with one of those medical bulbs in it, and I stuck the ashes on with glue . . . all you'd see was just one gleam."*

Earlier in the year, publisher-producer William Randolph Hearst had written to Hays: "Your advice and authority are made effective only because of the fear that producers have of getting into government difficulties. . . . Remove that fear of disaster and your department would not last as long as a drink of whiskey in Kentucky." By year's end, Hays was defending himself against an onslaught of criticism. A nondenominational religious journal called *The Christian Century* charged that "the three prominent Protestants—Messrs. Hays, [Carl E.] Milliken, and Joy—employed by the producers to man their office of public relations have no authority whatever to clean up a single film." James Wingate confirmed that the New York board had indeed made 1,000 more cuts than in 1930.

For reinforcement, Hays looked to Joseph I. Breen, who had proven himself a combative defender. When a Philadelphia priest had questioned the integrity of the International Federation of Catholic Alumnae, Breen had written him with the salutation "My dear Bozo" and the conclusion "I respectfully suggest that both yourself and Dr. Pace are fat-heads. I don't even hope that you are well. But I do hope that you get fired out of that soft job at the Seminary and have to go to work. I say,

again, that you are a fat-head." Breen had appealed to Hays in August: "The responsible heads of the studios are a cowardly lot. They are, too, an ignorant lot—in the sense that they don't know just what to do to clean the situation up." Breen had pitched the idea of finding a crusading administrator to make them tow the line. "We ought to try to get the best man in America to seriously take off his coat and go to work." He added: "Who that man is, I do not know." A few months later, and with some trepidation, Will Hays assigned Joe Breen to the SRC as director of public relations—and as a spy. What Hays did not know was that Breen would report his findings to the Midwest Catholics, too.

Jason Joy prepared Breen for the studio situation: "With crime practically denied them, with box-office figures down, with high pressure being employed back home to spur the studios on to get a little more cash, it was almost inevitable that sex, the nearest thing at hand and pretty generally surefire, should be seized on. It was." Nothing prepared the SRC for *Possessed.*

Lamar Trotti sent a telegram to Jason Joy: "My fear is we have another *Common Law* or *Strangers May Kiss* on our hands." Joy was incredulous. How had a kept-woman story gotten by them? "We didn't get a script on it," replied Trotti. "Mr. Thalberg was very understanding of our worry, but he holds that they have a perfect right to use the theme provided they do it with care." In deference, Thalberg cut these lines:

"I haven't anything to sell for pennies."
"All they have got is their brains and their bodies and they're not afraid to use them."
"Will sell her virtue to the highest bidder."

54

"And a yielding body."

"This bimbo's only a pick-up. He'll give me twenty bucks and then give his wife a bracelet."

Possessed was the artfully told story of Marian (Joan Crawford), a beautiful girl who works in a paper-box factory. When a train stops near her side of the tracks, Marian glimpses the enameled life she can never attain. A fey playboy, Wally (Skeets Gallagher), pours her a glass of champagne from the observation deck, gives her his card, and feigns shock when she crashes his Manhattan apartment. Once she decides that he is of no use to her, she goes after his friend, a wealthy politician named Mark Whitney (Clark Gable). Mark sets Marian up in a penthouse, educates her, and all is well until Marian wants to get married and Mark wants to get elected governor. With a minimum of "compensating moral values," Lenore Coffee's script saves Marian's honor and Mark's ballots. If Marian had been played by Constance Bennett, Loretta Young, or any of a dozen other players, the film would have gotten by the bluenoses, but Joan Crawford's films had begun to outgross Norma Shearer's, and Crawford became the more prominent target. Now Crawford was paired with Clark Gable, with whom she promptly fell in love. Their extramarital chemistry amplified the power of *Possessed.*

"You will be interested to hear the comment of two young girls sitting next to me when I previewed the picture," wrote Mrs. Alonzo Richardson, a member of the Atlanta Board of Review. "One said to the other, 'I would live with him too, under any conditions.' " A preview card from the same theater read: "What are the moral standards of writers and producers when they produce a picture of this tipe [sic]? The story is awful disgusting." Film critic

Photographer Milton Brown captured Greta Garbo and Robert Montgomery at dusk in the Bel Air Country Club, filming M-G-M's Inspiration.

Creighton Peet singled out Joan Crawford and Norma Shearer, laying at their feet the responsibility for "all modern thought in matters of morals and marriage" and saying that "school girls and serving maids will pay Metro hundreds of thousands of dollars to watch this film, and dream about it for days afterward." Daniel Lord charged that "Norma Shearer and Joan Crawford introduce our little girls to the 'romance' of kept women." Another critic wrote: "Norma Shearer's success was only mediocre until she came along as the reckless girl in 'Divorcee.' In every film since then . . . she has been ravishing and revealing, almost a torchbearer for the [single] standard. And the fans have flocked into her camp."

Perhaps in response to her critics, Norma Shearer gave Gladys Hall of *Motion Picture Magazine* a freely quoted interview. "Economic independence has put woman on exactly the same footing as man," said Shearer. "A woman today is good, or she is bad, according to the way she does a thing—and not because of the thing itself. An adventure may be worn as a muddy spot or it may be worn as a proud insignia. It is the woman wearing it who makes it the one thing or the other."

Father Daniel Lord warned the MPPDA that the SRC was wasting time on details and missing the larger picture. "Your authors have injected into the basic stories an underlying philosophy of life. The stories are now concerned with problems. They discuss morals, divorce, free love, unborn children, relationships outside of marriage, single and double standards, the relationship of sex to religion, marriage and its effects upon the freedom of women." Lord was emphatic: "These subjects are fundamentally dangerous." They were also profitable, as 1932 would prove.

56

A Mack Elliott portrait of Barbara Stanwyck
for Warner Bros.' Illicit.

Marlene Dietrich masquerades as a peasant
girl in Dishonored.

Lynn Fontanne models an Adrian creation
for M-G-M's The Guardsman.

A Hal Phyfe portrait of Sally O'Neil
as The Brat.

Joan Crawford personifies This Modern Age.
Photograph by George Hommel.

The Strangers May Kiss *souvenir program described
Norma Shearer's character as "The woman who was more than
a woman . . . one whose mind guided her love . . .
a superior creature whom strangers might kiss . . .
without fear of bondage!"*

"I'm in an orgy—wallowing—and I love it!" exclaims Norma Shearer to Robert Montgomery in M-G-M's Strangers May Kiss.

Hale Hamilton, Greta Garbo, and Clark Gable in a scene designed for Susan Lenox: Her Fall and Rise *by cinematographer William Daniels. Since most of the film was reshot, the scene exists only in this photograph by Milton Brown.*

60

Joan Crawford's performance as Sadie Thompson in Rain *should have been the pinnacle of her career (and a censor's field day),*
but Lewis Milestone's direction made the film a soggy flop. Photograph by John Miehle.

ART AND PROPRIETY

J anuary 1932 brought chills to Hollywood. M-G-M was insulated by a $12 million profit, but the eight other majors shivered with apprehension. They had reason. The Great Depression had worsened. Since 1929, weekly movie attendance had dropped from 10 million to 6 million. Warner Bros. posted losses of $7,918,604, and Fox Film more than $3 million. Universal Pictures laid off hundreds of employees. RKO-Radio Pictures went into receivership, its president, Merlin Aylesworth, predicting that the entire industry would be bankrupt in ninety days. When Paramount's profit margin plunged from $18 million to $6 million, it started selling off its theaters. A power struggle ousted sales chief Sidney R. Kent, who went to the Fox Film Corporation, leaving a sinking ship for a drifting one.

"Here's the shy Kentucky refugee!" says Sadie to the motley crew in Pago Pago.

Samuel Goldwyn was one of a handful of independent producers who released films through the United Artists Corporation (UA). He entered 1932 with a Zöe Akins play, *The Greeks Had a Word for It*, after persuading Joe Schenck, the head of UA: "It will really be different from anything attempted in Hollywood before by way of clothes, sets and women." It was the women who worried John Wilson of the SRC. There were three of them—Jean, Schatze, and Polaire—and their profession was unspecified. He wrote Schenck: "[If] the girls are portrayed as mere gold diggers who get all they can for nothing, it ought to be pretty clear that they are giving nothing and are essentially decent girls." Sam

Goldwyn changed the title to *The Greeks Had a Word for Them*, and Sidney Howard's script turned the "Three Musketeers of Riverside Drive" into showgirls, but their modus operandi remained the same.

At RKO, another single-minded producer tackled another Broadway success. David O. Selznick made no secret of his desire to produce "adult fare." He tried an exotic project, *Bird of Paradise*. Jason Joy tried to help him with the state boards, suggesting that a breast-feeding scene, native dance scenes (choreographed by Busby Berkeley), and Dolores Del Rio's nude swimming scene be cut. The Pennsylvania board cut a scene of Johnny (Joel McCrea) and a "small boy with Johnny's shirt on, standing with back to camera, when you see a shadow of his sex on the shirt."

More exotic movies came from RKO: *The Most Dangerous Game, Thirteen Women,* and *Panama Flo,* which featured Helen Twelvetrees as a Canal Zone dancer. Flo is laid off by a blonde-wigged old battle-ax called Sadie (Maude Eburne), who tells her performers: "If you gals wanta stick around the joint and pick up what you can from the customers, I have *no* objections." Another frustrated madam in a curly blonde wig could be glimpsed in Fox Film Corp.'s *While Paris Sleeps.* Madame Golden Bonnet (Lucille La Verne) dolls up innocent Manon (Helen Mack) for the leering patrons of her dive. The studio had neglected to submit the script for approval, so when the SRC saw it, alarms went off. Director Allan Dwan had to reshoot scenes showing Manon being gulled into "white slavery."

The taste for exotic tawdriness ended with UA's *Rain.* Will Hays okayed the infamous John Colton play after screenwriter Maxwell Anderson changed

Somerset Maugham's "Reverend Davidson" to a secular reformer, "Mr. Davidson" (Walter Huston). The real problem was transforming M-G-M's glamorous Joan Crawford into a sleazy Honolulu hooker, Sadie Thompson. Lewis Milestone rehearsed the cast to numbness, but his self-conscious camera movement botched the crucial scene in which the reformer bullies the hooker into praying. Milestone said: "I remember audiences greeting with a belly laugh a scene in which Huston pursued Crawford down a staircase while reciting the Lord's Prayer." The film that could have sparked a religious backlash was snuffed by Milestone's artistic pretensions.

At Universal, Carl Laemmle, Jr., cast Bela Lugosi as Doctor Mirakle in Robert Florey's *Murders in the Rue Morgue.* Admittedly not a horror fan, Jason Joy objected to a scene with a "Woman of the Streets," played by Arlene Francis: "Because the victim is a woman in this instance, which has not heretofore been the case in the other so-called 'horror' pictures recently produced, censor boards are very likely to think that this scene is overdone in gruesomeness. We therefore suggest . . . reducing the constant loud shrieking to lower moans and an occasional modified shriek." The film's discussion of evolution offended some censor boards more than Lugosi's torture scenes. Boris Karloff, meanwhile, was relegated to a low-budget film that had something to offend everyone. To conceal its lack of plot, *Night World* tacked on a series of gratuitous Code violations: suggestive dialogue, excessive drinking, racist caricatures, underwear shots, bathroom jokes, and even an effeminate man loitering seductively in the men's room.

Boris Karloff had a better showcase in James Whale's *The Old Dark House,* which was adapted by playwright Benn Levy from J. B. Priestley's novel *Benighted.* Whale's version was subtle enough to avoid censorship, but the ambisexual ambience of the "Femm" family was still there. Horace Femm

In Panama Flo, *another "Sadie" (Maude Eburne) responds to pleas for back pay: "Okay, kiddies. Sue me." Photograph by Elwood Bredell.*

(Ernest Thesiger) is a prissy skeleton. His sister Rebecca (Eva Moore) is an aged fanatic obsessed with rotting things. Their brutish servant, Morgan (Boris Karloff), jealously guards their cackling pyromaniac brother, Saul (Brember Wills). The weirdest sequence in the film has Rebecca unnerving a visitor, Margaret Waverton (Gloria Stuart): "You think of nothing but your long straight legs and your white body—and how to please your man. You revel in the joys of fleshly love, don't you? (Points to satin gown.) That's fine stuff, but it'll rot. (Points to Margaret's décolletage.) That's finer stuff still, but it'll rot too—in time!"

Universal's best horror film of the year was *The Mummy.* Its blend of sex and religion would have upset Daniel Lord, but it was cut severely before its release. John Balderston adapted a story called *Cagliostro* by Nina Wilcox Putnam and studio story editor Richard Schayer. Its premise was that love can last beyond death and through many incarnations. In the shooting script, now called *Im-ho-tep,* an Egyptian high priest is executed for the sacrilege of trying to revive a deceased vestal virgin, Anck-es-en-Amon, with whom he has had a forbidden love affair. The girl goes through a sequence of incarnations: a Saxon princess of the eighth century, a Christian martyr, a thirteenth-century noblewoman, and an eighteenth-century aristocrat. In 1922, an expedition digs up Im-ho-tep's mummified body, and a rash archaeologist reads the spell that revives him. Ten years later, the mummy, disguised as "Ardath Bey," finds his beloved in the form of a young Anglo-Egyptian woman, Helen Grosvenor. He plans to kill, mummify, and revive her with the same spell that had both doomed and immortalized him.

James Whale was busy with other things, so Junior Laemmle assigned cinematographer Karl Freund to direct the film. Freund was well suited to interpret this mystical tale, but he had little diplomacy. When he cast Zita Johann as the Egyptian girl

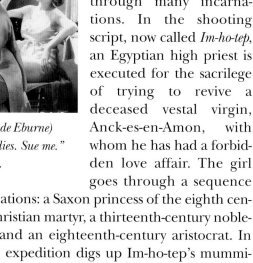

Geneva Mitchell, Mae Clarke, and Russell Hopton in a scene from Universal's Night World. *Photograph by Sherman Clark.*

Leslie Banks as Count Zaroff, who wrecks ships so he can hunt the survivors in RKO-Radio's The Most Dangerous Game. *Photograph by Gaston Longet.*

Doctor Mirakle (Bela Lugosi) rails at The Woman of the Street (Arlene Francis) in a gruesome scene from Universal's Murders in the Rue Morgue.

In ancient Egypt, a vestal virgin (Zita Johann) and a high priest (Boris Karloff) share a sacrilegious love; Universal's The Mummy *follows them through various incarnations. The setting was by Willy Pogany. Photograph by Fred Archer.*

Howard Hughes cast Paul Muni as a Borgia-like Scarface. *The usually diplomatic Jason Joy warned Hughes: "If you should be foolhardy enough to make* Scarface, *this office will make certain it is never released." Photograph by Eugene Kornman.*

and her modern incarnation, she invited him to dinner. Johann remembered: "Without a 'hello' or a name—his or mine—he said: 'In vone scene you haff to blay it from the vaist up—NOOD!' I believe he expected me to say: 'The hell I will!' Instead I said: 'Well, it's all right with me if you can get it past the censors.'" His bluff called, Freund made life difficult for the actress, who actually believed in reincarnation. She worked so many sixteen-hour days that she finally collapsed on the set. There was no nude scene, just transparent costumes and a love scene in the temple with Boris Karloff. If one mention of evolution could upset censors, what could a whole reincarnation sequence do? Junior Laemmle did not wait for angry letters; he cut the love scene and the reincarnation sequences, ostensibly to improve "the pace" of the film. Propriety had compromised another work of art.

BLOOD IN THE GUTTER

Father Daniel Lord watched Hollywood with alarm in 1932: "There rose on the horizon of the land a sinister figure by the name of Howard Hughes." In this city of arrogant, egotistical moguls, Howard Hughes was different. He was not Jewish, self-made, or sociable. He was twenty-six and he had millions of dollars, and nobody was going to tell him how to spend it. Having shocked Father Lord and Martin Quigley with brutal and tasteless films such as *Hell's Angels* and *Cock of the Air*, Hughes now ignored the ban on crime films. He hired director Howard Hawks, who with Ben Hecht wrote a script that turned the Capone family into the Borgias of Chicago, incest and all. According

Some of Scarface*'s graphic violence was indeed never released. The film itself was not seen from 1932 to 1980, when Universal, which acquired it following Hughes's death, released the longest available version.*

to Hughes biographer John Keats, the script "conveyed visions of illegal wealth, speed, lust, and violence, and wound up with blood in the gutter." It was simply called *Scarface*.

When Jason Joy read it, he did his best not to panic. He advised Will Hays that *Scarface* would be "the most harsh and frank gangster picture we ever had." When Howard Hughes ignored his letters, Joy got tough: "Under no circumstances is this film to be made. The American public and all conscientious State Boards of Censorship find mobsters and hoodlums repugnant. Gangsterism must not be mentioned in the cinema. If you should be foolhardy enough to make *Scarface*, this office will make certain it is never released." Howard Hughes sent a memo to Howard Hawks: "Screw the Hays Office. Start the picture and make it as realistic, as exciting, as grisly as possible." Hawks cast Paul Muni as Tony "Scarface" Camonte and did as he was told.

Two months later, Hughes tried a different approach with the SRC. He showed Joy a rough cut of *Scarface*. Joy made numerous suggestions. Surprisingly cooperative, Hughes reshot the ending of the film to show Camonte turning coward when deprived of his gun. Encouraged, Joy guessed that this second version would be passed by the state boards. Hughes, as was his wont, grew tired of conferences and went undercover. His publicity director, Lincoln Quarberg, took over and sent Joy to show the film to the boards. He showed it to all but James Wingate. This strategy, probably Will Hays's, had Joy return to Quarberg, pretending that Wingate would not pass the film. Joy then made Quarberg cut "inferences of incest" and hire uncredited technicians to shoot new sequences, including an ending in which Scarface goes to the gallows. After four months of knuckling under, Hughes got an unexpected reward: James Wingate rejected the film in total.

Quarberg wrote Hughes: "As you undoubtedly realize by now, the men who are actually running the picture business, including Will Hays and the Big-Shot Jews, particularly the M-G-M moguls, are secretly hoping you have made your last picture. They are jealous of your successful pictures, and have resented your independence, and your entrance into the industry from the start." As if to verify this, UA prepared a third version of the film.

The resilient Hughes had Quarberg arrange press screenings of the second version. The *Hollywood Reporter* called it "a masterpiece" and called the Hays Office "hysterical." On March 31, 1932, Hughes opened *Scarface* in New Orleans, which had a lax censor board. After the film got good press and attendance, Hughes retrieved all prints of the third version and tried to release the second version. The Ohio board passed the film, but others, including Pennsylvania and Chicago, did not. Hughes lashed out at the censor boards in a press release: "I am convinced that the determined opposition to SCARFACE is actuated by political motives." Hays pressured UA, and Schenck submitted the third version to Wingate—without Hughes's approval. In early May, Wingate approved it for exhibition in the state of New York. All this politicking did not go unnoticed. The *Christian Century* published an article, "Movie Censors Hear Their Master's Voice." It described the "grim determination of the industry to defeat the agencies which the public has set up to defend its children from vicious pictures."

In mid-May, after nearly six months of fighting, Hughes decided to open the third version in New York. It did well, but according to Hawks biographer Todd McCarthy, "discerning New York critics and viewers wanting to see the unexpurgated version merely crossed the Hudson River into New Jersey." Howard Hughes crossed the Los Angeles

River, opened Hughes Aircraft in Glendale, and turned his back on Hollywood.

THE FOX FILM CORPORATION

In 1932, a flickering star went to a faltering studio. Clara Bow had been off the screen for more than a year following a nervous breakdown. The "It Girl" was still in demand, but unsure where to make her comeback, she rejected Universal's *Impatient Maiden* and Goldwyn's *The Greeks Had a Word for Them.* When the Fox Film Corporation offered her $75,000 for one film, with approval of script, director, and cast, she accepted. The offer was an unusual one, but so was the studio.

The Fox Film Corporation spared no adjective in the ad campaign for Call Her Savage.

Its president was another Paramount refugee, Sidney R. Kent, an ex-boiler stoker whom Darryl Zanuck characterized as "an absolutely honest man." Its production chief was cofounder Winfield Sheehan, "a good discoverer of talent." Fox's stars included Janet Gaynor, Will Rogers, and Warner Baxter. Directing them were such talents as John Ford, Frank Borzage, and Raoul Walsh. They all labored in "Movietone City," ninety-six acres of Art Deco soundstages and virgin backlots in the "Westwood Hills" (which were flat). "Winnie" Sheehan's daily arrival at the facility was heralded by guards who stood at attention and saluted him. For Clara Bow's comeback film, he reopened the old "Fox Hills" studio at Sunset and Western in Hollywood (also flat), and assigned studio manager Sol Wurtzel to run it.

Director Erich von Stroheim described Sol Wurtzel as "a lowbrow if there ever was one." Shirley Temple said that he reminded her of "Reynard the Fox, with his arrowhead face, broad across the top, narrow at the bottom, with big, expressionless eyes, and a long, sharp nose." In 1932, Wurtzel gave Budd Schulberg, son of Paramount's B. P. Schulberg, a pointed lecture: "To hell with unhappy endings, offbeat material. I hear these directors bitching about what they really wanna make. Fuck 'em. What they wanna make, maybe five thousand highbrows in the whole country will pay their four bits t' see. I don't give a shit about art."

Wurtzel was obviously criticizing his own studio's output. Since the ouster of William Fox, it had no clear-cut image. One reason for its lack of identity was the failure of Kent and Sheehan to work as a team. "Fox in the early 1930s lacked positive studio leadership and a clearly defined policy," wrote film historian William K. Everson. "Offbeat, basically uncommercial properties slipped through because there was, in essence, no one to stop them." Darryl Zanuck was more blunt: "Fox had the best distribution organization in the business—and the worst films." Even so, five of them grossed a million dollars in 1931.

In 1932, the studio released forty films. Many were quality projects, including Raoul Walsh's *Me and My Gal,* William Cameron Menzies and Marcel Varnel's *Chandu the Magician,* and William K. Howard's *Sherlock Holmes.* William Dieterle's imaginative, compelling *Six Hours to Live* ran into trouble with the SRC because it depicted an international trade convention more interested in graft than commerce. Jason Joy advised against undermining the public's respect for disarmament conferences. His concern was valid. Fox Film told foreign stories with authority. Its huge sets and backlot gave its films an almost documentary quality. Still evident were the extravagance and German expressionism of its silent films. Fox Film ignored the Depression, releasing tasteful, costly fare.

The studio also released exploitative films such as Sidney Lanfield's *Hat Check Girl.* Maurine Watkins's script described this setting:

> OPEN WITH HOT MUSIC . . . atmosphere and character of the Embassy Club . . . colored orchestra in agonizing ecstasy . . . floor show of high-yaller girls in back-to-Africa dance . . . at a corner table sit three college kids, well under way, and a couple of cuties, one of whom slumps across the table as a flask drops to the floor unheeded . . . at another table, an elderly, bankerish gentleman is paying a check of $60.00 and gazing lasciviously into the gaping bodice of a young girl with innocent bangs

and false eyelashes. He thinks he's getting a lot for his money, but the coolly appraising gaze of that professional virgin indicates he hasn't *started* to pay!

Hat-check girls Sally Eilers and Ginger Rogers, besides braving this milieu, had to undress at regular intervals, without any plot motivation. When Jason Joy saw the film, it was too late to reshoot these scenes. He wrote: "It is becoming more and more general for directors to 'dress up' such dialogue scenes by undressing the women participants." Fox Film paid no attention; it was spending a quarter of a million dollars on Clara Bow, and it was not going to put her in coveralls. M-G-M was enjoying success with *Red-Headed Woman,* and MPPDA secretary Carl E. Milliken wrote to Joy: "Fox [is] strongly tempted to do something similar."

For Bow's comeback vehicle, Fox Film submitted the Tiffany Thayer novel *Call Her Savage,* a book that any other studio would have dropped with singed fingers. Jason Joy wrote to Hays: "The book is about as far wrong as it is possible to be." Besides having such elements as incest, masturbation, transvestism, and venereal disease, the book was patently racist, blaming its heroine's personality problems on her Native American blood. Thayer averred that "the background and local color, and some of the incidents, were all based on the life of my wife, who was a resident of Texas and is one-half Osage Indian." Independent producer Sam Rork bought the book for Bow, and sold it to Fox Film, who "took most of the real flavor of the story out of the first treatment, with the result that only another stupid picture was in prospect," said Joy. "Somewhere in between there lies a good film." Rork and producer Al Rockett worked with screenwriter Edwin Burke to find it.

The approved version was still pungent. In it, Nasa Springer (Clara Bow) is the tempestuous daughter of a rich Texas rancher (Willard Robertson). She does not know that her real father was an "Injun" (Weldon Heyburn) who killed himself after her mother (Estelle Taylor) gave him up. Nasa's temper propels her through a series of imbroglios that end only when she learns the truth about herself at her mother's deathbed. She resigns herself to a quiet life with Moonglow (Gilbert Roland), a "half-breed" who works for her father. Lamentable

TOP:
Clara Bow as Nasa "Dynamite" Springer in Call Her Savage.

CENTER:
Larry Crosby (Monroe Owsley) informs Sunny DuLane (Thelma Todd) that he is moving out, then knocks her down. "You'll be back," she responds. "I understand your little peculiarities."

BOTTOM:
Nasa returns from the street to find her baby dead in a fire and an old friend, Moonglow (Gilbert Roland), waiting with news of an inheritance. "I'll get even with life," she says. This is one of the powerful images created by cinematographer Lee Garmes.

OPPOSITE:
Thelma Todd gives a wickedly funny performance in Call Her Savage.

After her millionaire boyfriend calls her a savage, Nasa spends a drunken Art Deco evening.
Lighting by Lee Garmes, on-the-set photograph by Max Munn Autrey.

Clara Bow embodies "sin in soft focus" in this Max Munn Autrey portrait.

though it was, the plot gave Bow what most actors crave, a role with multiple identities. In one fast-paced film, Bow plays a wild teenager, an impulsive debutante, a jilted newlywed, a thrill-seeking party girl, a young mother, a prostitute, an aloof society gal, a slumming brawler, a sexy drunk, and a repentant daughter.

Jason Joy sent a letter to each state board: "Because it is a new Clara Bow that the screen is presenting . . . we are all very hopeful that the picture will be judged as a whole for the character study that it is, all parts of which inter-link importantly." In *Call Her Savage*, Fox mounted more titillating scenes than Paramount, more production value than M-G-M, and more topicality than Warner Bros. What it forgot was taste. The *Los Angeles Times* said: "*Call Her Savage* has been condemned by the more discriminating as a flashy, trashy, tasteless and unpleasant exhibit, but not even the most captious deny its superficial appeal to the larger public." In the winter of 1932, with 20 percent of theaters closed, *Call Her Savage* only made a profit of $17,407.

THE WARNERS GRIT

In 1932, Warner Bros. stayed afloat by making fifty films as quickly and as cheaply as possible. Jack Warner made a weekly inspection of the studio's 135 acres with Darryl Zanuck, earmarking used sets as the basis for new films. The studio spent the minimum on literary properties; Zanuck's policy was to wrest scenarios from newsprint: "[A scenario] . . . must have the punch and smash that would entitle it to be a headline on the front page of any successful metropolitan daily." Supervisor Robert Lord said that the only rule at the studio was: "Don't bore the audience: anything goes as long as it's entertaining and interesting."

William Dieterle's *Scarlet Dawn* was the story of a licentious young baron (Douglas Fairbanks, Jr.) caught in the Russian Revolution. The film opens with Baron Nikita's off-duty revelry, which includes a visit to his mistress, Vera Zimina (Lilyan Tashman). Fairbanks recalled the filming: "Lilyan Tashman [and I] had a torrid love scene to do. Dieterle would not let us go to lunch until the scene was finally concluded—about two hours later. His theory was that one could not and should not make love on a full stomach." The SRC cut part of the scene. Zanuck was incensed: "I want to go officially on record now as saying that we have less eliminations and less cuts made by the censorship boards than any other company in the business. We have never violated the Code at any time in any picture and we have never produced a condemned or barred novel or play, either in the open or by subterfuge, or by alteration of title."

This was technically true, because the studio did not spend money on hit plays or novels; the stories it developed from cheap properties or original stories, however, were sufficiently spicy. In *The Rich Are Always with Us*, Ruth Chatterton confronts the Other Woman: "Sex attraction and sex congeniality are two entirely different things. Perhaps you've already found that out. I neither know nor want to know." In *Blessed Event*, veteran actress Emma Dunn says: "Well, I'll be damned!" In the fast-moving Lee Tracy vehicle *The Strange Love of Molly Louvain*, he calls Ann Dvorak a tramp repeatedly, and a dance-hall girl tells a customer that a former dancer "and another dame got an apartment over on Thirty-eighth Street and they're doin' *all right*."

Specializing in raw urban melodramas, Warner Bros. soon established itself as the fastest-moving studio, prompting the rumor that Michael Curtiz and William Dieterle sometimes cut one frame from every shot in a film to tighten its pace. Actors had to be fast to keep up, and few were faster than Warren William, who came out of nowhere and quickly became the house seducer, exerting his oleaginous charms in *Under Eighteen, Beauty and the Boss, The Dark Horse,* and *The Match King*. Mervyn LeRoy's *Three on a Match* was the quintessential Warner Bros. film of 1932, cramming headlines, history, sociology, sex, alcohol, drugs, adultery, kidnapping, blackmail, and suicide into sixty-three busy minutes, as well as Joan Blondell, Ann Dvorak, Bette Davis, Humphrey Bogart, Glenda Farrell, Allen Jenkins, Lyle Talbot, and, of course, Warren William. Zanuck felt that *Three on a Match* could be a "box-office knockout" if the SRC allowed kidnapping scenes, because they showed that "kidnapping is a very unhealthy occupation from which nothing comes but misery, grief and no reward whatsoever." The SRC concurred and passed *Three on a Match*, along with *Union Depot, They Call It Sin, Play Girl, Week End Marriage, The Purchase Price,* and *Doctor X*. It also passed the violent Cagney

Joan Blondell (left) takes Buster Phelps away from his neglectful mother, Ann Dvorak, in Warner Bros.'
Three on a Match. *This scene was trimmed to preserve the film's frantic pace.*

After a series of flops at Paramount, Tallulah Bankhead gave Hollywood one last try. In M-G-M's Faithless,
she played both a kept woman and a fallen woman, then returned to Broadway. Faithless *was a hit, thanks in part to
the M-G-M glamour treatment, evident in this portrait by C. S. Bull.*

film *Taxi* and the grim Robinson film *Two Seconds*.

Warner's biggest problem of the year was *I Am a Fugitive from a Chain Gang*, which starred Paul Muni as real-life fugitive Robert E. Burns, who slipped into the studio under an alias to advise Zanuck. Mervyn LeRoy's film was a harrowing indictment of the Georgia penal system. Jason Joy tried to make him blur the film's locale and cut flogging scenes, for fear of offending the Old South: "While it may be true that the systems are wrong, I very much doubt if it is our business as an entertainment force to clear it up." The scenes remained, and Georgia sued Warner. The case was settled out of court, and Georgia finally removed chains from its prisoners. The film made money, but by the end of 1932, Warner Bros. had lost $14,095,054.

Meanwhile, MPPDA publicist Joseph Breen stood on the sidelines, recording every detail of the Hollywood scene.

THE M-G-M GLOSS

In the early twentieth century, Catholic schools taught students that "the Jews" were responsible for the death of Jesus. They did not differentiate between biblical Pharisees and Hollywood producers. Neither did Joe Breen. His confidential reports to the Midwest Catholics were rife with anti-Semitism. In a letter to Father Wilfred Parsons, editor of *America*, he slammed Will Hays for believing that "these lousy Jews will abide by the Code's provisions." He went on to say: "These Jews seem to think of nothing but money making and sexual indulgence. The vilest kind of sin is a common indulgence hereabouts and the men and women who engage in this sort of business are the men and women who decide what the film fare of the nation is to be." His reports to Hays omitted bigotry in favor of "business":

One very prominent lady star told a group of correspondents who were interviewing her that she is a lesbian. . . . The head of a prominent studio was caught in bed fornicating with his neighbor's wife by his own wife, who came into the room, revolver in hand, and failed to kill both of the bed-fellows simply because, in her excitement, she failed to quickly unfasten the lock on the pistol. . . . Name cards at [a

birthday] dinner were condrums [sic] for the men and cotex [sic], on which was a dash of ketchup, for the women. . . . A studio head whom you and I know personally very well is just now the laugh of the town because of his conspicuous and public liaison with a star who is reputed to be the most notorious pervert in all Hollywood. And so it goes.

Breen's moral indignation found an obvious target, which he confided to Parsons: "Ninety-five percent of these folks are Jews of an Eastern European lineage. They are, probably, the scum of the earth." Irving Thalberg was of German-Jewish descent and sensitive to the undercurrents of anti-Semitism in the American press. A fan magazine interviewer said to him: "Mr. Thalberg, I realize that you are of the new order in films—a young man with ideals."

"If you mean that I think I'm superior to the so-called cloak and shoe and glove manufacturers who have really given their lives and their pocketbooks to this business in order to allow us something to build on, why then, you are wrong. I respect them very much. They had ideals also."

The successes of 1931 allowed Thalberg to act on his ideals. He believed that the box office, not the Hays Office, decided what was suitable for the American public. In 1932, Metro presented the most diverse catalogue of entertainment in its eight-year history. Thalberg could take credit for this. His taste ran to adult subjects, to explorations of human nature and abnormal psychology.

His first hit of the year was also the first "all-star" film. *Grand Hotel* featured John and Lionel Barrymore, Joan Crawford, Greta Garbo, and Wallace Beery. In the opening scene, Doctor Otternschlag (Lewis Stone) tells the audience: "Grand Hotel. People coming, going. Nothing ever happens." A lot happens, but not to him, because he has been ruined by the Great War. "A grenade in my face. Diphtheria bacilli in the wound until 1920. Isolation for two years." Now he wanders the hotel, his face hideously scarred, waiting for mail that never comes, counseling shabby, pathetic Otto Kringelein (Lionel Barrymore): "Believe me, Mr. Kringelein, a man who is not with a woman is a dead man."

Grand Hotel's theme is that money destroys relationships. Baron von Gaigern (John Barrymore) tries to steal Grusinskaya's (Garbo) pearls, then

George Hurrell's portraits of Billie Dove for Blondie of the Follies *caused a Chicago censor to write Jason Joy: "I'm determined to see Dove's dress of beads!"*

relents when she is about to commit suicide. He comforts her, then sleeps with her. Meanwhile, he has spurned "stenographress" Flaemmchen (Joan Crawford), who decides to become the mistress of vulgar industrialist Preysing (Wallace Beery). Before she can sleep with him, a burglar distracts him. It is the Baron, trying to raise money so he can leave for a new life with Grusinskaya. Preysing kills the Baron with a telephone. Flaemmchen finds the body and runs into the hotel corridor.

Edmund Goulding, who directed the film, was probably one of the "perverts" Breen mentioned. "Eddie" was too careless to cover his indiscreet drinking, drug-taking, and homosexuality, and too absent-minded to remember the dazzling ideas he devised, so Thalberg had them transcribed. This excerpt is from the murder scene: "Flaemmchen looks this way and that. After all, it is Flaemmchen and not Lillian Gish running across the ice in 'Way Down East'—it is Flaemmchen, the Berlin girl. She pauses to try and clear her brain. 'What the hell is this—what is it?' The impulse naturally is to

scream in alarm. She doesn't—Flaemmchens don't."

Grand Hotel was convincing because of the way it handled its adult themes. During an early story conference, Thalberg told Goulding how to rewrite the scene of the Baron watching Grusinskaya undressing: "When he's on a sex thing, he's perfectly within his rights. When he has seen a naked woman, he can suddenly, very honestly, have a sex desire come over him. . . .Why does a man want one woman and another man [want] another? That's the kick of it, God damn it!" Jason Joy's reaction to the script was positive: "I know the picture will be great." He suggested removing eight lines, one of which was: "By the way, are you looking for a woman? You'll get what you're looking for—a masculine paradise—drink, women, dancing." Scenarist Hans Kraly cut the lines. As Thalberg had hoped, *Grand Hotel* was "full of life, a painted carpet upon which the figures walk." It was also a huge financial success.

The other blockbuster of the year was as far from the Berlin hotel as the jungles of Africa. The studio's answer to its own *Trader Horn* was W. S. Van Dyke's *Tarzan the Ape Man*, which proposed that a hero raised by apes was morally superior to civilized

George Hurrell's portraits of Joan Crawford for Grand Hotel *caught the spirit of a "stenographress" who did more than take dictation.*

profiteers. Johnny Weissmuller's Tarzan wrestled with alligators, killed natives, and met Jane Parker (Maureen O'Sullivan). O'Sullivan remembered: "It was a man who'd never seen a woman before. He didn't know what it was when he found her. Was it a monkey? He didn't know what to do with a woman. I guess he found out pretty quickly. It was a lovely, innocent concept, and yet very sexy." Thanks to the SRC, Tarzan and Jane got to live together at the fade-out.

In Clarence Brown's *Letty Lynton*, Joan Crawford got away with murder. It was excused by a woman's need to defend her honor, even if she had tossed it overboard many reels earlier. If Letty Lynton was immoral, the provenance of her story was equally dubious. M-G-M had first tried to buy Edward Sheldon's play, *Dishonored Lady*, which was based on the case of Madeleine Smith, the so-called Edinburgh poisoner, but the Hays Office said the play could never be adapted, due to its "lubricious" title. The studio then bought the novel *Letty Lynton* by Marie Belloc Lowndes. In the process of adaptation, its plot somehow came to resemble the unavailable Sheldon play.* Jason Joy warned M-G-M of the sim-

In Letty Lynton, *Joan Crawford was for once not playing a shopgirl on the rise. Letty is a spoiled rich girl enslaved by an oily* homme fatal *(Nils Asther). Photograph by Sam Manatt.*

ilarities between the script and the play: "The woman in both has affairs because of the sex urge, not out of love." Confirming Daniel Lord's concern, the film did not violate the Code in dialogue or costume, but in its "underlying philosophy of life."

Leticia Lynton, a sex-beset sophisticate, is enslaved by a sloe-eyed *homme fatal*, Emile Renaul (Nils Asther). Letty decides to kill herself because Emile plans to stop her from marrying wholesome Jerry Darrow (Robert Montgomery). She prepares poison, but Emile drinks it instead; of course, she doesn't stop him. At the inquest, she is accused of murder. Jerry saves her by saying that because he spent the night with her, and because he knew of her past, she had no motive. British censors would not pass the film because it "justified homicide without penalty." Angry letters appeared in newspapers such as the *Pittsburgh Press*: "The wicked prosecuting attorney is foiled by a parcel of lies . . . and the M-G-M lion yawns a benign blessing upon the impending nuptials. This talkie is typical of the

Still photographer Fred Archer made this famous portrait of Greta Garbo and John Barrymore on the set of Grand Hotel. *(The photograph is usually misattributed to George Hurrell.)*

case against Hollywood's concept of morals." Lamar Trotti wrote to Will Hays that "most of the M-G-M pictures have escaped drastic censorship action in this country because of the very fine manner in which the alleged dubious themes are handled." These themes made money, so Thalberg persisted with them.

His next film had an inside joke. *Blondie of the Follies* was the story of a cheerful New York girl whom the Ziegfeld Follies leads to an oil magnate. Playing Blondie was Marion Davies, the cheerful New York girl whom the Follies had led to newspaper magnate William Randolph Hearst—the producer of the film.

At a story conference, Edmund Goulding told Thalberg: "I want to soft-pedal it if we can. But you do know she is kept. Murchison [the oil magnate, played by Douglas Dumbrille] is after Blondie. He's

a climber. He's a Joe Kennedy. She's a chicken. He's definitely after her." Goulding also wanted to have transvestites in the film. He was a habitué of the popular Ship's Cafe in Venice, California. One of its attractions was a drag act starring the Rocky Twins. Goulding wanted to use it in the Follies setting: "We have a very funny routine worked out with Blondie and the Rocky Twins. The act is that the boys are dressed up in skirts and so forth to look like girls. Marion is the gendarme and comes on the scene to stop an argument."

The bilateral gender-bending was no doubt conceived to honor William Randolph Hearst's requirement that every Marion Davies film feature a sequence in which Davies could don men's clothes. The Rocky Twins idea never materialized. They performed more conventional chorus boy routines, but Davies got to satisfy Hearst. She and

The Mask of Fu Manchu *presented Boris Karloff as a Chinese megalomaniac on a crusade to* "kill the white man and mate with his women!" *If this was not bad enough, the film also had Myrna Loy as his "ugly and insignificant daughter." Photograph by C. S. Bull.*

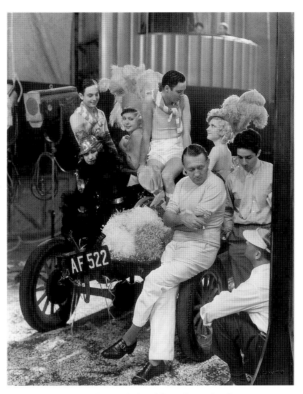

*Director Edmund Goulding brought the gay
nightlife of Hollywood to* Blondie of the Follies; *behind
him are the notorious Rocky Twins.*

In Kongo, *Virginia Bruce (left) shrinks from a
drugged-out voodoo party whose participants include Lupe
Velez and Conrad Nagel.*

her best friend, Lurline (Billie Dove), fall off a yacht, and Blondie replaces her wet clothes with a captain's uniform.

For his next project, *Rasputin,* Thalberg snatched an idea from RKO's David O. Selznick: why not star three Barrymores in one movie? This would be pure showmanship, "like a circus with three white whales," as John Barrymore put it. The analogy proved true, for Ethel, Lionel, and John were as cranky as albino leviathans after waiting two months for a finished script. It was not ready because the SRC had warned that the first six drafts made the Romanovs look stupid and unsympathetic. Ethel charged into Thalberg's office to recommend the man best qualified to write the fall of the House of Romanov, then rushed to Charles MacArthur's house and threw furniture at him until he submitted.

MacArthur could not understand Thalberg's revisions. "The Romanovs kicked your people around for three hundred years. Now you're trying to make a hero out of that stupid Nicholas."

"The tsarina was the granddaughter of Queen Victoria," said Thalberg. "Fifty percent of our foreign receipts come from England. I am not going to risk harming our foreign market because I'm a Jew. It wouldn't be fair to the stockholders."

MacArthur concentrated on Rasputin, creating the most licentious character ever written for an M-G-M film, a crude, lip-smacking lecher. When Joy saw the film, he immediately urged cuts. Because the film's cost would be further bloated by inevitable censorship problems, Thalberg agreed. Gone was John's line to Lionel: "I'm not interested in your anatomy." Also cut was a sequence that takes place in Rasputin's St. Petersburg lair (faithfully re-created by art director Alexander Toluboff, even to its flowered wallpaper pattern). In it, Rasputin's demented, scantily clad female disciples are shown to be living with him.

The assassination scene was a problem. This was to be the reward for all of Rasputin's sins. In a radical departure from history, MacArthur had contrived to have the Prince (John) murder Rasputin (Lionel) alone, and had him saying: "Die, you wallowing hog! You unclean horror! You belching swill!" Joy drew a blue pencil through most of this but hardly diluted the horror of the scene. After using the poker to knock Lionel down, John had to beat him and beat him—and beat him. At one point, John turned away and spat out a glob of vomit. Joy cut most of the beating but left everything else. What remained was more scary than what was cut. Cecil Holland's makeup was so grisly that the still man was not allowed to shoot it.

After being poisoned, beaten, and bludgeoned, the satanic Rasputin is dead. Or is he? The Prince, escaping Rasputin's disciples, looks over his shoulder to see the mad monk rise from the floor, his face caked with blood and brains. He staggers forward, muttering in a sepulchral voice, "Babylon has fallen . . . *fallen!* The great Day of Wrath is coming . . . the Tsar, Aloysha, all of them will go! You'll see their bodies, lying in the snow."

John Barrymore, eyes bugging, crosses himself and screams: "Get back in hell!" He throws Lionel in the Neva River, cursing: "Anti-Christ! Drown in the lake of hell! *Anti-Christ!*" Exhaling backlit bubbles, Rasputin finally expires.

Thalberg borrowed Boris Karloff from Universal to create more horrors. The *Mask of Fu Manchu* presented Karloff as a Chinese megalomaniac on a crusade to "kill the white man and mate with his women!" If this was not bad enough, the film also had Myrna Loy as his "ugly and insignificant daughter." Vexing to both the SRC and Loy was the daughter's character. Loy protested: "I've done a lot of terrible things in films, but this girl's a sadistic nymphomaniac!" In one scene she has handsome hero Terry Granville (Charles Starrett) stripped to the waist and whipped, as she cries out for him to be whipped "faster, faster, faster!" In another scene, Loy asks Karloff about the drugged, supine, half-naked Starrett: "He is not entirely unhandsome, is he, my father?"

"For a white man, no," Karloff replies somberly.

The Mask of Fu Manchu resonates with racial slurs. "A Chinaman beat me?" asks Jean Hersholt. "He couldn't do it!" Lewis Stone asks: "Will we ever understand these Eastern races? Will we ever learn anything?" Karen Morley shrieks at Karloff: "You hideous yellow monster!" According to M-G-M assistant editor Chester W. Schaeffer, the Chinese consulate requested a screening of *The Mask of Fu Manchu.* Schaeffer had to report to work on a Sunday and hastily remove offensive lines. When the consul saw the edited print, he didn't realize what the frequent "bup" of splices meant. At New York's Capitol Theater, the film's excesses drew laughs, but no one complained, and it was profitable.

William Cowen's *Kongo* was another exercise in perversity. It told the grim tale of "Deadlegs" Flint (Walter Huston), crippled ruler of a planting empire deep in the African jungle. Huston, re-creating his stage role, portrays a demented, sadistic man plotting revenge against another planter. C. Henry Gordon plays Gregg, the man sought by Flint, "the man who stole my wife. The man who kicked my spine in. The man who sneered! (He throws his crutch.) *That's* what he made me! Half a man! You *are* flesh and blood, Gregg! Degraded! Polluted! Her name smoldering from the Cameroons to Zanzibar!"

Flint's scheme pulls Gregg's daughter, Ann (Virginia Bruce), out of a convent and into a brothel. "There was a 'house,'" she relates. "From a convent to a house in Zanzibar . . . I 'graduated.'" Flint makes Ann an alcoholic, fever-ridden prisoner. A bleary-eyed doctor, Kingston (Conrad Nagel), staggers into Flint's preserve: "You've been chewing on the Byang root," says Flint. "You're a 'dope.'"

Kingston replies: "Well, what if I am? A man's gotta have something." Kingston tries to befriend Ann. She derides him, then softens: "You're a friendly fool. And that's something new. Maybe the rest of it won't be . . . *ugly.*"

The rest of the film is very ugly, with juju rituals and drugged orgies. When Flint's Portuguese mistress, Tula (Lupe Velez), lies to him, he threatens to wrap a wire around her tongue. She has already been sleeping with every male on the compound; even Flint's pet ape "Kong" hops on her regularly. Despite its grimness, *Kongo* was a success.

Kongo was not the studio's most horrifying film of 1932. Thalberg summoned writer Willis Goldbeck and told him to write a vehicle for Tod Browning, who had returned to M-G-M after the success of *Dracula*. Thalberg asked for something "even more horrible" than *Dracula* or *Frankenstein*. As was usual at M-G-M, Goldbeck's work merged with that of several others. Thalberg read it, and according to Goldbeck: "He looked at me sadly, shook his head and sighed, 'Well, it's horrible.'" He put the film into production, bringing real sideshow freaks onto the lot. There was an immediate outcry from the rest of the studio. "People run out of the commissary and throw up," complained supervisor Harry Rapf. Thalberg refused to shut the film down, saying, "If it's a mistake, I'll take the blame."

In *Freaks*, Thalberg and Browning created a world even more self-contained than that of *Grand Hotel, Kongo*, or *Rasputin. Freaks* inhabits the garish, warped world of the circus sideshow, complete with bearded lady, human skeleton, simpering pinheads, Siamese twins, a hermaphrodite named Josephine Joseph ("Don't get her sore—or *he'll* bust you in the nose!"), and an armless, legless man. The hero is a midget named Hans (Harry Earles). The villain is a narcissistic strongman, Hercules (Henry Victor), who plots with vain acrobat Cleopatra (Olga Baclanova) to murder the frugal midget—after she marries him. In the film's prologue, a barker (Murray Kinnell) sets the stage for tragedy: "We didn't lie to you, folks. We told you we had living, breathing monstrosities. You laughed at them. Shuddered at them. And yet, but for the accident of birth . . . you might be even as they are. They did not ask to be brought into the world, but into the world they came. Their code is a law unto themselves. *Offend one and you offend them all!*"

At her wedding feast, Cleopatra insults the sideshow family after they try to initiate her: "Dirty, slimy—*freaks!* Make *me* one of you, will you?!" When they see her poisoning Hans, the jig is up. During a horrendous storm, they track down her and Hercules. We see the freaks crawling through rain and mud, and, if they have no arms or legs, their knives are clenched between their teeth.

According to M-G-M art director Merrill Pye, when the film was previewed in an outlying district of Los Angeles, Thalberg knew they were in trouble: "Halfway through the preview, a lot of people got up and ran out. They didn't walk out. They *ran* out." Thalberg cut twenty-five minutes from the film. *Freaks* premiered in Los Angeles, where word of mouth killed it after two weeks. Patrons in Atlanta never got a chance to decide, thanks to Mrs. Alonzo Richardson of the Atlanta Board of Review, who labeled *Freaks* "loathsome, obscene, grotesque, and bizarre." Her board banned it, as did those in San Francisco and Great Britain; all this after a happy ending had been substituted. M-G-M pulled *Freaks* from circulation. It lost $158,607.

Two of the forty films that Irving Thalberg shepherded in 1932 starred his wife, Norma Shearer. *Strange Interlude* wowed audiences with its daringly modern theme of a woman who has a child by a man other than her husband to keep insanity out of the child's blood. Sidney Franklin's *Smilin' Through* was a sentimental change of pace for the

Greta Garbo submits to sadistic Erich von Stroheim in As You Desire Me.
Photograph by Milton Brown.

The sensitivity of W. S. Van Dyke's direction gave Tarzan the Ape Man's
lovemaking a fairy-tale quality. Photograph by Clifton L. Kling.

Conrad Nagel and Virginia Bruce find romance in the hellish jungle plantation of
Kongo; *lighting by Hal Rosson.*

Thelma Todd was a stylishly ubiquitous figure in pre-Code films; this is an
uncredited portrait from Speak Easily.

Superficial Carol Morgan (Tallulah Bankhead) is mesmerized by the roulette wheel in Faithless.

In The Mask of Fu Manchu, *the evil Fu (Boris Karloff) bedevils Sir Nayland Smith (Lewis Stone) with the image of Fu's nymphomaniac daughter (Myrna Loy) ravishing clean-cut Terry (Charles Starrett). Miscegenation was not allowed by the Code, so the scene was discarded.*

Norma Shearer was M-G-M's most daring star, whether for her transparent gowns or her willingness to age onscreen. She is seen here with Ralph Morgan in Strange Interlude. *Photograph by William Grimes.*

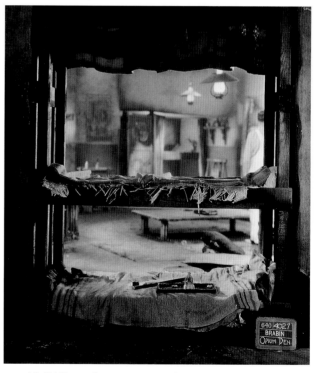

M-G-M's set decorators meticulously created an opium den for The Mask of Fu Manchu.

Rasputin and the Empress *was the first (and only) teaming of the Royal Family of Broadway, John, Ethel, and Lionel Barrymore; Lionel stole the show. Photograph by Milton Brown.*

torchbearer of the single standard, but even it defied the Code. As Shearer's sweetheart departs for the Front, she sits on a running board with him, imploring him to sleep with her first. Shearer's drawing power made massive hits of both films, but both she and Joan Crawford had a new rival on the lot.

SEEING "RED"

Howard Hughes had made Jean Harlow a celebrity, but did not know how to make her a star. M-G-M wanted to. Lewis Milestone advised Hughes: "She hasn't the slightest idea about acting. She has a wonderful body, a ridiculous head, and $60,000 is much more than you have a right to expect for her contract. Sell it." On April 20, 1932, Metro got Harlow—for $30,000.

After inquiring how she "made out with Howard Hughes," Irving Thalberg asked Harlow, "Do you think you can make an audience laugh?"

"*With* me or *at* me?"

"*At* you."

"Why not? People have been laughing at me all my life."

Harlow's claim to fame was her platinum blonde hair, so Thalberg cast her as the *Red-Headed Woman*. While supervisor Paul Bern worked with director Jack Conway to improve Harlow's acting, Thalberg worked with Anita Loos on the script, instructing her to "make fun of its sex element, just as you did in *Gentlemen Prefer Blondes*." In her script, "Lil," a.k.a. "Red," an amoral girl from the wrong side of the tracks, pursues her married boss, wrecks his home, takes up with his boss and his chauffeur, and, when he objects, she shoots him. How does she pay for her sins? She winds up in Paris, kept by a rich man, with the amorous chauffeur in her employ.

Lamar Trotti's April 27 report said: "This is in my mind the most awful script I have ever read." Thalberg was summoned to the SRC offices. According to Trotti, "He and I went into a session which lasted literally far into the night while my wife and his wife sat outside in the anteroom and starved. Thalberg, of course, is a man of persuasive powers and he used the usual high pressure salesmanship methods on me." Trotti, who had writing aspirations of his own, wasn't buying. "His contention is that they are playing it as a broad burlesque and that the audience will laugh at the situations as broad comedy. Maybe so; but that isn't in the script."

Red-Headed Woman's first preview was held in Glendale, and the audience did not know whether to laugh with it, at it, or at all. Even Thalberg was perplexed: "Well, you know, that girl's so bad, she might just be good." He added a prologue establishing Lil as a sexy cutup, and then previewed the new version in Pasadena. "That did it!" wrote Loos. "Laughs began at once and never ceased." Word of mouth reached the women's clubs and they fussed at Will Hays. When Jason Joy returned from his *Scarface* campaign, he screened the film, once at Metro and then at a theater: "My feeling is that this picture is either very good or very bad, dependent on the point of view of the spectator who sees it as [either] farce or as heavy sex."

One scene has the boss's wife (Leila Hyams) rebuke Lil: "You caught him with sex. But sex isn't the only thing in life. And it doesn't last forever. And when it's gone, you'll lose him. Because then he'll want love. And love is one thing you don't know anything about—and never will!" Joy reported: "When we saw the picture with an audience we got a definite impression that the audience was laughing *at* the girl and . . . when the wife turned on the girl, the audience applauded."

While Joy was persuading Hays to pass the film, Mrs. Alonzo Richardson of Atlanta was doing the opposite: "We have been working for years for clean decent pictures and here in 1932 we have THIS . . . Sex! Sex! Sex! The picture just reeks with it until one is positively nauseated." Joy answered: "In the cold projection room it seemed entirely contrary to the Code . . . when seeing it with an audience, it took on an entirely different flavor. So farcical did it seem that I was convinced that it was not contrary to the Code." On July 1, the SRC passed *Red-Headed Woman*, Metro released it, and the reviews rolled in.

The *Hollywood Citizen-News* wrote: "Somehow M-G-M, more than any other producing company, has a way of getting around the critical prejudices of Will Hays." P. S. Harrison, conservative editor of the trade paper *Harrison's Reports*, wrote: "Pictures of this kind, instead of attracting customers to the theatres, will drive them away." A Pittsburgh mother, Florence Fisher Parry, wrote: "'Red-Headed Woman,' without doubt, is the most depraved picture that has yet come out of Hollywood. . . . That old-fashioned principle of sexual restraint is still active on this wise old earth, and coat labels are still to be found on most of life's experiences."

Massachusetts and Pennsylvania cut most scenes of Lil's romance with her chauffeur (Charles Boyer). Ohio cut the unrepentant ending. England banned the film altogether, but one print found its way into the private collection of King George V. When Darryl Zanuck heard that Joy had used audience reaction as an argument, he wrote the SRC: "I insist that you give Warner Bros. the same privileges you gave Metro-Goldwyn-Mayer." Joy could not, and admitted to Carl Milliken: "I am in for it because probably right now half of the other companies are trying to figure out ways of topping this particular picture, and when the results of their planning get to me, it will require all of our strength to dissuade them." Sure enough, Fox Film was planning *Call Her Savage,* Warner Bros. was planning *Baby Face,* and M-G-M was planning *Red Dust.* In August, Martin Quigley wrote Hays: "It is my belief that the whole Code scheme has practically become a wash-out during the past few months. I am astounded at the things that have been getting by."

To capitalize on Harlow's new stardom, Thalberg cast her as a Saigon prostitute in an exotic sex drama called *Red Dust.* On July 2, twenty-one-year-old Harlow married forty-two-year-old Paul Bern. Shooting started on July 22. Even easygoing Clark Gable found the first few scenes vulgar. On September 5, Paul Bern was found dead of a bullet wound. The production shut down. When Harlow recovered sufficiently, the first scenes were reshot. Her costumes had more modest necklines, especially for the prostitute she was playing.

When Jason Joy reviewed the film, he mentioned "the extremely harassing circumstances which attended its delivery," and said, "The sex element has, on the whole, we believe, been handled

The Beast of the City, *policeman Wallace Ford, wants to ask gang moll Jean Harlow some questions. She replies: "Sure. If you don't ask them in Yiddish." The line was cut by numerous censor boards.*

extremely well." But he wanted Hunt Stromberg to remove the "derogatory speech by Harlow concerning the French, in which she refers to them as 'Frogs,' and goes on to make some crack about their hiding under the bed and singing the Marseillaise." He also pointed out "Harlow's line, spoken to the parrot when she is cleaning its cage, to the effect that it must have been eating cement." Stromberg had Harlow "loop" the words "Sweet Adeline" onto the soundtrack to replace the Marseillaise, but argued his way out of the other changes.

By this time, Jason Joy had endured five years of arguments, and he was growing weary. According to Geoffrey Shurlock, who was still at Paramount, Joy "saw the Code was not working. It had no teeth, and he was not going to spend his life fighting losing battles." He told Will Hays—off the record—that he wanted to resign, but would wait until Hays found someone to replace him. Hays approached the MPPDA's Carl Milliken, the former governor of Maine, who politely but firmly declined. Hays started sniffing around the state boards. *Red Dust* opened October 22, and *Time* said: "Given *Red Dust*'s brazen moral values, Gable and Harlow have full play for their curiously similar sort of good-natured toughness." They ended 1932 as stars, and M-G-M ended it with a profit of $8 million.

On Christmas Eve, L. B. Mayer made a rash announcement to his employees: "I say the country has emerged from the Depression, and so we have!" After he went home, M-G-M exploded in celebration. According to story editor Samuel Marx, "bacchanalia reigned." Bootleg liquor flowed like film developer, and offices were turned into trysting places, confirming Joe Breen's image of Hollywood as a hedonist enclave. Irving Thalberg, whose heart had been damaged in childhood by rheumatic fever, allowed himself the dangerous

"Poison gin" sends Jean Harlow on a rampage, and not even Una Merkel can stop her in the outrageous Red-Headed Woman.

The rowdy interplay of plantation owner Clark Gable and prostitute Jean Harlow made Red Dust *a huge success in the grim winter of 1932. It also brought letters of protest from women's clubs.*

92

On a rubber plantation in Indochina, a lady's undergarments give Hoy (Willie Fung) something to model. Vanteen (Jean Harlow) has seen transvestites in Saigon, but she marvels: "You find them even in the jungle!" This was a frequently censored scene from Red Dust.

Red Dust *had its gritty scenes. Here Jean Harlow cleans out a bullet wound Clark Gable has gotten from a spurned girlfriend.*

Paramount's Marlene Dietrich luxuriates in a Eugene Robert Richee portrait. The sitting was supervised by her mentor, Josef von Sternberg, who made soft focus a seductive signature.

luxury of a few cocktails. The year's pace, Paul Bern's death, and the stress of recent battles with Mayer suddenly took their toll. The thirty-three-year-old executive suffered a heart attack. Doctors ordered him to rest for six months, and Norma Shearer put aside her career to care for him. While Thalberg slowly recovered, he watched another studio surpass his "adult" films.

THE PARAMOUNT GLOW

In 1932, the studio in the center of Hollywood made films with a unique look. Director Josef von Sternberg, cinematographer Lee Garmes, and portrait photographer Eugene Robert Richee had created a style recognizable by its diffused golden glow. Paramount's glow was on the screen and not in its coffers; the studio was in trouble. By April, Paramount had already lost $2,450,211. As it slid toward insolvency, Paramount produced fifty-seven features, at least eight of which would be acknowledged as works of cinematic art.

Two men were responsible for the quality of Paramount's best films: expansive vice president Jesse Lasky, who had cofounded Paramount with Adolph Zukor, and industrious production head B. P. Schulberg. As the financial crisis edged him out, Schulberg said: "Successful production depends on novelty, not past performance. Production must look forward, not backward." His advice went unheeded, and many of the year's releases were Janus-faced flops. Most of Tallulah Bankhead's films reeked of Dietrich. In *Thunder Below* and *Devil and the Deep*, Bankhead played a languid vamp stuck in a turgid zone; neither film showed her unique gifts. After making *Faithless* a hit for M-G-M, she left Hollywood.

Paramount borrowed Clark Gable from M-G-M and teamed him with Carole Lombard in *No Man of Her Own*. Edmund Goulding's story had gambler Gable visiting the small, dull town where Lombard works as a librarian. The story editor noted: "The story is essentially a brutal one—a sock on the nose—and we are going to sacrifice its best values if we try to soften it, make it nice, or whitewash it." The finished film was a light comedy, a bit cynical, but hardly brutal. Its main attraction was the chemistry between Lombard and Gable.

After Father Daniel Lord saw *No Man of Her Own*

in St. Louis on a Sunday afternoon, he "burned up the typewriter" with a letter to Will Hays, claiming that the film violated every tenet of the Production Code, dismayed that the people in the audience "seemed to thoroughly enjoy themselves." In his clerical opinion, seeing this film "was a sin." This opinion was shared by Martin Quigley, who warned Hays that he risked the wrath of "thousands of persons important in various religious, social, and educational activities." Apparently it did not occur to Hays that a priest declaring a film sinful could have serious consequences at the box office. Lamar Trotti had already advised Hays about conditions at the studio: "There seems to me to be a very real and distressing tendency at Paramount to go for the sex stuff on a heavy scale. One gets the feeling not only in the scripts but in the conversations in the studio where talk about pictures having to have 'guts' and about 'having to do this or do that to make a little money to pay our salaries' is too frequently heard."

Paramount did well with sexy comedies: W. C. Fields in *Million Dollar Legs*, the Marx Brothers in *Horse Feathers*, and Harold Lloyd in *Movie Crazy*. There was also Alison Skipworth as an elderly con artist in *Madame Racketeer*, and as a teacher lost in a speakeasy in *Night After Night*. *The Big Broadcast* was Paramount's acknowledgment of the medium that, along with the Depression, was emptying theaters. Sixteen million Americans owned radio sets, so Frank Tuttle's film had more than a dozen radio acts, including Cab Calloway, who did a musical number, "Kickin' That Gong Around." In it, the loose-limbed singer deplores "Minnie the Moocher's" drug habit and then mimics her inhaling cocaine.

Taking a cue from Ernst Lubitsch, sketch-artist-turned-production-designer Jean Negulesco invested *The Big Broadcast* with a visual vocabulary that became as unique to Paramount as its cloth diffusion filters. His use of slow motion, musical transitions, cartoonlike choruses, and artfully designed montages was first seen in *This Is the Night*, a comedy full of "non-stars" whose ensemble playing matched the film's agile editing. It had Lili Damita, Charlie Ruggles, Thelma Todd, Roland Young, and, in his first featured role, Cary Grant. One running gag has an evening gown torn off Claire (Thelma Todd) by a limousine. Jason Joy wrote: "When Claire's coat flies open and Gerald [Roland Young] looks down on a 'vista' afforded by the open coat, he gasps—with a great intake of breath. The assumption is that he has seen a great deal." Schulberg made cuts without ruining the rhythm of the sequence. In its playing, innuendo, and purely cinematic idiom, the film was a template for Paramount's sophisticated comedies, and now Jason Joy could praise it. "The risqué situations and dialogue have been handled with delicacy and without offense." *This Is the Night* was an economically made film (it used UA's standing set of the Venice canals at Goldwyn Studios), but, sad to say, it did not make money.

A companion film could be seen in Ernst Lubitsch's *One Hour with You*, which reunited *The Love Parade*'s Jeanette MacDonald and Maurice Chevalier. In it, Lubitsch and his longtime collaborator, Samson Raphaelson, took a wry look at adultery. Lamar Trotti was worried: "It has the continental flavor that I fear will be dangerous." That "flavor" was the best thing the studio had going for it. As Lubitsch said, "There is Paramount Paris and Metro Paris, and of course, the real Paris. Paramount's is the most Parisian of all." Jason Joy found the finished film beguiling, too. He praised "the delicate and charming manner in which the subject matter has been treated." The *Los Angeles Times* credited the "Lubitsch touch, which has become more than a legend." Jeanette MacDonald remembered: "The first pictures I made were very 'naughty.' . . . I was flaunting around in sleazy negligees and slinky gowns. Oh, yes! The famous 'Lubitsch touch.' [It had] an amusing kind of naughtiness. Not 'dirty.' Not really 'sexy' . . . it really had great *whimsy*." *One Hour with You* played in "tinted and toned" prints: amber for night interiors, blue for night exteriors. A costly production, it lost money.

Lubitsch's next film economized with its cast (Herbert Marshall, Kay Francis, and Miriam Hopkins) and sets (Busch Gardens, UA's Venice canal, and standing sets at Paramount), but its imagina-

In Horse Feathers, *Zeppo Marx woos Thelma Todd, while Harpo Marx provides a silent chorus. Photograph by Gordon Head.*

tion was rich beyond Hollywood's most extravagant budget. Even Geoffrey Shurlock, a new SRC reviewer, had to say that *Trouble in Paradise* was "the most sparkling and entertaining of Lubitsch's comedies since the advent of talkies." Then he added: "For adults." After all, it was the story of two jewel thieves (living together, of course) who fleece a rich, glamorous widow. As in all Lubitsch films, the seeming meanness of the plot belied the smiling sympathy of its director. Lubitsch later said: "As for pure style, I have done nothing better or as good as *Trouble in Paradise*." Neither the critics nor the public agreed; there was red ink in paradise.

Ernst Lubitsch either could not or would not direct the next MacDonald-Chevalier vehicle, so Paramount anxiously approached Rouben Mamoulian: "They had no book, no theme, and I'd have to find one in a hurry because they had the two stars on five thousand a week, there was no picture, and the money was mounting up." The resulting film, *Love Me Tonight*, drew on a lot full of talents, including screenwriter Samuel Hoffenstein and composers Richard Rodgers and Lorenz Hart. Trotti made a few suggestions to Schulberg about risqué lyrics, then finished: "May I add that this is one of the most delightful scripts that I have ever read." *Love Me Tonight* showed the continental studio at its most harmonious, but it, too, lost money. What did make money at Paramount in 1932?

Shanghai Express, Marlene Dietrich's first film of the year, was as eagerly awaited as Greta Garbo's *Grand Hotel*, and it, too, had a diverse group of characters thrown together in an exotic setting. Josef von Sternberg used light, shadow, and innuendo to create Dietrich's newest permutation, "Shanghai Lily," but "the notorious White Flower of China" chugged through the SRC without a hitch. *Shanghai Express* only had problems because of a religious fanatic named Dr. Carmichael (Lawrence Grant) who acts like an angry censor, a French officer named Major Lenard (Emile Chautard) who has been "discharged for a minor offense," and a revolutionary named Chang (Warner Oland) who says: "I'm not proud of my white blood." Many boards cut Carmichael's ranting, France cut Lenard's line, and China banned the film altogether.

Shanghai Express made $33,000, so Paramount gave in to Josef von Sternberg on his next script, *Blonde Venus.* As Jason Joy wrote Will Hays: "The argument started because the original script was too raw for Schulberg. A perfectly safe version of the script was developed, but now that von Sternberg and Schulberg have patched up their differences, the rewrite on the script seems to indicate that Schulberg has compromised pretty much with von Sternberg." The film has Helen Faraday (Marlene Dietrich) sell her favors to a rich politician (Cary Grant) to pay for the medical treatment of her husband, Ned (Herbert Marshall). Joy explained to a Paramount executive why he had passed the film: "Never are infidelity and prostitution themselves made attractive." Attractive, no; amusing, maybe. "My name's Taxi Belle Hooper," says Rita La Roy. "'Taxi' for short." Dietrich asks her: "Do you charge for the first mile?" *Blonde Venus* should have. It lost money.

In early 1932, Jesse Lasky made a deal to bring Cecil B. DeMille back to Paramount. After a series of flops at M-G-M, DeMille wanted to return to religious sagas. Paramount agreed to let him make *The Sign of the Cross.* In April, Paramount's New York directors pushed Lasky out. In June, they ousted B. P. Schulberg. Emanuel Cohen was now at the Paramount throttle, determined to turn the company around. He signed Bing Crosby and Mae West. He bought Ernest Hemingway's *A Farewell to Arms,* hired Frank Borzage to direct, borrowed Helen Hayes from M-G-M to play Catherine Barkley, and cast Gary Cooper as Frederic Henry. Trotti wrote Hays that the new executives were

In this scene from Night After Night, *an unbilled hatcheck girl exclaims: "Goodness, what beautiful diamonds!" Maudie Triplett (Mae West) replies: "Goodness had nothing to do with it, dearie." Photograph by Gordon Head.*

going to "live or die by this picture and that they are going to be as daring as possible." The production took two months and cost $900,000, but the result was well worth it. Borzage had crafted an epic, and people wanted to see it. Before they could, there was the matter of the Code. The film had an illicit love scene on the pedestal of a horseman's statue, an illicit love scene in a hospital bed, an "unofficial marriage," graphic scenes of childbirth, and the retreat of the Italian army, which could be the biggest problem of all. What would Jason Joy do?

Nothing; Jason Joy had already succumbed to the blandishments of the Fox Film Corporation, where Sidney Kent and Winfield Sheehan had been courting him for six months. He was now ensconced in a luxurious office, making sure that Fox Film's scripts would be approved. His SRC successor was none other than his former nemesis, the New York State censor, Dr. James Wingate. Assisted by new reviewer Geoffrey Shurlock, Wingate took a look at *A Farewell to Arms.* True to form, he rejected it, then went to his quarters at the Hollywood Athletic Club. He was in for a rude awakening.

Paramount, which had already cooperated with the SRC to the extent of placating the Italian Embassy and shooting two endings, appealed his decision, and presented the film to the AMPP jury. On December 7, 1932, Carl Laemmle, Sr., Sol Wurtzel, and Joseph Schenck ruled in favor of Paramount, saying that "because of the greatness of the picture and the excellence of direction and treatment the childbirth sequence was not in violation of Article II of the Production Code." *A Farewell to Arms* premiered a day later, and within weeks, it was making the money that the rest of the films in the Paramount calendar had not. Yet Paramount ended 1932 with a deficit of $15,857,544.

As Dr. Wingate settled into the SRC, Lamar Trotti quit and went to Fox Film to work as Jason Joy's

Still photographer Bert Longworth made tantalizing tableaux of Tallulah Bankhead and Charles Bickford for Thunder Below, *but the film did not deliver the drama of his images.*

This Is the Night *was a delightfully sexy comedy that had no stars. It featured Roland Young and Lili Damita (pictured), plus Charlie Ruggles, Thelma Todd, and newcomer Cary Grant. Photograph by Fred Archer.*

Carole Lombard and Clark Gable in a Eugene Robert Richee portrait for No Man of Her Own. *The film outraged Daniel Lord, coauthor of the 1930 Code.*

The SRC gave raves, not cuts, to the brilliant musical comedy Love Me Tonight, *which starred Jeanette MacDonald and Maurice Chevalier. Photograph by Bert Longworth.*

In Love Me Tonight, *Myrna Loy sings a stanza from "Mimi."*
The SRC remarked on the transparency of her negligee, but passed the scene.
In 1949, the Production Code Administration (PCA) permanently
deleted this shot, as well as a song in which Jeanette MacDonald's doctor
(Joseph Cawthorn) tells her: "A peach must be eaten. / A drum
must be beaten. / And a woman needs something like that!"
Photograph by Bert Longworth.

Maurice Chevalier sings "I'm an Apache" in Love Me Tonight. *State*
censor boards cut the line "Nuts to you!" Photograph by Bert Longworth.

Paramount's Trouble in Paradise *enchanted its SRC reviewer, but in the fall of 1932, Depression-poor audiences spent their dimes on M-G-M's* Red Dust *and* Smilin' Through. *This portrait of Miriam Hopkins, Herbert Marshall, and Kay Francis was made by Eugene Robert Richee. When Paramount later submitted the film for reissue, the PCA turned it down; fortunately so, for it escaped intact.*

Still photographer Earl Crowley made this beautifully lit portrait of Gary Cooper and Tallulah Bankhead for The Devil and the Deep.

Jeanette MacDonald and Maurice Chevalier host a dinner party in One Hour with You. *Photograph by Bert Longworth.*

The chauffeur (Irving Bacon) presents the gown that the door has torn off Claire (Thelma Todd), mistress of Gerald (Roland Young), in This Is the Night. *Photograph by Fred Archer.*

In Blonde Venus, *Marlene Dietrich cuts a swath through a soft-focus South.*
Photograph by Don English (designed by Josef von Sternberg).

Marlene Dietrich emerges from a gorilla costume to sing
"Hot Voodoo / Black as mud / Hot Voodoo / In my blood!" in Blonde Venus.
Photograph by Don English (designed by Josef von Sternberg).

Jean Negulesco's sketch art for A Farewell to Arms *was faithfully reproduced by art director Hans Dreier and cinematographer Charles Lang, Jr. Photograph by Sherman Clark.*

The love scene between Gary Cooper and Helen Hayes that took place on a pedestal was more poignant than sensual. This scene was cut from the negative in 1938. (A complete print of A Farewell to Arms *resides at the University of Texas.)*

*An Otto Dyar portrait of Anna May Wong made for
Paramount's* Shanghai Express. *Courtesy Roy Windham.*

*A Don English portrait of Marlene Dietrich as Shanghai Lily
in* Shanghai Express. *Courtesy Roy Windham.*

This Don English portrait of Clive Brook and Marlene Dietrich captures Lee Garmes's shimmering
camerawork on Shanghai Express.

assistant. Paramount was shooting *She Done Him Wrong* and about to release *The Sign of the Cross*. For the next few months, Wingate would be very busy.

"UNDER THE NAKED MOON"

At fifty-one, Cecil Blount DeMille was perhaps the best-known film director in the world, whether for sex fables such as *Male and Female* or biblical epics such as *The King of Kings* (on which Father Daniel Lord had served as technical adviser). DeMille's eminence meant nothing to the new regime at Paramount Pictures. Emanuel Cohen only cared that *The Sign of the Cross* be made economically: "Remember, Cecil, you are on trial with this picture." DeMille's interest in the film was not purely aesthetic; he had raised half of its budget of $650,000.

The Sign of the Cross was a time-tested play by Wilson Barrett, a powerful tale of Christian endurance in Nero's Rome. DeMille submitted the script not only to the SRC but also to Daniel Lord, hoping to get the inside track with Will Hays. Lord cautioned DeMille against making the Romans too "nightclubbish" and the Christians too dull, so DeMille trimmed the script of most of its pagan elements. To finish the film within budget, DeMille enlisted the talents of costume and set designer Mitchell Leisen. Leisen was bisexual, with a reputation for decadence. He embellished the spiritual story with authentically pagan detail. As time grew shorter and the job more demanding, DeMille let Leisen codirect much of the film. Before long, they had turned the venerable play into a catalogue of Hollywood's private life. With a straight face, DeMille asked a reporter: "Do you realize the close analogy between conditions today in the United States and the Roman Empire prior to the fall?"

In *The Sign of the Cross*, DeMille cast ladies' man Fredric March as the womanizing Roman, Marcus Superbus, but was unsure who could play the Empress Poppaea. At the time, Claudette Colbert had played mostly "bright young things." DeMille called to her from his office window one day: "How would you like to play the wickedest woman in the world?"

"I'd love it," she answered.

For her screen test, an actor upbraided her: "You harlot!"

"I love you" was her reply. The way she said it assured DeMille that he had made the right choice. Leisen said: "Making the costumes for Claudette was a real pleasure. . . . I slit her skirts right up to the hip to show her marvelous legs. She didn't have a stitch on underneath." Colbert's Sapphic bias brought another dimension to the role, but no one could compete with Charles Laughton for depravity. When asked by a reporter how he was portraying Nero, he said: "I play him straight." In contrast to Laughton's undulant, triple-jointed emperor, Leisen cast muscular Georges Bruggeman as his ever-present male slave. Their seminude propinquity brought new meaning to the line "Delicious debauchery."

For the obligatory bath scene, DeMille put Poppaea in a huge pool of asses' milk. Leisen said: "DeMille wanted the milk to just barely cover her nipples, so the day before, I had Claudette stand in the pool and I measured her to get the level just right." The studio technicians filled the pool with powdered milk. In a few days, the heat of the lights turned it sour. Cinematographer Karl Struss recalled: "Oh, boy! It smelled to heaven! It was there for a week. Claudette was really nude, so she couldn't get out too often." When she did, DeMille tried to get a free look; a technician inadvertently blocked it, and DeMille cursed him.

DeMille's voyeurism aside, Struss remembered the film as a "great challenge. I used gauze throughout, to give the feeling of a world remembered; it wasn't much used then, as it had been in the silent period. I shot the whole black-and-white picture through bright red gauze." Some of his finest work, as well as that of Leisen and art director Hans Dreier, was in two sequences, the Circus Maximus and the orgy scene. The Circus Maximus scene re-created in sadistic detail the excesses of the "Arena Games." The orgy scene had as its centerpiece the "Dance of the Naked Moon." Dissolute Marcus has failed to seduce innocent Mercia (Elissa Landi), so he asks Ancaria (Joyzelle Joyner), the "most wicked and, uh, *talented* woman in Rome," to perform a dance that will "warm her into life." As conceived by Leisen, directed by DeMille, and shot by Struss, the scene was something that had never been done before, a narcotic ode to sex.

DeMille was in the sands of the arena, filming an

Amazon beheading a pygmy, when his business manager ran up to him: "We've just used up the budget. You haven't got a dime." DeMille stopped filming. He had managed to make his epic within budget. Now he had to get it past the Hays Office. Jason Joy was still working at the SRC when the film came up for approval, but James Wingate was there, too, learning the ropes. They looked at *The Sign of the Cross* and collaborated on a letter to Paramount: "Ordinarily we would have been concerned about those portions of the dance sequence in which the Roman dancer executes the 'Kootch' Movement. But since the director obviously used the dancing to show the conflict between paganism and Christianity, we are agreed that there is justification for its use under the Code."

The SRC may have found justification, but many Catholic publications, including *Our Sunday Visitor, Commonweal,* and *America,* saw pornography. Martin Quigley's *Motion Picture Herald* could recommend the film only to people whose "sensibilities survive the odors of Lesbos and de Sade." The *Hollywood Citizen-News* lambasted it as a "vicious excursion in eroticism, cloaked in religion." Ancaria's dance was described by one scandalized Catholic as "the most unpleasant bit of footage ever passed by the Hollywood censors." Daniel Lord told DeMille that it smacked of "sex perversion." Martin Quigley referred to it with great distaste as "that lesbian dance," and declared: "The scene is objectionable because it transgresses the limits of legitimate dramatic requirements and becomes an incident liable to an evil audience effect."

DeMille had not expected this response from the usually well-disposed Catholic press. When Protestant and Jewish leaders also voiced disapproval, he asked Paramount: "Are there many people who will stay away from a theater today because of a sensational dance?" Before he got an answer, Will Hays called him.

"I am with Martin Quigley. What are you going to do about that dance?"

"Will, listen carefully to my words because you may want to quote them. Not a damn thing."

"Not a damn thing?"

"Not a damn thing."

Paramount shipped the film to the censor boards. The few who did cut it concentrated on

An Otto Dyar portrait of Charles Laughton as Nero for Paramount's The Sign of the Cross.

gorillas, alligators, and asses' milk. Not one board cut the "lesbian dance." *Harrison's Reports* speculated that no one knew what it meant. Whether they knew what it meant or not, the Midwest Catholics knew impure love when they saw it. Hollywood had defiled their mythology of Christians vs. lions, and they would not forget.

OPPOSITE:
In The Sign of the Cross,
*Fredric March introduces Joyzelle Joyner as
"Ancaria, the most wicked and, uh,
talented woman in Rome." Photograph
by William Thomas.*

TOP:
*Ancaria (Joyzelle Joyner) performs the
"Dance of the Naked Moon," at the urging of
Marcus Superbus (Fredric March), to
seduce Mercia (Elissa Landi), the innocent
Christian girl. This scene was cut from
the negative of* The Sign of the Cross *for a
1935 reissue, but restored by MCA-Universal
for its 1993 video release.*

BOTTOM:
*Charles Laughton as Nero and
Georges Bruggeman as his all-too-willing
slave in a scene designed by Mitchell Leisen
for* The Sign of the Cross.

ENTER MAE WEST

In spite of the Depression, or perhaps because of it, *The Sign of the Cross* was a bigger hit than anyone expected. To see Rome in soft focus, destitute people offered theaters handwritten I.O.U.s. "Nearly every one of them was redeemed when cash began to flow again," wrote C. B. DeMille. But Paramount could not cash these little pieces of paper, and on February 4, 1933, the company went into receivership. Six weeks later, it declared bankruptcy. Watching this with no little interest was the SRC's next challenge, a plump forty-year-old woman from Brooklyn. Mae West's first starring film, *She Done Him Wrong*, had been released January 27. Years later, she recalled the Hollywood of early 1933: "It was a world that came awake with an economic hangover, and instead of being thankful it was being saved, tried to assault its rescue teams." Before the year was over, she would be credited with saving Paramount Pictures—and denounced as an evil influence.

Mae West had come to Hollywood seven months earlier, at the invitation of supervisor William LeBaron. Another loyal friend, George Raft, was making his first starring vehicle, *Night After Night*, and wanted West to play a supporting role. After waiting eight weeks for a script, she was crestfallen: "My part was very unimportant and banal. The dialogue did nothing for me." She offered to repay the $40,000 she had already collected. LeBaron told her she could rewrite her lines. She did, and her scenes were the only lively part of the film. Suddenly everyone remembered Mae West, the playwright—and star—of the infamous *Diamond Lil*. Paramount already owned *Diamond Lil*, and though it was on the SRC's "banned" list, the studio decided to film it, disguising it as *Ruby Red*.

The SRC's John Wilson wrote: "There is no objection to Mae West writing any story she wants, but they must stay away from the basic plot of 'Diamond Lil.'" Paramount continued with the project, hiring writer John Bright to work with West and worldly wise Lowell Sherman to direct. Other studios caught wind of it. Harry Warner sent Hays a telegram, hinting that if Paramount could film a banned play, so could he. Hays quickly responded that "there is no danger of their violation of the agreement."

As Jason Joy was leaving for his new job at Fox Film, Paramount defied the SRC and scheduled a start date for the film, which was now called *She Done Him Wrong*. James Wingate was ill-prepared to deal with this crisis, so Hays stepped in. He wrote to company president Adolph Zukor: "By all means this ought to be stopped as it is a direct violation by Paramount of its most solemn agreement." Filming started on November 23, 1932. On November 28, Hays ordered an emergency meeting. Zukor agreed to abide by the Code and not mention *Diamond Lil* in any advertising. The MPPDA told him that Lowell Sherman could continue filming. He had never stopped.

On November 29, in one of his first official acts as new SRC director, James Wingate wrote to Paramount, suggesting changes: "In order to remove even the slightest suspicion of white slavery, we suggest that you include inserts of the photographs of the girls indicated in sequence A-14, in order to show the audience that these girls are dancers, singers, etc." He also advised that they "develop the comedy elements [and] invest the picture with such exaggerated qualities as automatically to take care of possible offensiveness." He need not have worried on that account.

From the moment Mae West swaggered across the screen, audiences knew they were in the presence of a master—a master of exaggeration, innuendo, and humor. The ribaldry she had flashed in *Night After Night* came to sexy fruition in *She Done Him Wrong*, the story of a Gay Nineties saloon singer who says: "Always remember to smile. You'll never have anything to worry about." Lady Lou (Mae West) is always smiling; every man she meets falls for her and showers her with diamonds, the real love of her life.

Mae West's onscreen struggle with Russian Rita (Rafaela Ottiano) was as picturesque as it was violent. Photograph by El Bredell.

TOP:
When Cary Grant declines Mae West's offer of a cigarette, she thinks better of it: "Yes, I guess smoking is going to make a man look effeminate." A photograph from She Done Him Wrong *by El Bredell.*

BOTTOM:
Quoth Mae West: "Always remember to smile. You'll never have anything to worry about." She worried the women's clubs of America. According to censor Geoffrey Shurlock: "She rubbed them the wrong way. We were not used to having sex kidded." Portrait by Eugene Robert Richee.

OPPOSITE:
Making She Done Him Wrong *brought Mae West into conflict with director Lowell Sherman. Screenwriter John Bright, who had also been vetoed by West, asked for help. Sherman declined: "Sorry, baby, but I have to handle the bitch-goddess on the set." Cinematographer Charles Lang, Jr., is at left.*

For five years the screen had been dominated by languid foreign stars such as Marlene Dietrich and Greta Garbo. Garbo thrilled her fans by reacting to situations; she rarely initiated them. "The drama comes in how she rides them out," said Irving Thalberg. Mae West was different. She wrote her stories, and in them she ran the show. "She was the strong, confident woman, always in command," said Adolph Zukor. "And that was the real Mae." In *She Done Him Wrong*, Lady Lou says: "Men's all alike, married or single. It's their game. I just happen to be smart enough to play it their way." She plays it with sex, but tempers it with humor, striding through every scene with the rhythmic tread of a transvestite dinosaur, bursting out of a wardrobe so tight that she never sits. She sells her humor with a mellifluous voice, humming one-liners such as:

"The wolf at my door? Why, I remember when he came into my room and had pups."

"There was a time when I didn't know where my next husband was comin' from."

"Why, he'd be the kind a woman'd hafta marry ta get rid of."

"Why, a boy with a gift like that oughta be workin' at it."

"When women go wrong, men go *right after them.*"

There was, of course, the line that became a catch phrase, the endlessly quoted (and misquoted) "Why doncha come up sometime an' see me?" Two other lines barely made the final cut: "Say, you can be had," and "Hands ain't everything." James Wingate tried to delete them from prints after the initial release, but only succeeded in cutting one verse from the song "A Guy What Takes His Time." *She Done Him Wrong* was Mae West triumphant. Wingate confided nervously to Hays: "We are not sure that this type of picture will do the industry any good." Sidney Kent wrote Hays: "I believe it is worse than 'Red-Headed Woman' from the standpoint of the industry—it is far more suggestive in word and what is not said is suggested in action. I cannot understand how your people on the Coast could let this get by." Critical response was equally strong.

Elizabeth Yeaman of the *Hollywood Citizen-News* described the film as "the most flagrant and utterly abandoned morsel of sin ever attempted on the screen, and I must confess that I enjoyed it enormously." Louella Parsons said that West was "just as naughty as she was on stage and perhaps just a shade more flirtatious." John S. Cohen, Jr., wrote in the *New York Sun*: "She is humorously brazen. She is brazenly humorous. Comedy saves her and her rôles." Best of all was the item in the *Los Angeles Review*: "*She Done Him Wrong* . . . has turned into a golden gusher for Paramount. Exhibitors can't pry it loose from their screens." The film made $2 million in less than two months. With *A Farewell to Arms, The Sign of the Cross,* and *She Done Him Wrong,* Paramount was out of the quicksand, but not out of the woods. Neither was Hollywood.

The first week of March was the worst. Two thousand studio employees were out of work. Franklin D. Roosevelt took office and declared March 6 a bank holiday. On Friday, March 10, as the moguls convened in an angry clump to debate salary cuts, nature provided a punctuation mark: the Long Beach earthquake. On Monday, March 13, the studios shut down until 50 percent salary cuts were agreed upon. The next morning, in studio after studio, the moguls broke the news. At M-G-M, L. B. Mayer was unshaven and weeping. At Warner Bros., Darryl Zanuck promised to restore salaries within a month. Warner contract player Aline MacMahon recalled: "That night I went to the Brown Derby, and waiters were carrying large bowls of caviar behind a screen. And behind the screen were the Warner families, celebrating with caviar. It was a great break for them." The crisis, however, was real; the bank holiday cost the studios $14 million and they had only enough finished films to last two weeks.

As if this were not enough, Will Hays was on a rampage. Worried by a rash of bad publicity, he made the MPPDA directors sign a document in which they promised to abide by the Code, then went to Hollywood to make it stick. On April 20, he told a group of executives: "There is no use referring to pictures made by other companies, such as *She Done Him Wrong,* and say[ing], 'See, look what *they* got away with—we can do the same.' " According to Hays, this document was all that stood between them and federal censorship. But films had to be made, and federal censorship was a distant threat, about as likely as a boycott by Roman Catholics. All that stood between the producers and racier movies was James Wingate.

SEX IN SOFT FOCUS

Dr. James Wingate had been a school administrator since 1900, but not even the New York school system could prepare him for a job as a Hollywood censor. He was sadly miscast. Morris L. Ernst and Pare Lorentz described him: "Middle-aged, slightly pompous yet evasive, and given to long-winded and meaningless speeches. His spectacles and severe garb give him the appearance of a clergyman or a Y.M.C.A. organizer."

Wingate tried to organize the SRC, but producers were used to Jason Joy's creativity. Wingate could not think like a writer and he was slow. Darryl Zanuck wrote him: "Your reports are coming in so slowly that very often half of the picture is finished photographing when we get it. . . . Please give us as quick action as you possibly can." Wingate's assistant, Geoffrey Shurlock, remembered: "He couldn't explain what needed to be done in a given script to make it acceptable to the Code. He was quite simple-minded and logical about things, really quite square . . . and he didn't get on very well with these emotional Jewish producers. They had wild ideas about doing it their way. He'd say, 'No, no! Cut it out!' And what they wanted was not to cut it out but to do it differently."

In April, Will Hays borrowed Joy back from Fox Film in an attempt to balance Wingate's "narrower considerations" with Joy's concern for "the general flavor of pictures." While Joy tried to work in two places, Wingate tried to keep up. To appease Hays, the studios promised not only to cut back on problem films, but also to offer uplifting material, beginning with *Alice in Wonderland, Little Women, State Fair,* and *Pilgrimage.* The "clean pictures" were well received, but there were too few of them, and "dirty pictures" still had a following. Darryl Zanuck said: "Love stories and sex stories make very good headlines, and sometimes very good pictures." One of his best was both, with music.

Dr. James Wingate's transition from the New York State censor board to the SRC was not a smooth one. Photograph by Patch Bros., New York. Courtesy the Bison Archive.

In late 1932, Zanuck had suggested bringing musical pictures back. Jack Warner had answered: "Oh, Christ, no! We can't give 'em away!" Undeterred, Zanuck put a backstage story into production on the Burbank lot, while Busby Berkeley surreptitiously shot its musical numbers at the Vitagraph lot on Sunset Boulevard in Hollywood. Zanuck screened the film for Warner: "Jack went out of his mind! He never knew until it was screened that it was a musical." Wingate also liked it, but suggested a few deletions, including: "The reference to 'Any Time Annie—she only said "no" once, and then she didn't hear the question.' " The line stayed in, and *42nd Street* was a wisecracking, tune-filled, visually innovative hit.

Warner Bros.' next musical, *Gold Diggers of 1933,* was another showcase for Busby Berkeley's production numbers. In "Pettin' in the Park" and "We're in the Money," Berkeley created abstractions of female anatomy that were both lyrical and lewd. *Gold Diggers of 1933* was one of the first films with "alternate footage." The state boards had become so troublesome that a number of studios were shooting slightly different versions of censorable scenes. When the film was edited, the toned-down reels were labeled according to district. In this way, one version could be shipped to New York, another to the South, and another to British territories. In one version of *Gold Diggers,* the rocky romance between Warren William and Joan Blondell (whom he calls "cheap and vulgar") is resolved backstage after the "Forgotten Man" number; in another, the film ends with the number.

In *Employees' Entrance,* Warren William played a rapacious boss, but not even he was as bad as the local ads said he was. Reformers complained about the salacious, misleading publicity posters commissioned by exhibitors. For this film, the company's New York advertising department made up flyers that read:

Department Store Girls—This is *your* picture—about *your* lives and *your* problems!

See what happens in department store aisles and offices after closing hours!

Girls who couldn't have been touched with a 100-ft. yacht—ready to do anything to get a job!

Beautiful models who whisper their dread of the "Boss" who can "make" or break more women than a sultan!

Zanuck told Wingate that the New York executives made him reserve 20 percent of the year's calendar for "women's pictures, which inevitably means sex pictures." The best of these starred Ruth Chatterton, who brought her clipped elegance to some piquant proceedings. In *Frisco Jenny* she was an unwed mother, a prostitute, a madam, and a murderer. In *Lilly Turner* she was a carnival dancer. Her best was Michael Curtiz's *Female*, in which she runs an auto factory and emulates Catherine the Great. Wingate wrote:

It is made very plain that she has been in the habit of sustaining her freedom from marriage, and at the same time satisfying a too definitely indicated sex hunger, by frequently inviting any young man who may appeal to her to her home and there bringing about a seduction. After having satisfied her desires with these various males, she pays no further attention to them other than to reward them with bonuses. And in the event that they become importunate, she has them transferred.

Warner Bros. told Wingate that Chatterton's antics would be adjusted, but made no changes. Another unconventional film was *Ex-Lady*, the story of a career woman who wants a trial marriage. Its newly elevated star, Bette Davis, described her character: "Well, what she wants, of course, is freedom. She never will be satisfied until she has every right that a man has. . . . The exceptional woman should have the same opportunities and the same freedom to develop them that the exceptional man has."

In Columbia's *Cocktail Hour*, Bebe Daniels is a highly paid commercial artist who also prizes her freedom. In RKO's *Christopher Strong*, Katharine Hepburn is a free-spirited test pilot who becomes pregnant by a married man. Dorothy Arzner's film has a postcoital scene similar to those in *All Quiet on*

the Western Front and *Mata Hari*. We see a clock on a nightstand and hear Lady Cynthia Darrington (Hepburn) whisper to Sir Christopher Strong (Colin Clive) that she will give up flying to please him. In these films, the errant career woman gets a worse comeuppance than a kept woman—not from the censors, but from the script. Ruth Chatterton is on her way to the altar at the end of *Female*, clutching an incongruous piglet, cured of her female supremacist notions. Bette Davis and Bebe Daniels also end their respective films as "reformed" feminists. In *Christopher Strong*, Hepburn commits suicide (and, by implication, abortion) in her beloved monoplane.

At Columbia Pictures, Frank Borzage filmed another of his meditations on the transcendence of love. *A Man's Castle* has an innocent waif (Loretta Young) literally "shacking up" with a cynical hobo (Spencer Tracy) in a shantytown. Cinematographer Joseph August used soft focus to give this homely setting a glowing aura, and Borzage's vision of romance was so persuasive that the principals fell in love, carrying on a romance in full view of Hollywood. Also in full view was Spencer Tracy's backside; in one scene in *A Man's Castle*, he jumps naked into the East River.

Frank Capra's *The Bitter Tea of General Yen* was an unusually lavish film for Columbia, which was a small studio known for mounting entire films around one set. Its parsimonious owner, Harry Cohn, was also its head of production. The film was an odd choice for Capra, whose films were usually explorations of Americana. It told the story of a missionary (Barbara Stanwyck) who falls in love with a Chinese warlord (Nils Asther). Capra fell in love with the concept and ignored the miscegenation laws of thirty states, including California.

After reading the script, Joy was less worried about the sexual angle than about the political one: "Just because the Chinese themselves prefer it, I wonder if you would want to refer to them as Chinese rather than as Chinamen as is now indicated in several parts of the story." Capra made the changes and proceeded with his interracial romance. Cinematographer Joseph Walker shot it in dreamlike soft focus: "The nature of the film lent itself to a new invention I had just completed: the Variable Diffusion." This enabled him to shoot the entire film, including tracking shots, in the softest of soft focus. His visual poetry did not soften audi-

In M-G-M's Today We Live, *Gary Cooper (off scene) discovers Joan Crawford living with his friend. She admits: "We didn't wait." Photograph by Frank Tanner.*

42nd Street *returned musicals to favor with backstage scenes such as this one between Ruby Keeler and Dick Powell.*

Lynn Browning was one of the two hundred chorines who graced the stages of 42nd Street.

Before teaming with Fred Astaire, Ginger Rogers was a presence in numerous naughty musicals. This scene from Gold Diggers of 1933, *in which she sang "I've Got to Sing a Torch Song," was deleted by Warner Bros. before its release; it slowed the film. Photograph by Bert Longworth.*

This "art still" of Guy Kibbee and Joan Blondell was posed exclusively for the artist who painted the posters for Gold Diggers of 1933.

Joel McCrea and Constance Bennett are a sensual couple in RKO's Bed of Roses.

Nils Asther and Barbara Stanwyck try not to fall in love in Columbia's Bitter Tea of General Yen. *Joseph Walker made it the most soft-focused of all the pre-Code films.*

Marion Davies and Bing Crosby try not to throw up on the set of M-G-M's Going Hollywood. *Photograph by James Manatt.*

Jean Harlow and Clark Gable in the opening (door) sequence of M-G-M's Hold Your Man.

Warner Bros.' Goodbye Again *has a funny scene in which Hugh Herbert and Joan Blondell wear themselves out while waiting for his wife and her boss to return from a "meeting."*

In A Man's Castle, *cinematographer Joseph August's soft focus makes Loretta Young and Spencer Tracy look less sinful.*

In Parachute Jumper, *Douglas Fairbanks, Jr., is a flier who unknowingly transports drugs between the United States and Mexico.*

Sing, Sinner, Sing *was made by tiny Majestic Studios, which did not submit its scripts to the SRC; hence this scene of Paul Lukas and Jill Dennett in a story that exploited the life of torch singer Libby Holman.*

Gloria Stuart and Eddie Cantor (in a tasteless disguise) in Goldwyn's Roman Scandals.
Photograph by Kenneth Alexander.

Georges Bruggeman and Elissa Landi in a William Cameron Menzies setting for Fox Film's
I Loved You Wednesday.

Bette Davis and Gene Raymond essay a trial marriage in Warner Bros.' Ex-Lady.

Lawyer Frank Morgan wonders if his wife, Nancy Carroll, is deceiving him in
Universal's A Kiss Before the Mirror.

Mae West "tosses discretion to the wind and her hips to the North, East, South, and West" in Paramount's I'm No Angel.

"Tired of it all?" asks Ginger Rogers. "No. Just tired," replies overworked Joan Blondell in Fox Film's Broadway Bad.

ence reactions. According to Barbara Stanwyck: "The story was far ahead of its time in that the missionary comes to respect the 'heathen' attitudes of the Oriental. Before the General drinks his poisoned tea, she touches him in farewell—and worse—actually kisses his hand. His hand! Women's groups all over the country protested, wrote letters to exhibitors, saying we were condoning miscegenation." The film had the honor of opening Radio City Music Hall as a movie palace*; it was pulled one week later for lack of attendance.

The Fox Film Corporation pointed proudly to the success of Frank Lloyd's film of Noël Coward's *Cavalcade.* Apart from a few "damns" and "hells," this was family entertainment and it was making money. On the other hand, the studio was grinding out more than its share of sexy movies. One was the last entry in the Victor McLaglen–Edmund Lowe series that had begun with *What Price Glory?* John

Blystone's *Hot Pepper* was not as vulgar as *The Cock-eyed World* or *Women of All Nations,* but it had the irrepressible Lupe Velez running around in a satin sheet. James Wingate assured Will Hays that "both the sex elements and the rough language, which hitherto have given unfortunate notoriety to this series, have been considerably toned down." *Variety* described the film as "a little dirtier and a little rougher" than its predecessors.

The better Fox films included *Walls of Gold, Zoo in Budapest,* and *The Devil's in Love. I Loved You Wednesday* was codirected by Henry King and William Cameron Menzies. In it, Elissa Landi plays Vicki, a ballet dancer whose live-in lover, Ran (Victor Jory), dumps her when his wife, Cynthia (Miriam Jordan), shows up. Wingate disliked the script and asked for cuts. To his surprise, Winfield Sheehan replied: "These lines seem vital to the dramatic action of the story and, to us, not offensive nor do

127

The wickedest Warner Bros. star, Warren William, in a Bert Longworth study from The Mind Reader.

On the set of M-G-M's Dinner at Eight, *assistant film editor Chester Schaeffer overheard twenty-two-year-old Jean Harlow say to costar Marie Dressler, who was sixty-two: "I can't imagine being old. I don't want to get old." Dressler gently chided her: "Don't be silly. It isn't fun 'til you're forty." Portrait by Harvey White.*

we feel at the studio that they are out of the line of good taste. We are, therefore, not eliminating these." Only Maryland and Pennsylvania cut the "scene in which Vicki is shown on the rubbing table in such a way as to reveal a generous portion of her breast."

In Sidney Lanfield's *Broadway Bad,* Joan Blondell plays a showgirl who secretly raises a child so that her scandal-loving public will not be disillusioned. The first-draft script by William R. Lipman and A. W. Pezet used a poem to establish its atmosphere:

> From the lives of————
> sad-hearted dolls and lonely guys,
> who pull burning torches from the
> fires of love: : :
> Playboys on the make, who substitute
> checks' appeal for sex appeal: : :
> Gals, whose heels are round, because
> their heads were soft and their
> hearts were warm . . . once: : : . . .
> Wits to whom credit for a wise crack
> is more sacred than a reputation: : :
> Pals, who make a business of friendship . . .
> and always cash in by selling it short: : :
> And the rest of the mob to whom life has
> become a gag: : :
> And whose answer to Fate's chuckle
> is 'Nuts!'
> ————this story is drawn.

In Frank Tuttle's *Pleasure Cruise,* Genevieve Tobin awaits a suitor (Ralph Forbes) in her darkened stateroom. Her husband (Roland Young) locks up the would-be suitor and enters the stateroom himself. In the morning, the suitor comes to apologize to Tobin for not showing up. Her startled expression asks: Then who *did* make love to me in the dark?

At Paramount, Mae West's next film was Wesley Ruggles's *I'm No Angel,* in which she realized her lifelong ambition of playing a lion tamer. In this witty, bawdy film, she also tames every man in sight, cracking one-liners like whips. Martin Quigley wrote: "A vehicle for a notorious characterization of a scarlet woman whose amatory instincts are confined exclusively to the physical. There is no more pretense here of romance than on a stud-farm . . . its sportive wise-cracking tends to create tolerance

In RKO's Christopher Strong, *Katharine Hepburn wears a chain mail "moth costume" to symbolize her independence—and self-destructiveness.*

if not acceptance of things essentially evil." Surprisingly, its critics were in the minority, and *I'm No Angel* surpassed even *She Done Him Wrong* at the box office. A Louisiana exhibitor affirmed: "The church people clamor for clean pictures, but they all come out to see Mae West."

At M-G-M, Louis B. Mayer took advantage of Irving Thalberg's absence to remove him from his post and make him one of a group of "independent producers" on the lot. Thalberg's recuperation stretched to nine months, and without him to guide them, the newly elevated producers veered toward adult subjects. Mayer also installed his son-in-law, David O. Selznick, as a producer. Selznick's first move was to do his own all-star film, *Dinner at Eight*. Playwrights George S. Kaufman and Edna Ferber were afraid that the censors would spoil it. Frances Marion, Herman Mankiewicz, and Donald Ogden Stewart adapted it, but it lost little of its magic.

Stewart played a game with the SRC: "You would learn to put in . . . incidents or bits of dialogue that they could take out, so that they would let you leave in other things." Thus, in one of Marie Dressler's speeches, "son of a bitch" became "son of a—" but Jean Harlow's lines to Wallace Beery were left intact: "You couldn't get into politics! You couldn't get in anywhere! You couldn't even get in the men's room at the Astor!" According to Stewart, "[Joy and Wingate] wouldn't want to take out too much, so you'd give them five things to take out to satisfy the Hays Office—and you'd get away with murder with what they left in."

The most scandalous behavior in an M-G-M film was not censored or even commented on by James Wingate; he had no idea what he was seeing. Marion Davies, who was earning $10,000 a week, and Bing Crosby, who was earning $6,000 per film, were knocking themselves out on the set of *Going Hollywood*—but not with hard work. They were partying daily in Miss Davies's fourteen-room bungalow. When it was time to film the musical number "We'll Make Hay While the Sun Shines," Davies and Crosby emerged from the palatial structure and took their places in a field of cellophane daisies. The three-foot-high flowers were motorized, swaying from side to side in time to the music. Davies looked at the flowers, and her head also swayed from side to side. She blurted to Crosby: "Don't watch 'em! You'll get sick!" She took a deep breath,

concentrated on a spotlight, and froze her features in a semblance of romantic abandon. No one knew that she was dead drunk.

"BLACK MOONLIGHT"

Irving Thalberg returned to M-G-M in August 1933. He saw films made on redressed sets with rehashed ideas and redundant sex. After a preview of one such film, a new producer crowed: "It's a smash!"

"Yes," said Thalberg coldly. "A few more like it and we'll smash the company!"

This film could have been any of a dozen that betokened the studio's new avarice. Thalberg wanted successful films, too, but never sacrificed taste for profit. He had bought Rose Franken's play *Another Language* for Norma Shearer, only to see Walter Wanger produce it with Helen Hayes. In this version, director Edward H. Griffith shot an art-class scene using a totally nude woman.

Producer Lawrence Weingarten tempted censors with Harry Beaumont's *Should Ladies Behave*. In it, an aging artist (Conway Tearle) dumps his mistress (Katharine Alexander) for her teenage niece (Mary Carlisle). His mistress tells him: "I'd like to meet you ten years from now. I'll have my revenge." Producer Lucien Hubbard used sets and music from *Dinner at Eight* for William Wellman's *Midnight Mary*, an underworld film in which playboy Franchot Tone, apropos of nothing, asks gangster moll Loretta Young: "Now *what* do you suppose made me think of sex?" In another scene, Young whispers in Ricardo Cortez's ear what she will do with him when they are alone. Years later, Loretta Young said: "I didn't know she was living with that man. . . . If I had, I think I would have put it out of my mind." In Sam Wood's *The Barbarian*, Myrna Loy and Ramon Novarro enjoy sadomasochism in Egypt, complete with slapping, whipping, and kidnapping. This volatility is excused by the revelation that Loy is half Arab.

Sexual irregularities were not limited to M-G-M. In Fox Film's *Hoopla*, Clara Bow was "Lou," a hard-boiled carnival dancer accused of seducing a pathetically homely teenager to get a cheap ring. After her boss, Nifty (Preston Foster), gets her off, she goes after his son, Chris (Richard Cromwell), lifting her skirt and saying, "Take a *good* look. It won't cost you anything." Then she and Nifty's cast-off mistress, Carrie (Minna Gombell), lure Chris into a disturbingly realistic drinking bout. "Is that the real stuff?" he asks, pointing to a bottle of "white mule."

"If it isn't, I've been gypped outa two bucks." answers Carrie.

"Hoop-*la!*" exclaims Lou after a lusty swig. "That'd make ya run upstairs an' rob your own trunk!" More dirty laughs follow as she gets Chris stupidly, stinking drunk.

The film rolls into nastier territory when Carrie pays Lou $100 to seduce Chris, and Lou swims nude in front of him. James Wingate wrote to producer Al Rockett: "We recommend . . . that the scene be re-edited, so as to indicate that Miss Bow has some clothes on when swimming . . . and eliminating the fade-out in which the couple fall over backwards." *Hoopla* opened in New York without cuts, and Will Hays stepped in, writing to Fox: "I know you will want to take steps immediately to correct this mistake." Two weeks later, Wingate wired a new review: "No exposure of intimate parts of body and no more exposure than has been portrayed in several other recent pictures." The film was well-received, but Clara Bow retired, saying: "I don't wanna be remembered as somebody who couldn't do nothin' but take her clothes off."

The most offbeat film at 1933's most offbeat studio was Erich von Stroheim's *Walking Down Broadway.* Stroheim was known as the most perverse and extravagant director in Hollywood, and he was con-

Barbara Stanwyck in Ladies They Talk About. *Portrait by Homer Van Pelt.*

Clara Bow in Hoopla. *Portrait by Otto Dyar. Clara Bow Estate, courtesy Rex Bell, Jr.*

sequently unemployable. Winfield Sheehan hoped that a small film set in America would be a successful change of pace for Stroheim, but according to screenwriter Leonard Spigelgass, Stroheim was "chiefly interested in the neuroses" of lower-class New Yorkers and "turned the simple American characters into far more complicated ones, Vienna-oriented." Their script was subtitled "An Inconsequential Story concerning small people along THE GREAT WHITE WAY." Its first scene has a young man picking up a girl with this line: "Well—if it ain't Gloria [Swanson]—I didn't know you with your clothes on . . . Say!—with what I've got in my head—an' them—(looks at girl's hips)—we'll produce! Catch on?"

Jason Joy had been the first to review the script, writing to Hays: "Von Stroheim . . . kicked like a steer about seeing us, but I was very much pleased yesterday to hear that he thinks we aren't so bad . . . this man has always been a hard one to handle." His actors would agree. He slapped Boots Mallory when she could not cry after working for more than twenty hours, and Terrance Ray "was supposed to laugh, and he couldn't," recalled cameraman Charles van Enger. "And so what von Stroheim did, he had a guy tie a string around the end of his pecker. He put it down his pants . . . and he would pull this string and that made the guy laugh." As usual, Hollywood did not tolerate Stroheim for long. When Winfield Sheehan and Sol Wurtzel previewed *Walking Down Broadway,* they decided that it was too aberrant even for Fox Film.

They fired Stroheim and reshot the entire film, releasing it as a shambles called *Hello, Sister!*

RKO-Radio Pictures saved its hide with that of a supersimian. *King Kong* was the most perverse love story of all, right down to the giant ape's olfactory inspection of his love object, Fay Wray. Perversity also emerged from the jungles at Paramount. *The Island of Lost Souls* was a rich man's *Freaks*. Adapted from the H. G. Wells novel *The Island of Dr. Moreau*, it was photographed by Karl Struss and directed by Erle C. Kenton, both of whom were recognized portrait photographers. As Sternberg had made the American South a glistening backdrop for Dietrich, Kenton turned Catalina Island and the Paramount backlot into a foggy nest of horrors. "Luckily, we had a real fog," remembered Struss. When they did not, Struss gave the film the Paramount treatment, making hot light fall through bamboo slats onto steaming white stucco. What takes place in this dreamlike setting is not so pretty: Dr. Moreau (Charles Laughton) is trying to transform animals into humans. Laughton plays the blasphemous vivisectionist as an effete, purring host. When a young visitor to his island reviles him for his experiments, he answers, ever so coolly: "Mr. Parker, spare me these youthful horrors." The film, which played up the sexual attraction of the animals for the humans, was rejected by no less than fourteen local censor boards, but Paramount persisted with jungle oddities.

Edward Sutherland's *Murders in the Zoo* opens in Indochina with Lionel Atwill tying up a man whom he suspects of cuckolding him. Atwill and his henchmen leave the man, who staggers into a wide-angle close-up that reveals a hideous sight—his mouth has been sewn shut. *King of the Jungle* has Buster Crabbe as Kaspa, the Lion Man, whose exposed buttocks are upstaged only by animals escaping a circus fire. Charles Laughton is upstaged by no one in *White Woman*, a sweaty jungle film in which he torments an atypically passive Carole Lombard. *Tonight Is Ours* was adapted from Noël Coward's *The Queen Was in the Parlour*, and its perversity takes place in a Ruritanian flashback. Claudette Colbert marries the King of Kroya, only to discover that he is a bit kinky: "You pretend that you're my slave and I'll chase you around the room, and then—" *Girl Without a Room* had Parisian perversity. Ralph Murphy's stylishly directed film features a dance by Joyzelle. In it, she wears nothing

but a coat of metallic body paint. Its setting is a Paris bistro, but it could be any dive in the "twilight world" of Manhattan.

Something queer was happening in 1933. Films were introducing audiences to "lavender men" and "mannish" women. *Sign of the Cross* had its frankly erotic lesbian dance. *Cavalcade* had a shot in which one willowy young man affixes a slave bracelet to the wrist of another. *Call Her Savage* had a scene in which Clara Bow goes slumming in Greenwich Village. The restaurant she visits has a floor show of two young men dressed as chambermaids, singing these lyrics:

> *If a sailor in pajamas I should see*
> *I'm sure 'twould scare the life out of me!*
> *But on a great big battleship we'd like to be*
> *Working as chambermaids!*

In his book *Gay New York*, historian George Chauncey describes the "pansy craze" that swept New York in the early 1930s. Coming as it did on the heels of the so-called Negro craze, it first captured the attention of novelists such as Tiffany Thayer and Carl Van Vechten and then of Hollywood. Flouting Article II, Section 4 of the Code, screenwriters began to insinuate sex perversion into their work. They began with the "nance comedy" of actors Grady Sutton, Ferdinand Gottschalk, and Franklin Pangborn. In Paramount's *Hot Saturday*, Sutton plays a bank teller whom any girl can safely date because he is *so* harmless. In *Female*, Gottschalk plays a wicked, mocking little man who can say with prissy insolence: "The dominant *male*, my dear." In Paramount's *International House*, Franklin Pangborn plays a hotel manager who has nerves of steel, provided he gets his cup of tea. When W. C. Fields lands an autogyro on the terrace of the hotel, Pangborn waves effusively at him. Fields frowns, pulls the flower from his lapel, and says: "Don't let the posy fool ya!" Publicity for RKO's *Professional Sweetheart* said: "Pangborn is famous for his portrayals of 'sissified' characters . . . those chaps usually known as Adelbert, who go in for arched eyebrows and a mincing walk." At this same studio, *Our Betters* had a character who was more cartoon than human, a dance instructor (Tyrrell Davis) who wears as much lip rouge as the socialites he tyrannizes.

In 1933, the studios turned a corner, transforming caricatures into characters. At Warner Bros., in Lloyd Bacon's *Footlight Parade,* Francis (Frank McHugh) asks Kent (James Cagney) to audition a special friend: "I simply had to tell you. This boy, Scott Blair. He's a discovery. Just loads of talent and personality."

"He sounds fascinating," replies Kent. "Bring him up some time. Maybe the three of us could knit some doilies." Wingate wrote Warner: "You should be very careful to avoid characterizing Francis as a 'pansy.' It seems to us that it is all right to show him as being rather fluttery and temperamental, but the various remarks made about him by Kent are likely to over-emphasize the characterization."

At Universal, John Stahl's *Only Yesterday* has Franklin Pangborn as a vivid but respectable interior designer who brings a handsome young man (Barry Norton) to a party at a penthouse he has decorated, on the way admiring a painting in a shop window: "Look! That heavenly blue against that mauve curtain. Doesn't it *excite* you? You know, blue like that does something to me!"

The Fox Film Corporation had the distinction of being the first studio to use the word "gay" to denote homosexuality in a film. In David Butler's *My Weakness,* Charles Butterworth and Sid Silvers are both hopelessly in love with Lilian Harvey. Butterworth suggests a solution: "Let's be gay!" The SRC mandated that the line be muffled in the soundtrack of all release prints. At the same studio, Raoul Walsh's *Sailor's Luck* included a splashily effeminate swimming pool attendant (Frank Atkinson). Sailor Jimmy (James Dunn) spies him and says to his pals: "Et-gay the ansy-pay!" The attendant waves at them: "Bye, sailors!" Walter Lang's *The Warrior's Husband* went further. It told the story of Pontus, an ancient country where women are warlike, and men are sylphlike, raised only to procreate. Sapiens (Ernest Truex) is prepared by his father, Sapiens Major (Ferdinand Gottschalk), and mother, Pomposia (Helen Ware), for presentation to Hippolyta (Marjorie Rambeau).

SAPIENS MAJOR: Do you want your son to go in there with his ankles showing?

POMPOSIA: Bosh! Hippolyta's mind isn't on his ankles.

SAPIENS: No—she probably has *higher* thoughts.

SAPIENS MAJOR: (reprovingly) Sapiens!

The Warrior's Husband used gender role reversal to get its pansy past the SRC, but films showing lesbians were more direct.

At Warner Bros., *Ladies They Talk About* put Barbara Stanwyck in prison. In a neighboring cell is a beefy gal who delights her cellmate with the size of her biceps. "You're just always exercising!" coos the cellmate. United Artists released a bizarre film by Rowland Brown called *Blood Money.* Its plot concerns a powerful bailbondsman (George Bancroft). His girlfriend, Ruby (Judith Anderson), runs a nightclub. When she advises her brother, Drury (Chick Chandler), against going out with trashy women, he defends his new girlfriend.

"This one is nothing but class," says Drury. "Wears a monocle and a man's tuxedo."

"Then you're safe," laughs Ruby.

"That's just where you're wrong. She dresses that way for laughs. Got a great sense of humor."

The girlfriend, played by Kathlyn Williams, is waiting at the bar. A woman sits down nearby, and Williams looks her up and down.

As the year wore on, this type of scene became more prevalent. Martin Quigley wrote to Will Hays: "It may be noted that the angle of perverted sex . . . has crept so broadly into several items of recent product that it will be fortunate indeed if it escapes notice in the newspapers." What concerned Hollywood's critics most was how matter-of-factly it presented homosexual characters. Director William K. Howard planned to film *The Power and the Glory.* In Preston Sturges's script, a railroad magnate (Spencer Tracy) endures the unspoken love of his best friend (Ralph Morgan). Howard got resistance from both the Hays Office and Fox Film. Sidney Kent wrote to Winfield Sheehan: "If there is in this story a sex relationship such as Mr. Hays mentions, it will have to come out. I think the quicker we get away from degenerates and fairies in our stories, the better off we are going to be and I do not want any of them in Fox pictures." Nevertheless, Fox Film was the only studio besides M-G-M that showed a profit in 1933; the queer folk remained.

At Paramount, one musical number captured the decadence of New York and the depravity of Hollywood. It appeared in a Bing Crosby vehicle called *Too Much Harmony.* The film's centerpiece was a revue, *Cocktails of 1933,* which was written by Arthur Johnston and Sam Coslow. Its best production number was "Black Moonlight." At the time,

Carrie (Minna Gombell) agrees to pay Lou (Clara Bow) one hundred dollars to seduce the carnival boss's teenage son in Hoopla.

In Hoopla, *Clara Bow assumes Harlow's hard-boiled gaze and Dietrich's aggressiveness. Portrait by Otto Dyar of Bow and Richard Cromwell. Clara Bow Estate, courtesy Rex Bell, Jr.*

In Fox Film's Walking Down Broadway, *Mac (Terrance Ray) shows Mona (Minna Gombell) dirty postcards. Mona exclaims:* "Burn *my* clothes!" *This scene was discarded when the film was taken from Erich von Stroheim and reshot as* Hello, Sister!

Charles Bickford makes a sweaty pass at Carole Lombard in Paramount's jungle melodrama White Woman.

Harlem was a place where New Yorkers could find all-night jazz, drag bars, and drugs. Its unique attractions had been celebrated in novels such as Carl Van Vechten's *Nigger Heaven,* but the evanescence of its escapes was rarely mentioned.

As Shirley Grey sings on a darkened stage, a drugged-out girl walks across a bridge high above, enacting a sad pantomime.

Lost in the shuffle, I've drifted and strayed,
Bruised by the city, bewildered, betrayed,
With a heart heavy laden, with faltering strides,
I have come to the bridge, to the line that divides.

Shirley Grey sings "Black Moonlight" in Paramount's
Too Much Harmony.

The girl sees a man approaching, a rough-looking workman. She sidles up to him, and tries to pick him up. He laughs in her face, pushes the palm of his hand in it, and shoves her away from him. She slams into the railing. As he saunters off, she throws her purse to the ground, and looks down.

What am I doing up here in a daze,
As I gaze at the cold river bed,

The girl climbs the railing and starts to jump from it. A policeman stops her. The girl steps down and looks behind her, where curtains part and reveal the beckoning lights of Harlem.

Why do I ask myself "Shall I go back?"
When I seem to be going ahead . . .

The girl walks toward the lights, and the scene changes to a dream. Shirley Grey sings in a sequined pavilion as rows of fluffy-haired dancers advance in somber, measured steps.

To Black moonlight,
Where ev'rything reflects your color.
Darkness that is endless,
Nights that leave me friendless, blue.

The dancers thrust, wriggle, and writhe. A silhouette of a naked arm pounding a drum is superimposed over them, and a montage flashes images of weary black musicians. As lights move, the dancers' skin color changes from white to black, and their dancing becomes overtly sexual.

Black moonlight, you make the lights of
*   Harlem duller,*
Just like me you're faded,
Jaded and degraded too.

As the dancers retreat from the stage, their skin still metamorphosing, Shirley Grey ends her song.

Black moonlight, I've lost all power to resist you,
Madly I await you,
Even though I hate you!
Black moonlight!

This scene was cut only by the Massachusetts and Pennsylvania censors, but its significance was far-reaching. In four minutes, it told a persuasive story of drug addiction, prostitution, and suicide, and showed the commingling of races in one body—all in a popular family film. If a scene as corrupting as this could be planted in a harmless plot, Hollywood was capable of anything. Someone stronger than James Wingate was needed, and Joe Breen was available.

Charles Laughton as H. G. Wells's Dr. Moreau
in Paramount's Island of Lost Souls. *Portrait by Mack Elliott.*

Sadism in soft focus: Ramon Novarro subjugates Myrna Loy
in M-G-M's The Barbarian.

137

While strolling through Busch Gardens, Nora Cecil and Mabel Stark encounter Kaspa, the Lion Man (Larry "Buster" Crabbe) in Paramount's King of the Jungle.

Frances Dee and Larry "Buster" Crabbe return circus lions to a soft-focus jungle in King of the Jungle.

A camera crane was needed for this close-up of the star of RKO-Radio's King Kong.

Fay Wray wears little more than a shamed expression after Kong removes her dress and sniffs his fingers. This scene was removed at the behest of the PCA in 1938 but restored by Janus Films in 1969.

139

Frances Dee is a restless nymphomaniac in Blood Money,
a Twentieth Century Pictures production.

Kathleen Burke will soon feed Lionel Atwill's alligators in Paramount's
Murders in the Zoo. *Photograph by Sherman Clark.*

When Joyzelle Joyner dances in Paramount's Girl Without a Room, *she wears naught but body paint.*

Lionel Atwill is a sculptor whose obsession with his work is more than artistic in Warner Bros.'
The Mystery of the Wax Museum. *Photograph by Scotty Welbourne.*

TOP:
*William Farnum, Helen Hayes,
and Robert Montgomery are upstaged by an
unbilled model in this Milton Brown
photograph from M-G-M's*
Another Language.

BOTTOM:
In M-G-M's Black Orange
Blossoms, *Jean Harlow wore Clark Gable's
bathrobe in this "morning after"
scene. Before the film was released as* Hold
Your Man, *the scene was reshot to show
her wearing street clothes.*

OPPOSITE:
*"You're young and fresh, and I'm burnt
out." John Barrymore's speech to Madge Evans
in M-G-M's* Dinner at Eight *was prophetic,
both for the character and for the actor.
Photograph by Frank Tanner.*

Franklin Pangborn usually played a fussy, flustered sissy.

In Fox Film's The Warrior's Husband, *Elissa Landi played the Warrior. Ernest Truex usually played a purse-lipped, put-upon "pansy."*

Ferdinand Gottschalk always played a bitchy old queen.

"You don't know much about women, do you?" Ruth Chatterton asks Philip Reed in Warner Bros.' Female. *Her expression betrays the realization that her intended conquest is an invert.*

In RKO's Our Betters, *mincing, made-up Tyrrell Davis kisses Violet Kemble-Cooper's hand.
It is a prelude, not to romance but to a torturous tango lesson.*

In Blood Money, *Kathlyn Williams plays "The Mannish Woman," less interested in
George Bancroft than in the unbilled blonde at right.*

Busby Berkeley was well-suited to choreograph a lustful slave auction in Goldwyn's Roman Scandals.
Settings by Richard Day. Photograph by Kenneth Alexander. Courtesy the Kobal Collection.

"Do you know what it means to feel like God?" asks Dr. Moreau (Charles Laughton) in the stylishly scary Island of Lost Souls.

"THREE CHEERS
FOR SIN!"

The winter of 1933 was a frustrating time for Joe Breen. He could see James Wingate failing, but there was little he could do about it. When he did help with films such as *A Man's Castle,* he was hamstrung by irresolute policies. Breen turned to the Midwest Catholics for moral support. He wrote Father Wilfred Parsons that "nobody out here cares a damn for the Code or any of its provisions." He wrote Father FitzGeorge Dinneen that the Hollywood producers were "a foul bunch, crazed with sex, dirty-minded and ignorant in all matters having to do with sound morals." He wrote Martin Quigley that Will Hays was in "abject fear" of the moguls. He wrote Father Daniel Lord that the March crisis had caused the studios to go after "quick money."

When Lord wrote Quigley that Wingate was a "complete washout," Quigley decided to see for himself. Breen noted his reaction: "I never saw him so down in the mouth about anything." Hays tried to rekindle Quigley's enthusiasm, but failed. For Quigley and the Midwest Catholics, there was only one conclusion: they had been had. The first defection came in May. Lord told Hays that Hollywood could go "merrily to hell." The next was Dinneen, who began naming indecent films from the pulpit. In his opinion, what the movies needed was a "legion of decency." Alice Ames Winter of the General Federation of Women's Clubs also resigned, but Hays talked her into remaining. In May, he assigned Breen to work with the studios on three controversial films, *Baby Face, The Story of Temple Drake,* and *Ann Vickers.*

Baby Face was Darryl Zanuck's answer to *Red-Headed Woman.* He wrote the treatment and sold it to Warner Bros. for a dollar; with a weekly salary of $3,500, he hardly needed the money. He then had a story conference with Barbara Stanwyck and screenwriter Howard Smith, who confirmed it with a memo:

> Following up the conference with Stanwyck, I am sending you this note to remind you of the things she suggested, and which you suggested during the conference, for amplification and

improvement of the story.

> 1. The idea of Baby Face's father forcing the girl to dance at stag parties and to have affairs with the different men at the start of the story . . . how her father forces her to dance in the almost nude for the few shekels which the men give her, and which shekels the father immediately, brutally takes away from her.

The script of *Baby Face,* by Gene Markey and Kathryn Scola, was tougher than anything Warner Bros. had submitted to Wingate, who quickly notified Hays: "The theme is sordid and of a troublesome nature. However, we will do our best to clean it up as much as possible, and the fact that Barbara Stanwyck is destined for the leading role will probably mitigate some of the dangers in view of her sincere and restrained acting."

Baby Face was Lily Powers, an ambitious girl who escapes a degrading existence in a steel town by exploiting the men who want to exploit her. The only trustworthy man she knows, an old cobbler, advises her:

> A woman, young, beautiful like you, can get anything she wants in the world. Because you have power over men. But you must use men, not let them use you. You must be a master, not a slave. Look here—Nietzsche says, "All life, no matter how we idealize it, is nothing more nor less than exploitation." That's what I'm telling you. Exploit yourself. Go to some big city where you will find opportunities. Use men! Be strong! Defiant! Use men to get the things you want!

In a note not meant for the SRC, the screenwriters planned one of Lily's many seductions: "We go as far in this scene as the censors will allow." To show Lily sleeping her way to the top, the script has the camera crane up a skyscraper to the saxophone wail of "The St. Louis Blues."

Wingate ingenuously asked Zanuck to downplay "the element of sex" and to punish Lily by having her lose her money and her husband, the bank president whom she genuinely loves. "That is, if Lily is shown at the end to be no better off than she was when she left the steel town, you may lessen the chance of drastic censorship action by this strengthening of the moral value of the story."

Zanuck agreed and the film went into production. Director Alfred E. Green finished it just in time for Hays's emergency visit to Hollywood.

Hays looked at *Baby Face* and told Wingate to order changes. Wingate drafted Breen; Breen wrote a letter and Wingate signed it. Zanuck reluctantly made the changes and shipped the film to the New York board. Irwin Esmond, Wingate's successor in New York, promptly rejected it. Zanuck lost patience: "I deleted and altered the lines you objected to—such as 'Is it your first?' and 'I know you have had many lovers before.' Elimination of both these lines weakened both situations. . . . I shot a new ending to the picture, which gave it a more wholesome and brighter finish."

In mid-April, Zanuck suddenly had more pressing concerns. Jack Warner reneged on the studio's promise to restore salary cuts to its employees, making Zanuck look like a first-class liar. He sent a letter to Warner: "For many reasons with which you are cognizant, I hereby offer my resignation from all capacities in which I am employed by you." Hal Wallis succeeded Zanuck as head of production, and *Baby Face* became his problem.

Alfonse Ethier quotes Nietzsche to Barbara Stanwyck in Baby Face.

At this point Joe Breen reviewed the "Reasons Supporting the Code" and decided to invoke the concept of "morally compensating values." As historian Leonard Leff points out, this phrase is found nowhere in the Code: "Breen normally justified his use of the concept by citing a clause that allowed the 'presentation of evil' provided that in the end, 'the audience feels that evil is wrong and good is right.'" So armed, Breen wrote Warner: "Nowhere is the heroine denounced for her brazen method of using men to promote herself financially . . . we would suggest an attempt to use the cobbler in a few added scenes as the spokesman of morality."

The cobbler's dialogue was rewritten by Breen: "A woman, young, beautiful, like you are, can get anything she wants in the world. *But there is a right and a wrong way. Remember, the price of the wrong way is too great.* Go to some big city where you will find opportunities. *Don't let people mislead you.* You must be a master, not a slave. *Be clean, be strong, defiant, and you will be a success.*" (Emphasis added to indicate Breen's new lines.) Wallis dubbed the new lines onto an over-the-shoulder shot of the cobbler, and Esmond passed the film.

"Three cheers for Sin!" cried a review in *Liberty* magazine. "If you don't think it pays, get a load of Barbara Stanwyck as she sins her way to the top floor of Manhattan's swellest bank. . . . This is about the roughest story that has come to the screen, but done disarmingly well." Another review asked if the SRC had "been out to lunch all year." Somewhat apologetically, Stanwyck told the *New York Sun*: "Everyone else has glamour but me, so I played in *Baby Face*. Anything for glamour." Although the Ohio and Virginia censors would not pass the film, it played in more territories than anyone expected. Breen's use of "morally compensating values" had set a precedent.

He could not do as much with *The Story of Temple Drake*. Its source was the William Faulkner novel *Sanctuary*, reviewed by Lamar Trotti in 1931: "This is a sadistic story of horror—probably the most sickening novel ever written in this country. Important because of its brilliant style, it has had quite a large sale." It was the fable of a Southern society girl whose rebellious streak runs her afoul of inbred mountaineers and an impotent bootlegger. He rapes her with a corncob and makes her work in a brothel, which she eventually enjoys. Trotti was unable to finish the book, declaring it "utterly unthinkable as a motion picture." When Paramount's Emanuel Cohen attempted the unthinkable in early 1933, Will Hays told Breen: "We simply must not allow the production of a picture which will offend every right-thinking person who sees it." Cohen assigned Oliver H. P. Garrett to write the screenplay and Stephen Roberts to direct. James Wingate met with Cohen: "As a parting shot, I advised him that I would much appreciate their making a Sunday school story out of 'The Story of Temple Drake.'"

Not everyone took it so lightly. *Harrison's Reports* charged Cohen with doing "the greatest harm to the motion picture industry that has ever been done in its entire history." Paramount executives denied that George Raft had refused to appear in the film, but cast Jack LaRue as the twisted bootlegger. Cohen cast Miriam Hopkins as Temple Drake, who still went to "Miss Reba's house," not as an inductee but as a sex slave to Trigger, whom she ultimately murdered. In Garrett's script, Trigger was no longer impotent, so the infamous corncob was struck from the plot. Jean Negulesco, fresh from the successes of *The Big Broadcast* and *A Farewell to Arms,* made storyboard sketches, and then found himself awarded the dubious distinction of "technical adviser on the rape scene." He alluded to the unique rape with some subtle set decoration, but Will Hays insisted that a corncrib and even stray corncobs be removed. Negulesco then carefully set up each shot, fielding questions from Miriam Hopkins such as "Jean, are my legs open at the right angle? Shouldn't my dress be up higher? Do I scream?" As shot, the scene ends with Trigger leaving a menacing close-up, and as the image of a barn wall (painted with soft-focus shuttered light) fades out, there is a terrified scream.

Breen previewed *The Story of Temple Drake* in mid-March and pronounced it "sordid, base, and thoroughly unpleasant." He told Cohen to make changes in the film before submitting it to any censor boards. Cohen ignored him and submitted it to the New York board in mid-April. Esmond promptly rejected it, and the other state boards found out. For the first time in the history of the Code, it appeared that all eight boards might reject a film. In May, a nervous Cohen worked with Breen to make such changes as Esmond deemed necessary. Jump cuts, overly loud background music,

Dick Powell, Mary Astor, and Adolphe Menjou convey the tipsy frivolity of Convention City.

and claps of thunder muffled lewd dialogue, but the rape remained. Though it was only suggested by a fadeout and a scream, it was unprecedented. The film received mixed reviews. Many critics condemned it, but just as many conceded that it was powerfully written, directed, and acted. Its aesthetic merits, however, could not hush its bad publicity. Breen had predicted that it would earn the "wrathful condemnation of decent people everywhere." He was right, but these people did not have to see it to disapprove of it. Just seeing its lurid posters drove them to write outraged letters.

Breen also tried to squelch RKO's *Ann Vickers,* which was based on a Sinclair Lewis novel forbidden to Catholics because its feminist heroine has two affairs and one abortion. When he had read the script in May, he wrote: "This script simply *will not do.*" Producer Merian C. Cooper countered that the script had already cleaned up most of the book's problems and that it did not "pander to cheap sex, nor to cheap and vulgar emotions." But this was not enough for Breen. He insisted that the script have a "spokesman for accepted morality."

At this point, the film was already in production, and RKO president B. B. Kahane was less than willing to abide by precepts that were not in the text of the Code. After three weeks of revisions and an investment of $300,000, he wrote: "We cannot afford to risk this amount of money with a chance that after we finish the production, Dr. Wingate will renew his objections or make new ones." Kahane went on to say that RKO was "frankly doubtful that [Wingate] had a broad enough viewpoint regarding the Production Code." He then called Will Hays's bluff by asking for an AMPP jury to judge not the film but its script. Did Hays defend Breen's "voice for morality"?

Hays dodged the issue, spewing platitudes about the studios' responsibility "to establish in the minds of the audience that adultery is wrong, unjustified, and indefensible." Kahane then questioned the ability—indeed, the *authority*—of Wingate or Hays to interpret the Code in such a way that RKO would have to "affirmatively establish" that a character's actions were wrong. Hays responded by sending a letter to all the studios, telling them that "illicit sex relationships" were not to be filmed, regardless of good taste. The standoff between him and RKO ended, predictably enough, with a few token cuts, but its lessons to Joe Breen were invaluable: morally compensating values were needed, but Will Hays was not going to fight for them.

John Cromwell's *Ann Vickers* was only one of a dozen 1933 films with sexual elements. What Breen failed to acknowledge was that some of them—*King Kong, The Story of Temple Drake, The Song of Songs, The Bitter Tea of General Yen, Dancing Lady*— were works of art. As skilled a story editor as Jason Joy, he did not share Joy's respect for cinematic accomplishment. Joseph I. Breen only had one goal, to impose his moral values on the film industry. "The mainspring of his vitality," wrote Jack Vizzard, "was the fact that he nurtured not the slightest seed of self-doubt regarding his mission or his rectitude. He was right, the moviemakers were wrong, and that was that."

The film that got the most cuts of any since 1929 was *Convention City*. Years later, its producer, Henry Blanke, was known to boast: "Me. I was the one. Single-handedly I brought on the whole Code. Yeah. Ask Joe Breen. He'll tell you. Ask him about *Convention City*." Robert Lord's script for *Convention City* was nominally set in Atlantic City, but it took place in a universe devoted to only two activities: drinking and fornicating. When Wingate read it, he and Joy immediately held a conference with production head Hal Wallis, telling him that it "seemed to indicate a pretty rowdy picture, dealing largely with drunkenness, blackmail and lechery, and without any particularly sympathetic characters or elements."

In Convention City, *Guy Kibbee says to Joan Blondell:*
"You take off your dress and I'll take off my toupee."

Wallis hastened to assure them that the script would incorporate all thirty of their suggested changes. Among them were:

Page 27: We suggest modifying the line "stage our honeymoon in Macey's [sic] window" under the Code, perhaps replacing it with "our wedding."

Page 47: We suggest toning down this scene between Bill, Orchard, and the girls. We believe that under the Code it will be necessary to omit the final line "Take off his clothes," and the action of the girls going to work on Orchard . . .

Page 96: The word "slut" will probably be censorable . . .

Page 132: It will be necessary under the Code to handle this scene so that there is no indication that this is a house of assignation or brothel. We would recommend portraying it rather as a speakeasy, or something along that line. We also believe the line "the library staff upstairs" should be deleted under the Code.

Convention City was a series of indelicate episodes occasioned by a convention of the Honeywell Rubber Company. In one, salesman Ted (Adolphe Menjou) tries to edge salesman George (Guy Kibbee) out of a promotion by seducing Claire (Patricia Ellis), the boss's teenage daughter. Salesperson Arline (Mary Astor) disapproves: "Ted, she's only a child. You want to go to the pen?"

"She's old enough—almost, anyhow," laughs Ted. "I remember the year she was born."

Lord made every change suggested by Wingate and Joy, including "a comedy bit about a drunk who was chasing a sheep around the lobby of the hotel, trying to lure it up to his room." Lord changed the sheep to a goat, and moved the chase out of the hotel. In one day, he rewrote twenty-nine pages. At the top of one, he noted: "Mr. Wingate suggests that we handle the following drunken scenes with extreme delicacy." One character summed up these scenes: "I'm stinkin'—and I love it!"

Director Archie Mayo had a heavy hand, according to a memo from Jack Warner: "We must put brassieres on Joan Blondell and make her cover up her breasts because, otherwise, we are going to have these pictures stopped in a lot of places. I believe in showing their forms but, for Lord's sake, don't let those bulbs stick out." Blondell remembered the film: "That is the raunchiest thing there ever has been . . . we had so many hysterically dirty things in it . . . no dirty words or anything like that, just funny, burlesque-y." One of the most outrageous lines involved the conventioneers' product. A Honeywell Rubber Company employee says: "Let's place our goods in convenient slot machines. You never can tell when an emergency may arise!" When Wingate reviewed the finished film, he wrote to Hays: "While not as rough as the script indicated, it is nevertheless somewhat low-tone entertainment, long on drinking and rowdiness, but is fortunately free from any actual sex situations." The state boards did not agree. *Convention City* averaged twenty cuts per board.

Even in a choppy condensation, *Convention City* did respectable business—and gave reformers more fuel. Joe Breen stood at the edge of the SRC, seemingly powerless as Wingate passed one filthy film after another. Still, Breen's public relations job had made him some powerful allies. One was Bishop John J. Cantwell of Los Angeles. At Breen's urging, Cantwell visited each of the studios, contacted other bishops, and spoke with banker A. H. Giannini, chairman of the Bank of America. Breen thought the threat of a financial boycott would frighten Hollywood into compliance, so he brought Giannini to an AMPP meeting on August 1. He also invited a powerful Catholic lawyer, Joseph Scott, who was affiliated with the Los Angeles Chamber of Commerce.

After Will Hays introduced them to the assembled executives, Giannini said he would no longer underwrite films that were "prostituting the youth of America." Scott, whose wife was Jewish, warned against a backlash of anti-Semitism, contending that communists and film moguls were "serving to build up an enormous case against the Jews in the eyes of the American people." The implied threat was a Catholic boycott, which could in turn spawn a Christian revolt against Hollywood, the last thing the industry needed in this year of crisis.

Once again, the studio heads pledged cooperation, resolving to cleanse themselves of what Adolph Zukor admitted was "dirt and filth." Breen did not believe them. He did not know that Joseph Schenck had convened a second meeting—to denounce Scott and the reformers as "narrow-minded and bigoted" and convince his fellow moguls that they had the right to film mature subjects. But Breen knew that Hollywood, regardless of race or creed, spoke only one language: box office. He rallied the original Code group behind him: Dinneen, Mundelein, Parsons, Lord, and Quigley. For two months, they threw ideas back and forth. Then they had a brainstorm.

Quigley and Breen approached Reverend Amleto Giovanni Cicognani, a representative of the Pope, to speak to American Catholics on their behalf. At this time, the Roman Catholic population of the United States was 20,322,594.* The apostolic delegate spoke to the National Conference of Catholic Charities in New York on October 1, enjoining clergy and laity alike: "Catholics are called by God, the Pope, the bishops and the priests, to a united and vigorous campaign for the purification of the cinema, which has become a deadly menace to morals." He was especially solicitous about young movie fans: "What a massacre of innocent youth is taking place hour by hour!"

More than forty secular organizations had already voiced disapproval of 1933's films, galvanized by a sensational new book, Henry James Forman's *Our Movie Made Children*. First serialized in *McCall's* magazine, it was the culmination of the Payne Foundation Study, a three-year series of interviews and experiments conducted to measure the effect of films on children. That this study was backed by the pro-censorship Motion Picture Research Council did not faze Forman or the factions who cited it. All that mattered were its shocking statistics.

They stated that the weekly film audience was one-third children, and mostly unsupervised. In the films they watched, 87.5 percent of the characters smoked, 66 percent drank, 43 percent were drunk, and 43 percent enacted a bedroom scene. According to Forman, these films portrayed an unreal world where "apparently every human being over forty has been chloroformed . . . in that world, where few toil and none spin, these movie characters play their rôles preponderantly in full accoutrements of formal dress." Since the book claimed that youth retained 70 percent of what they viewed, that retention increased as time went by, and that sleep (and other nighttime activities) were severely affected, it relied heavily on adolescent testimony:

"Buddy Rogers and Rudy Vallee have kissed me oodles of times, but they don't know it, God bless 'em."

"When I see a fellow and a girl in a passionate love scene . . . I just have a *hot* feeling going through me and I want to do everything bad."

"After I have seen a romantic love scene, I feel as though I couldn't have just one fellow to love me, but I would like about five."

"When I see these movies, I . . . go out to some roadhouse or an apartment with my man and get my wants satisfied. Especially when I get all stirred up and my passion rises . . . I have a feeling that can't be expressed with words but with actions."

Another best-seller was Herbert Blumer's *Movies and Conduct*, which quoted an articulate high-school girl: "I imagined myself caressing the heroes with great passion and kissing them so they would stay osculated for ever . . . I practiced love scenes either with myself or with a girlfriend. We sometimes think we could beat Greta Garbo, but I doubt it." Both Forman and Blumer blamed the film industry for America's erotomania, never admitting that the public paid cash to make Garbo a star. At M-G-M, Walter Wanger was preparing a new Garbo film for this same eager public.

Garbo's friend Salka Viertel was writing a screenplay, *Christina*, based on the life of the seventeenth-century Swedish monarch, causing Hollywood sophisticates to wonder if she would hint at the queen's bisexuality. Irving Thalberg asked her if she had seen the German film *Mädchen in Uniform*, which had a lesbian subtext: "Does not Christina's affection for her lady-in-waiting indicate something like that?" Viertel recalled: "He wanted me to 'keep it in mind,' and perhaps if 'handled with taste it would give us some very interesting scenes.'" M-G-M submitted the script to the SRC, and Wingate promptly replied: "We assume that you will be careful to avoid anything in the portrayal of this scene which might be construed as lesbianism."

In the script, which also bore the handiwork of Ben Hecht and S. N. Behrman, Christina travels her country dressed as a man and must share a cozy room in a snowbound inn with a Spanish ambassador (John Gilbert). He, of course, discovers her true sex, and they spend several idyllic days together. In August, Joy got Wanger to agree that Rouben Mamoulian would shoot the scene at the inn several ways. However, Mamoulian had conceived the morning-after scene as a lyric poem, and shot it so that it could only be cut one way: "Garbo strokes the bedroom where she has been with her lover, so that she will remember every detail. . . . The scene was choreographed. She played it to a metronome. She had to roll over a bed, and move around the room in what was a kind of sonnet in action." Cinematographer William Daniels said: "All the light in the room came from the fire—or seemed to." The two artists had created a masterpiece of sensuality, and Mamoulian was not about to let the SRC tamper with it.

Jason Joy, meanwhile, was preoccupied with business at Fox, and Wingate was losing ground. According to Jack Vizzard: "Wingate took refuge in the Hollywood Athletic Club, where about all he was allowed to do was work out on the barbells. . . . He was not to be faulted if he took a second cup of cheer at cocktail time." Breen saw the SRC falling apart, unable to stop another "perverted" film. He became a man possessed. He rushed from diocese to diocese, asking each bishop to work with him. Then he wrote a speech for Cantwell to deliver at the annual bishops' meeting in November. His impassioned speech attacked such "vile and nauseating" films as *The Sign of the Cross*, and exhorted the bishops to organize against Hollywood: "The pest hole that infects the entire country with its obscene and lascivious moving pictures must be cleaned and disinfected." The bishops concurred.

On November 15 they elected the "Episcopal Committee on Motion Pictures." Its head, the Most Reverend John T. McNicholas, Archbishop of Cincinnati, worked with Bishop John Noll of Fort Wayne, Bishop Hugh Boyle of Pittsburgh, Bishop Cantwell, and Martin Quigley to create a "Catholic Legion of Decency." The Legion would perform three basic functions: pressure tactics, boycotts of proscribed films, and enforcement of the Code.

Wallace Beery eyes Pert Kelton in The Bowery, *Darryl Zanuck's first production for Twentieth Century Pictures. Photograph by Kenneth Alexander.*

Jesse Lasky's first production for the Fox Film Corporation was Zoo in Budapest, *which starred Loretta Young and Gene Raymond. It was distinguished by Lee Garmes's cinematography. Photograph by Anthony Ugrin. Courtesy the Kobal Collection.*

Breen's barnstorming ended in New York, where he met with Will Hays. Hays told him that he was returning Joy to Fox Film and that he was sending Wingate on a "vacation." Hays then asked Breen to head the Studio Relations Committee. Breen accepted, and returned to California to assume his new post. His first challenge was the M-G-M film now called *Queen Christina.*

Mamoulian knew that Breen would go after the scene in the inn. Mamoulian later said: "I always divide the world into two: those who like the scene and those who don't." Wingate had liked it, and advised cutting only two of Christina's lines from it: "Do you think the old saints would approve of us? Will we have their blessing?" and "This is how the Lord must have felt when He first beheld the finished world, with all His creatures—living, breathing, loving . . . " Mamoulian removed the first, but retained the second. Breen was taking office at the SRC as the film was being edited, but M-G-M was too fast for him.

According to Garbo biographer Karen Swenson, a studio representative worked with New York's Irwin Esmond to cut the film for its premiere—without Breen's approval. Esmond passed it and *Queen Christina* opened on December 26. Most reviews were highly laudatory. A dissenting review came from Martin Quigley, who singled out the scene at the inn "which registers with voluminous and unnecessary detail the fact of a sex affair. The sequence is emphasized and dwelt upon beyond all purposes legitimate to the telling of the story, thereby assuming a pornographic character."

Breen fumed to Mayer: "I know that the picture has been playing in New York for some days without our approval." Then he got down to business. The idea that the queen should invoke God's name on the morning after an illicit affair was repugnant. He planned to cut most of the scene at the inn: "I think Miss Garbo should be kept away from the bed entirely. The scene should be cut from the action at the spinning wheel, at least, and the business of lying across the bed fondling the pillow is, in my considered judgment, very offensive."

Wanger and Mamoulian thought otherwise. They bypassed the new head of the SRC and presented the film to an AMPP jury. Three days later, the secretary of the jury sent M-G-M its decision: "This jury, consisting of Messrs. B. B. Kahane, Jesse L. Lasky, and Carl Laemmle, Jr., saw this picture in your projection room yesterday afternoon and decided unanimously that the picture be approved as exhibited yesterday." *Queen Christina* was vindicated, the sixth SRC decision to be overturned in three years.

Breen did not raise a ruckus. He had lost the battle, but not the war. The state boards in Kansas, Maryland, Ohio, and Pennsylvania cut parts of the scene, and the Virginia board cut it entirely. The Detroit Council of Catholic Organizations condemned *Queen Christina* in the *Michigan Catholic*, describing Garbo as a "perverted creature." In dioceses across the country, bishops were mobilizing against Hollywood. A Catholic crusade was beginning.

"We'll have to get you off the snow—cold turkey," Irene Dunne tells cocaine addict Helyn Eby-Rock in RKO-Radio's Ann Vickers.

The depraved Baron von Mertzbach (Lionel Atwill) buys a work of art—and a model—in Paramount's The Song of Songs. *Photograph by Don English.*

From sentimental innocence to cynical glamour: the evolution of Marlene Dietrich in The Song of Songs. *Photograph by Irving Lippman.*

Bert Longworth makes a supine portrait of Barbara Stanwyck as the horizontally ascendant Lil Powers for Warner Bros.' Baby Face.

Barbara Stanwyck, aptly posed with a ladder, in a Bert Longworth portrait for Baby Face.

Ruby Lemarr (Florence Eldridge) does as little as possible to shelter Temple Drake (Miriam Hopkins) from the storm in The Story of Temple Drake. *Karl Struss's soft focus saved the Paramount film from being completely nightmarish.*

Trigger (Jack La Rue) shoots Tommy the Feeb (James Eagles)
so he can rape Temple Drake. The scene owed its effectiveness
to Jean Negulesco's design.

The infamous rape was reduced to a fade-out and
a scream, but it outraged reformers. The Story of Temple
Drake *became a cause célèbre.*

Greta Garbo played an ambiguous monarch in M-G-M's Queen Christina.

When Garbo ate grapes in Queen Christina, *sound engineer Douglas Shearer made
the sensual sound audible in the finished film.*

One of the most famous bedrooms in film history was nearly shut down by a newly prominent censor.
The scene between Greta Garbo and John Gilbert in Queen Christina *was directed by Rouben Mamoulian,*
lit by William Daniels, and assailed by Joseph Breen.

BREEN'S NEW BROOM

In early 1934, film companies noted an increase in box-office receipts. Franklin Roosevelt's New Deal policies were taking hold, and 70 million Americans a week were now attending the movies. They favored such whimsy as *Flying Down to Rio, Moulin Rouge,* and *Hips, Hips, Hooray.* No less whimsical was the scenario that Hollywood was living: a Catholic attack on the movies, sanctioned by the same people who had fostered the Production Code, the Midwest Catholics. Father Daniel Lord wrote: "I was only one of the many who had had hopes for the Code and was mad through and through." At first, the attack was more rhetorical than real, since the Episcopal Committee was still debating strategies. "We can settle on a common plan later," said Bishop Hugh Boyle of Pittsburgh. "In the meantime, it's best to swarm upon the enemy from all sides with all kinds of weapons."

These weapons included spot boycotts of local theaters, letters to local film exchanges, and letters to the studios. Lord published a pamphlet, *The Movies Betray America,* that accused the industry of "faking observance of the Code." It listed statistics of seduction, rape, murder, brutality, and vulgarity filmed since 1930. Although Martin Quigley and Will Hays thought Lord's pamphlet rash, it was cited by priests in most of the country's 103 dioceses. Catholics who were not already outraged were made to question what they saw at their local movie palace. The first diocese to formally blacklist films was that of Detroit. Monsignor John Hunt proscribed sixty-three films in *St. Leo* magazine, including *Convention City, The Story of Temple Drake, Queen Christina, Flying Down to Rio, Hips, Hips, Hooray!,* and *George White's Scandals.* By April, the air was thick with religious railing.

Joe Breen had taken over the SRC only a few months earlier, so most films in release had not been touched by him. They were a lively group. RKO released *Hips, Hips, Hooray!,* a silly comedy starring Bert Wheeler and Robert Woolsey. One musical number, "Keep Romance Alive," had a bevy of naked chorus girls bubbling in and out of glass-sided bathtubs. Fox Film Corp. tried to make a star of German actress Lilian Harvey in Rowland V. Lee's *I Am Suzanne!* One amazing scene had a marionette show in which Satan (Lionel Belmore) shouts "I pull the strings!" at each sinful puppet. A mannish woman puppet declares herself: "A woman, alas, by Nature's plan / But I like to dress up *like a man!*" Alas, both the puppet and Lilian Harvey were too rarefied for the public.

Universal did better with Frank Borzage's *Little Man, What Now?* The poignant story of a young couple's struggle to subsist in decadent Berlin was passed by Wingate, but the Massachusetts and Ohio boards did not care. They cut a scene of Douglass Montgomery rolling on top of Margaret Sullavan in the grass, even though the characters were married. They also cut the dialogue in which Montgomery's mother admits to him that a man is living with her: "Oh, look! He's shocked! Well, if you think I'm so wicked, why do you come here?" Columbia's *It Happened One Night* also sailed through the SRC, even though it showed Claudette Colbert undressing and sleeping in the same auto camp room as Clark Gable. M-G-M filmed Jerome Kern's *The Cat and the Fiddle,* in which Jeanette MacDonald and Ramon Novarro live together without benefit of clergy. Paramount also ignored Wingate, pushing Stephen Roberts's *The Trumpet Blows* and Mitchell Leisen's *Death Takes a Holiday* through production without changes.

Of the films blacklisted by the diocese of Detroit, twelve were Paramount's and twelve were Warner Bros.' No one offended Breen's sense of rectitude more than Jack Warner. In Breen's opinion, the typical Warner product was a "cheap, low-tone picture with lots of double-meaning wisecracks and no little filth." One film that got by him was Michael Curtiz's *Mandalay,* which had Ricardo Cortez selling his girlfriend, Kay Francis, to a "nightclub" owner, Warner Oland. Producer Hal Wallis knew what he could get away with. In a memo to writer

Robert Presnell, he said that the nightclub "should be shot carefully, that is, making it more of a nightclub and gambling house than . . . a hook shop. I don't feel we will sacrifice anything by doing this because people will put their own interpretation on it and know what kind of establishment it is and what Francis is doing there."

In a memo to director Curtiz, he was more cautious: "When you show Kay Francis in the bathtub with Cortez in the shot and a close-up of Kay Francis in the tub and show her stepping out of the tub and going into Cortez's arms, then you get me to the point where I am going to have to tell you to stick to the script and not to do anything else. For God's sake, Mike, you have been making pictures long enough to know that it is impossible to show a man and woman who are not married in a scene of this kind." The final version wasn't much improved; Kay Francis steps out of the tub, puts a towel around herself, and kisses Cortez through a window, at which point the towel falls to the floor.

Joseph I. Breen began 1934 as the new director of the SRC.

Another Warner film that slipped by Breen was Lloyd Bacon's *Wonder Bar,* an all-star musical with spectacular production numbers by Busby Berkeley. Story editor Robert Lord had submitted Earl Baldwin's script to the SRC in October 1933, and Wingate had recommended thirteen changes, including removal of the "irregular sex relationship" between dancer Dolores Del Rio and her partner, Ricardo Cortez, who whips her. Lord told Wallis: "The changes demanded by the Hays Office seem to me even more idiotic than usual. I would earnestly recommend that we go ahead and make the picture as is." Wallis made a few changes, submitted them to Wingate, then ignored him and charged ahead.

In December, *Wonder Bar* was running behind schedule. Lord was still preparing two musical numbers, one of which was "Goin' to Heaven on a Mule," a shamelessly racist picture of blacks enjoying such celestial pleasures as dancing and watermelons. He wrote Wallis: "Granted, no intelligent person could object to it [but] the various boards of censorship throughout the country have never been distinguished for their intelligence! Do you think it would be borrowing trouble to consult Col. Joy and His Happiness Boys before we went ahead with the number? Or would it be better to make the number, show it to them in the picture and trust to our abilities of salesmanship to overcome any of their objections?" Wallis chose a more devious course. He ran the film for Joy and Geoffrey Shurlock, but without the two musical numbers, assuring them that "there was nothing to worry about in the two numbers."

In the meantime, Breen took over the SRC. Two months later, Hays Office counsel Vincent Hart saw *Wonder Bar* and reported "one item which the audience did not seem to relish," but it was not one of the unseen musical numbers. It was in "the ballroom scene where a man and a woman are shown dancing. Into the scene comes an effeminate-looking youth who taps the dancing man on the shoulder and asks 'May I cut in?' whereupon the man dancing with the girl smiles, leaves her, and the two men dance off together." Breen checked his file copy of the script and there it was, on Page 25: "The man and the youth dance off together—the girl walks disgustedly off the floor."

Breen questioned Shurlock and phoned Joy at Fox; neither remembered the sequence. Growing angry, Breen fired off a letter to Warner, asking for a screening of the entire film. A week passed, and Breen had not gotten a reply. "Neither can I get any rise out of Mr. Warner by way of the telephone," he groused to the New York office. "It is quite evident that this gentleman is giving me the run-around. He evidently thinks that this is the smart thing to do." Breen had momentary satisfaction when the state boards in Ohio and Pennsylvania cut the scene, but he knew he would have to change the way he dealt with producers. He later told Jack Vizzard: "When I spoke to them politely, they thought I was a sissy. I had to show them that I meant what I said."

Vizzard remembered: "He was not a big man, about five foot eight. He was chesty, with an athletic spring in his legs. When he looked at you, it was as if he was saying: 'You wouldn't like to knock this chip off my shoulder, would you?' He was an intelligent man, so this was no dummy act. He was physically fearless."

Before long, the trade papers and even the *New York Times* were commenting on his pugnacious new approach: "Mr. Breen knew how Hollywood liked to argue. He adapted his Gaelic voice and temperament to the situation. He pounded desks as hard as any producer in town. His voice could be heard, on occasion, for miles, while theirs carried but for blocks. The studios were amazed. Could this be a Hays man? He didn't win all his arguments, but his average was excellent." On one occasion, Breen went to visit Harry Cohn at Columbia. He presented Cohn with his portfolio. Cohn was not impressed: "What's all this shit?"

"Mr. Cohn—I take that as a compliment."

"What does that mean?"

"My friends inform me that if there's any expert in this town on shit—it's you. So if I have to be judged, I'm glad it's by professionals."

Having tamed another filmland dragon, Breen returned to the SRC, where scripts were piling up, and there was news from the Episcopal Committee. On April 28, 1934, the Legion of Decency was incorporated. The crusade had begun in earnest.

A Busby Berkeley number, "Spin a Little Web of Dreams," from Warner Bros.' Fashions of 1934.

Lilian Harvey defies Satan (Lionel Belmore) and his dancing devils in Fox Film's I Am Suzanne!

Jeanette MacDonald and Ramon Novarro live together in M-G-M's The Cat and the Fiddle.

It Happened One Night *glistens with Frank Capra's humor and Joseph Walker's diffusion. In this scene,*
Claudette Colbert and Clark Gable share a delicious anticipation.

Miss Frisby (Thelma Todd) eyes the inane Andy (Bert Wheeler) in the RKO production
Hips, Hips, Hooray! *Walter Plunkett designed the office girls' costumes.*

In M-G-M's This Side of Heaven, *interior decorator Bobby Watson gives*
Mae Clarke the hard sell: "Don't you think this is an engaging design? It's been frightfully
admired. I made an overstuffed chair of it for Marjorie Delancey. Do you know her? She's
a precious old thing. She's frightfully fleshy. No matter what she puts on, she looks like
a busted sofa. . . ." His client frowns: "It strikes me as a bit too gay."

In Warner Bros.' Wonder Bar, *Dick Powell and Al Jolson put on brave faces as Bert Longworth captured this unusual scene, described by Joe Breen: "[A] man and a woman are shown dancing. Into the scene comes an effeminate-looking youth who taps the dancing man on the shoulder and asks 'May I cut in?', whereupon the man dancing with the girl smiles, leaves her, and the two men dance off together." Jolson comments: "Boys will be boys."*

169

The spring of 1934 saw films that used pre-Code freedom to explore social issues.
One of the best was Universal's Little Man, What Now? *Here are Douglass Montgomery*
and Margaret Sullavan in a Charles Hall setting. Photograph by Junius Estep.

OPPOSITE:
"To life. And to all brave illusion." Prince Sirki (Fredric March) makes a toast
in Paramount's Death Takes a Holiday. *Mitchell Leisen's film was a haunting blend of the*
spiritual and sensual, as shown in this uncredited portrait of March and Evelyn Venable.

THE FINAL BLOWOUT

The Legion of Decency was not so much an organization as it was a manifestation of Catholic will. By joining it, American Catholics showed their support for the Episcopal Committee. They did not have to attend meetings or vote. They only had to sign a pledge card placed in the church pew at Sunday Mass, and recite the pledge written by Archbishop John McNicholas.

> I wish to join the Legion of Decency, which condemns vile and unwholesome moving pictures. I unite with all who protest against them as a grave menace to youth, to home life, to country and to religion.
>
> I condemn absolutely those salacious motion pictures which, with other degrading agencies, are corrupting public morals and promoting a sex mania in our land.
>
> I shall do all I can to arouse public opinion against the portrayal of vice as a normal condition of affairs, against depicting criminals of any class as heroes and heroines, presenting their filthy philosophy of life as something acceptable to decent men and women.
>
> I unite with all who condemn the display of suggestive advertisements on bill-boards, at theatre entrances and the favorable notices given to immoral motion pictures.
>
> Considering these evils, I hereby promise to remain away from all motion pictures except those which do not offend decency and Christian morality. I promise further to secure as many members as possible for the Legion of Decency.
>
> I make this protest in a spirit of self-respect and with the conviction that the American public does not demand filthy pictures, but clean entertainment and educational features.

A number of cities were ready for the Legion: Chicago's Cardinal George Mundelein had joined with Father FitzGeorge Dinneen to educate their flock; Boston's Cardinal William O'Connell was using radio broadcasts to urge boycotts; and Detroit Catholics were displaying signs in their cars: "We Demand Clean Movies." With the Legion, bishops had a focus for their zeal and a tool for recruit-ment. Within a month, the Legion collected 300,000 signatures in each of the dioceses of Brooklyn, Philadelphia, and Los Angeles, 500,000 in Cleveland, 600,000 in Detroit, 1 million in Boston, and 1 million in Chicago. Meanwhile, Martin Quigley got the signal from Bishop McNicholas to formulate a plan for control of the movies, and he immediately consulted Joe Breen.

Though the Catholics were unanimous in their contempt for indecency, they disagreed on how to quash it. Over this issue, according to historian Gregory Black, they broke into two camps. The first camp comprised Archbishop McNicholas, Bishop John J. Cantwell, the Episcopal Committee, and Quigley. They believed that a show of strength and the mere threat of a boycott would force Will Hays to accept Joe Breen's interpretation of the Code. They favored the abolition of the AMPP jury, but opposed national boycotts, censorship, and blacklists.

The second camp comprised Cardinal Mundelein and his followers: Dinneen, Cardinal Dougherty of Philadelphia, Cardinal William O'Connell of Boston, and Daniel Lord. They, in turn, favored boycotts, letter-writing campaigns, and wildcat blacklists. That was where Lord went out on a limb. In May, he began printing lists of "Code Violators" in his magazine, *The Queen's Work*. His review of *The Trumpet Blows*, for example, ended with: "It is unfit for any decent person to see or approve, and it violates the Code in a dozen different ways. Protest to Paramount Studios, Hollywood. Protest to George Raft, same address." Neither his blacklist nor any of the dozen others in circulation had been cleared by the Episcopal Committee, and they created confusion for Catholic moviegoers. Even so, these blacklists fanned the flames of indignation and contributed to what was now a national crusade.

In Hollywood, it was business as usual. The studios continued to provoke Breen, and though his mind was on the Legion, he responded. Darryl Zanuck's dramatic departure from Warner Bros. had been followed by the equally showy founding of Twentieth Century Pictures, which released films through United Artists but did not belong to the MPPDA or its West Coast branch, the AMPP. At his new studio, Zanuck's randy nature influenced films such as Gregory LaCava's *The Affairs of Cellini*. Breen assailed its characters as "libidinous persons

*In the spring of 1934, the Fox Film Corporation engaged George Hurrell to make this portrait of Alice Faye,
who had created a sensation in* George White's Scandals.

Twentieth Century Pictures' The Affairs of Cellini *starred Fredric March as the lascivious Benvenuto Cellini and Constance Bennett as the depraved Duchess of Florence.*

who engage themselves in promiscuous sexuality."

Lowell Sherman's *Born to Be Bad* cast Loretta Young against type. She played Letty, an "escort" who uses her eight-year-old son Mickey (Jackie Kelk) to con married millionaire Malcolm (Cary Grant). The film has bookseller Fuzzy (Henry Travers) as the voice of morality, but it is a weak voice. Letty mocks it:

> All right. You've made your little speech. Now I'll make mine. . . . Honor and decency? That's a lotta hash. What'd it ever get *me?* I was reared right and my people taught me everything— except how to protect myself in the clinches.
>
> And what happened? The first time I met up with a real problem in life, I went down for the count. You know what happened. I wound up on your doorstep in the rain, cold and hungry. Fifteen years old, with a baby about to be born. No money, no husband, and nobody I could go to.

This speech was added at Breen's behest. He felt that it "did a great deal to make acceptable the heroine's peculiar psychology," but a "shot of Letty seated on the floor, with the upper part of her body covered with a dressing gown, and the crotch of her legs pointed four-square into the face of her child seated on the floor beside her, is very offensive to all four members of this staff [Breen, James Wingate, Geoffrey Shurlock, and Islin Auster]." When he rejected the film a second time, Zanuck wrote him: "We realize that recently you have been pressed by the . . . Catholic Church for clean pictures and that perhaps you have received stringent orders to reject many things that you would not even contemplate rejecting in the past. However, we of 20th Century feel that we are hardly the company to be made an example of."

Breen humbly replied: "We are not infallible. It may be that our judgment is all haywire." Zanuck, who had become the first non-Jewish mogul, could not submit the film to an AMPP jury because he was also the first nonsignatory of the MPPDA, but his releasing company, United Artists, had to have the SRC's approval, so he agreed to recut the film. Years later, Loretta Young remembered the film: "I hated it so. And disapproved of it. And when the picture came out, the review said, 'This picture is called *Born to Be Bad*. It is.' That's all it said! It never ran in first-run theaters. It went to second-run." And it lost money.

The Fox Film Corporation had a success in *George White's Scandals*. Broadway producer George White packed it full of suggestive musical numbers, one of which has a character walking to the bathroom with a Sears catalogue under his arm. Daniel Lord sniffed: "It is difficult for George White to produce any type of entertainment that he does not soil." Breen rejected the film, but an AMPP jury overrode him. He admitted: "I have learned very much in the past two or three months. One of the things I have learned is not to expect much help in the matter of clean pictures from a jury."

Of course, the local boards cut the jokes, as well as Alice Faye's show-stopping number, "Nasty Man," in which chorus girls gyrated in "nude look" costumes. The film was aptly named *Scandals*. The gossip columns had a field day when Alice Faye was named corespondent in a divorce suit filed by the wife of her costar, Rudy Vallee, and then sang "Foolin' with the Other Woman's Man" in Fox Film's *Now I'll Tell*. In another scene in that film, she tells Spencer Tracy that she was born in the Virgin Islands. "You must have left there when you were quite young," he says, smiling.

Breen's Catholic hackles were raised by Columbia's *Twentieth Century*. He wrote Harry Cohn: "We still believe there will be serious difficulty in inducing an anti-Semitic public to accept a [film] produced by an industry which is believed to be Jewish in which the Passion Play is used for comedy purposes." The sequence in question has Broadway producer Oscar Jaffe (John Barrymore) signing two out-of-work Oberammergau Passion Play performers (Herman Bing and Lee Kohlmar) for a comically overblown play about Mary Magdalene. Cohn agreed to eliminate the line in which one player proudly says: "I am der lead." Breen was otherwise uninterested in the film, which was a triumph for writers Ben Hecht and Charles MacArthur, director Howard Hawks, Carole Lombard, and John Barrymore, who considered Jaffe his best onscreen performance.

RKO-Radio Pictures filmed Somerset Maugham's *Of Human Bondage,* but not without resistance. After several postponements, Breen grudgingly acknowledged the book as "something of a classic," and allowed the film to proceed. "The picture will have to be watched very carefully," he said, "and we have reserved the right to reject certain scenes in the picture if, upon viewing it, we find these to be improper or offensive." He decreed that the cruel, slatternly Mildred (Bette Davis) should die of tuberculosis, not syphilis. Cuts to Maugham's story notwithstanding, the film was distinguished by John Cromwell's direction and by Davis's extraordinary performance. Breen was unimpressed by literary pedigrees. He once referred to Emile Zola as a "filthy Frenchman who grew rich writing pornographic literature." Samuel Goldwyn wanted Zola's *Nana* to introduce his Ukrainian discovery, Anna Sten. Breen told Goldwyn to rewrite *Nana* first. After Willard Mack and Harry Wagstaff Gribble finished with her, Nana was more petulant than passionate, but the Legion of Decency condemned her nonetheless.

Universal's *The Black Cat* was a film so frightful and twisted that every right-thinking Catholic should have picketed it, but not even Breen understood how perverted it was. After reading the script by Peter Ruric and director Edgar G. Ulmer, he had made perfunctory requests for cuts, including:

Sequence F-3: This scene of the corpse of a young girl suspended in a glass coffin . . . is rather gruesome and is open to serious objection.
Sequence H-32: In introducing the guests [at the Satanist ceremonies], care should be taken to avoid any suggestion of homosexuality or perversion.
Sequence I-36: Use of the inverted cross

here is definitely inadvisable. Throughout this celebration of the Black Mass of Poelzig's rituals, care should be taken to avoid any suggestion of a parody on any church ceremony.

The film told the story of a brilliant architect—and war criminal—Hjalmar Poelzig (Boris Karloff), who lives in the modernized fortress where he sold out his countrymen, including his best friend, Vitus Werdegast (Bela Lugosi). Living with him is Werdegast's daughter, Karen (Lucille Lund), who does not know that her husband killed her mother and keeps her embalmed corpse standing in a glass coffin in the bowels of the fortress. Werdegast's quest for vengeance is thwarted by his phobia of cats and by Poelzig's desire to involve an unwitting young visitor, Joan (Jacqueline Wells), in a Satanist rite.

Apparently, Breen had never read *Là-bas,* the 1891 novel by Joris-Karl Huysmans; he would have seen that Poelzig's real intent was to rape Joan on the altar and then kill her. In any case, after Universal made a few minor changes, Breen passed the film and let the censors have their way with it. But even they did not catch on. The Maryland, Ohio, and Chicago boards cut only the scene where Werdegast takes his revenge on Poelzig, skinning him alive, and neither Breen nor the Legion condemned *The Black Cat.*

As the Catholic crusade gained speed, Breen was often called away from the SRC. As a result, his beleaguered staff let some racy Paramount films

Joe Breen decreed that Mildred (Bette Davis) die from tuberculosis, not syphilis, in Of Human Bondage. *She is seen here with Reginald Sheffield, Reginald Denny, and Ethel Griffies. Photograph by Alex Kahle.*

out the door. Cecil B. DeMille shot *Four Frightened People* in Hawaii, much to the discomfort of his cast and crew. One scene literally made Claudette Colbert sick. To satisfy DeMille's fetish for bathing scenes, she had to shower under a mountain waterfall. She caught intestinal influenza from the water, and for naught: most censor boards cut the scene. DeMille said: "Motion pictures didn't start immodesty. Immodesty began when they put clothes on a woman's body." A rebuttal came from Daniel Lord: "He surely can be credited with an effort to set things back to the primal norm by reversal of the process."

Bolero, directed by Wesley Ruggles, captured the glamour of 1913 Europe with the dancing of Raoul (George Raft). Raoul treats his dance partner Leona (Frances Drake) shabbily, stringing her along until he finds someone better. When she threatens to leave the act, his brother (William Frawley) tells him to pacify her: "All she wants is love. I don't think she's fussy where she gets it." Leona is being kept by an elderly man (Phillips Smalley), whom she refers to as "an old fluff." She jealously complains to Raoul: "I'm tired of dancing with you while you screw your face out of shape for the benefit of every dame, while I go home with an old relic—because I can't afford to go home without him."

Breen was back at work when Paramount submitted the musical extravaganza *Murder at the Vanities.* Producer A. M. Botsford promised to change the script per Breen's request: "Throughout the stage directions in the script, considerable stress is laid upon the almost-nudity of the girls. We assume that in production you will take care that nothing offensive creeps in." Earl Carroll's *Vanities* was a Broadway show known for expanses of female flesh, so Breen was assuming in vain. Mitchell Leisen's film was almost as revealing as the show, and even had a musical number entitled "Sweet Marihuana." Breen warned Paramount about censorship problems, but passed the spectacular film. Only the Detroit board condemned it.

The same studio made a sexy comedy that rivaled *Convention City.* Erle C. Kenton's *Search for Beauty* had Robert Armstrong and James Gleason as con artists who dupe Olympic medalists (Ida Lupino and Buster Crabbe) into editing a near-defunct health magazine. Before long, the crooks have turned *Health and Exercise* into a skin-and-

Kay Francis attends to unhappily pregnant Jean Muir, but the SRC will not let Muir ask for an abortion in Warner Bros.' Dr. Monica.

confession magazine—"so hot you could fry an egg on it!" When Lupino objects to its "reeking" articles, Armstrong says: "My dear young lady, there can be no virtue without a knowledge of vice. You don't know a stove is hot until you touch it, do you? These stories all point a moral."

"Yes," she snaps. "Just enough moral to sneak them through the mails."

Armstrong reminds her that a board of censors must approve each story. In a scene that should have tweaked Breen, the film shows the censors as clubwomen who are titillated by the stories they review: "'I Loved an Artist' . . . Oh, those poets! What thrilling love lives they lead! Just leaping from one bed—of flowers—to another!"

"Don't you think it points a moral?" asks Armstrong.

One censor answers: "About one percent moral—and ninety-nine percent sex."

"There's nothing wrong with sex," says Armstrong. "As long as it leads to, uh, what it leads to."

"I got nothin' against sex," pipes up Gleason. "Either ya got it—or ya go lookin' for it."

The script thumbed its nose at Breen when teenagers Sally (Toby Wing) and Susie (Verna Hillie) compare notes on "I Loved an Artist."

SALLY: I sure wish I could meet a guy like that "dark, mysterious artist." Of course, you get a bill for it in the end.

SUSIE: Bill? Baloney! That "paying the price" stuff is the bunk. They just put that in to make

176

the yarn moral. I'll bet that dame is living on Park Avenue, riding around in an imported oil can—and splashing mud in the faces of pure working girls. If I *ever* get a chance—

SALLY: Me, too! And I don't care what his past was or his future is. As long as he's got a *present! Tee hee!*

Oddly, Breen did not bristle at this insult to his "voice for morality." He only warned Botsford about certain visual problems: "The shot of Crabbe seen through the woman's binoculars, concentrating on his loins, [and the] shot in the locker room, in which a couple of men run through naked." The film was released without cuts, but it only got through the Chicago and New York boards in the same condition. Every other board cut it, loins, locker room, and all.

Warner Bros. tried to get several adult films through the SRC. *Dr. Monica* was the story of a physician (Kay Francis) who cannot have a child. Her husband (Warren William) gets her friend Mary (Jean Muir) pregnant. When Mary faints, the unknowing Monica comforts her:

MARY: This is hideous! You've got to help me!
MONICA: Of course I will.
MARY: When? Right away?
MONICA: (sternly) Just what do you mean?
MARY: (desperately) You know!

Three of the Fox Film personnel responsible for its racy image in early 1934: dance director Sammy Lee, actress Alice Faye, and producer Sol Wurtzel.

MONICA: (angrily) Don't you ever talk that way again—don't you ever think that way again!

Before filming the scene, Hal Wallis deleted the lines from "Of course" to "away?" But that wasn't enough for Breen. He wanted no hint of abortion: "In the first bedroom scene between Monica and Mary, you will delete the following lines: 'Just what do you mean?' [and] 'You know!'" The film went out with a jarring negative cut, but was still condemned by the Legion.

The cuts made in Mervyn LeRoy's *Heat Lightning* were not as hurtful to the film, which starred Aline MacMahon as a bitter auto mechanic trying to protect her young sister (Ann Dvorak) from men. She fails, and, as Breen pointed out, three seductions take place in one film. Even with the eight cuts he required, the film was still effective. Warner Bros. invited German director G. W. Pabst, who was famous for *Die freudlose Gasse* and *Pandora's Box,* to direct Louis Bromfield's novel *A Modern Hero,* the story of an amoral young womanizer (Richard Barthelmess). The studio ignored Wingate's suggestion of thirteen cuts. Breen let the film go to the Pennsylvania board, where it sustained twenty-eight cuts. The Legion also condemned it.

In M-G-M's *Manhattan Melodrama,* Clark Gable's walk to the electric chair prompted a cable from Will Hays about the line "where he said that they should get the lace nightgown, black for him and 'lace for the next guy.' Word has come to me that the words were spoken as if he said 'lays' and it has actually caused laughs in different places [which] shows how careful we have to be." *Hollywood Party* had an effeminate ape, an uncouth Jimmy Durante, and an uncontrollable Lupe Velez, wearing a gown that revealed large vistas of her hips. Richard Boleslavsky's *Men in White* had Code problems, too. Breen refused to allow any suggestion that the peritonitis suffered by nurse Elizabeth Allan was due to an abortion performed by her lover, Clark Gable. M-G-M bypassed Breen, and, true to his prediction, the film was attacked by censor boards and denounced by the Legion of Decency. In Jack Conway's *Viva Villa!,* aristocrat Teresa (Fay Wray) tells Pancho Villa (Wallace Beery) that her father used to love the music of the "peons crying when he whipped them." When she refuses his crude advances, Villa whips her and then shoots her. The film was probably the year's most brutal, but Breen passed it and the Legion ignored it.

W. S. Van Dyke's surprise hit *The Thin Man* made M-G-M stars of William Powell and Myrna Loy. On a hunch, Van Dyke cast the well-known "heavies" as the bibulous, happily married, highly sexed detectives Nick and Nora Charles. "One-take Woody" Van Dyke shot the film in fourteen days. According to still man Ted Allan, the cast was so exhausted that they all got drunk at the wrap party. "Myrna Loy fell flat on her ass and we had to pick her up off the roof of the soundstage where we had the party." The SRC was not amused by the film. Breen was suspicious of an exit line: "Does that mean it's *bedtime?*" Even terrier Asta was suspect. Wingate called Hunt Stromberg about the "dog gag," in which an off-screen Asta stops at a fire hydrant, pulling the onscreen leash held by Loy. Another successful Metro film was Clarence Brown's *Sadie McKee,* in which Joan Crawford perfected her rags-to-riches formula. During the ragged part of the film, Sadie (Crawford) goes to New York with her boyfriend Tommy (Gene Raymond), and they nervously share a hotel room. After promising to sleep in a chair, Tommy sings "All I Do Is Dream of You" to Sadie, who is nestled in the bed. Of course, the song leads to a good-night kiss—on the bed. The Legion of Decency condemned *Sadie McKee.*

M-G-M tangled with Breen over Jack Conway's *Tarzan and His Mate.* The expensive sequel to *Tarzan the Ape Man* had taken two years to launch, and when previewed, it had 116 minutes of non-stop action. The *Hollywood Reporter* said: "New *Tarzan,* packed with showmanship, needs cuts." Breen agreed. The film had Tarzan and Jane in bed, and

Asta the dog contributed to the adult humor of M-G-M's The Thin Man. *William Powell and Myrna Loy made the unassuming production a sexy hit. Photograph by Ted Allan.*

*In 1934, Norma Shearer, the "First Lady of M-G-M,"
was a convenient target when* Riptide *displeased Daniel
Lord. Portrait by George Hurrell.*

*Joan Crawford was the most popular actress at M-G-M
in 1934, but the Legion of Decency condemned* Sadie McKee.
Portrait by George Hurrell.

"You ought to be more careful with your clothes when you go lovemaking," says Marjorie Rambeau, mother of the womanizing Richard Barthelmess, in Warner Bros.' A Modern Hero.

Anna Sten dismisses a smitten sailor in Goldwyn's Nana: *"Love? Dead. That's life."*

In Warner Bros.' Heat Lightning, *Aline MacMahon and Ann Dvorak cannot escape abusive males, even in the dusty outskirts of Vacaville, California.*

Jane in a very brief costume. Maureen O'Sullivan, who again played Jane, later recalled: "They tried different things to make Jane look pretty sexy. First of all they had the idea of wearing no bra, no brassiere at all, and that she would be always covered with a branch. They tried that, and that didn't work. So then they made a costume, and it wasn't that bad." There was, however, a nude swimming sequence. Because of it, Breen rejected the film. Louis B. Mayer appealed his decision. An AMPP jury, B. B. Kahane, Carl Laemmle, Jr., and Winfield Sheehan, met at M-G-M to look at the film.

Breen reported: "After a rather animated discussion between the jurors, the representatives of Metro, and Mr. Breen, the verdict of this office was sustained by the jury." The discussion included outraged protests by Mayer and Thalberg that films such as *Common Law* had gotten away with less tasteful nudity. When a print of *Common Law* was delivered from RKO, it revealed Constance Bennett's nude stand-in in the far corner of a very wide shot. This time, Breen had won the battle, but not the war. Scenes were reshot, recut, and eleven minutes were cut from the film—but which film?

According to historian Rudy Behlmer: "From all evidence, *three* versions of the sequence eventually went out to separate territories during the film's initial release. One with Jane clothed in her jungle loin cloth outfit, one with her topless, and one with her in the nude." Even the territories that did not see the nude scene thought that Jane's costume (which at one point popped open to reveal her crotch) was disgraceful. O'Sullivan said: "It started such a furor that the letters just came in. So it added up to thousands of women that [sic] were objecting to my costume. . . . I was offered all kinds of places where I could go in my shame, to hide from the cruel public who were ready to throw stones at me." The film was condemned, but even she did not take the drubbing that Daniel Lord reserved for the First Lady of M-G-M.

Irving Thalberg's first project for Norma Shearer after his return to M-G-M was to have been a remake of Michael Arlen's *The Green Hat,* but the Lost Generation novel suddenly looked dated, and with Breen running the SRC, it also looked risky; its plot included homosexuality, venereal disease, and illegitimacy. Thalberg instead had the multifaceted Edmund Goulding write an original story for Shearer's return to the screen. *Riptide* was a tasteful trifle about a woman driven to adultery by her husband's lack of faith in her. The film was passed without problems, and no one expected the vicious review that appeared in the June issue of Lord's *The Queen's Work*.

> *Riptide* is unfortunately typical of the pictures that have been built around Norma Shearer, the much-publicized wife of Irving Thalberg, who picks her plays and roles. It seems typical of Hollywood morality that a husband as production manager should constantly cast his wife in the role of a loose and immoral woman. . . . That the picture is beautifully mounted and the heroine elaborately gowned makes the plot that much more insidious. We advise strong guard over all pictures which feature Norma Shearer. They are doing more than almost any other type of picture to undermine the moral code and the Producers' Code.

Ironically, Thalberg and Shearer were finishing a film that was far removed from her glossy vehicles, *The Barretts of Wimpole Street*. Father Lord's article enraged Thalberg, and he complained volubly to Bishop Cantwell. Cantwell, backed by Quigley, told Archbishop McNicholas to rein in Lord: "His unwise and irresponsible statements are doing us harm in Hollywood, and creating much confusion." Indeed, Lord had allied himself with a Protestant contingent that favored the abolition of block-booking. In late May, he was but one of many factions raging at the movies. Quigley and Breen looked at the big picture. Quigley acknowledged that "our ideas of morality in entertainment differ radically from those held by the vast majority of the public in this country." Breen admitted: "I have no real authority to stop the dirty pictures." Changing their position, they agreed that these pictures had to be stopped at the script level, and that only box-office pressure would make the studios cooperate.

Breen sent a letter to Cardinal Dougherty in Philadelphia, proposing that the Cardinal use the Legion to institute a boycott of films in his city, where Warner Bros. had substantial holdings. This was the same Cardinal Dougherty who in 1927 had thrown *The Callahans and the Murphys* out of circulation with one fell swoop. On May 23, he declared from the pulpit that Catholics in his diocese were to boycott *all* motion pictures, and that this was a "pos-

The SRC forbade M-G-M to explain Elizabeth Allan's illness in this scene with Myrna Loy in Men in White. Director Richard Boleslavsky is at her bedside and cinematographer George Folsey is at the camera. Photograph by Ted Allan.

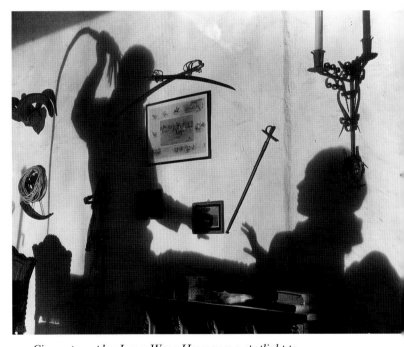

Cinematographer James Wong Howe uses a spotlight to convey Wallace Beery's brutality to Fay Wray in M-G-M's Viva Villa! Photograph by James Manatt.

itive command, binding all in conscience under pain of sin." Box-office receipts immediately fell 40 percent. Geoffrey Shurlock remembered: "Harry Warner, who owned the Stanley chain of theaters in

An on-the-set portrait by Alexander Kahle of Bette Davis in
RKO's Of Human Bondage.

A Hal Fraker portrait of Carole Lombard in
Columbia's Twentieth Century.

Philadelphia, was losing $175,000 a week."

Daniel Lord brought up the rear, asking five thousand high school students in Buffalo: "How would you like to clean up the movies?" *Variety* told of thousands of letters pouring in from children, teenagers, and church groups. More telling was their financial impact. Within weeks, Hollywood lost several million dollars. Lord wrote: "Hollywood knew it was licked—to its own salvation."

Frightened moguls turned to Will Hays. Harry Warner pleaded: "Will, you've got to save us. I'm being ruined by the hour. If anybody else does this thing, we're out of business." The potential loss of 7 million Catholic customers was bad enough, but it now appeared that Protestant and Jewish groups might join the crusade. The Federal Council of Churches made it known that its 22 million members were willing to join the Legion of Decency. The Catholic Church had Hays backed against a wall. He called Breen: "Joe, look! For the love of God, come over here! What can you do?"

"I've been telling you guys it's coming," Breen answered.

On May 28, Hays held a secret meeting with Quigley and Breen. Hays capitulated, saying: "The Catholic authorities can have anything they want." Breen relayed a message from Archbishop McNicholas: "You have a Code. Apply it. Implement it. You will have no problem at all with the Catholics if you do that simple thing." Hays agreed to let Quigley and Breen negotiate on his behalf with the Episcopal Committee. A meeting was planned for June 19 in Cincinnati. In the meantime, the Legion of Decency, which had already collected 3 million pledges, held its first rally. Addressing 50,000 people, Cleveland bishop Joseph Schrembs exhorted them: "Purify Hollywood or destroy Hollywood!" The stage was set for Joe Breen's ascendance.

A Mac Julian portrait of Kay Francis in Warner Bros.' Mandalay.

A LeRoy Robbins portrait of Loretta Young in Twentieth Century Pictures' Born to Be Bad.

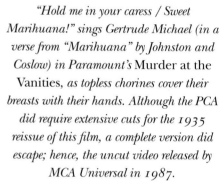

"Hold me in your caress / Sweet Marihuana!" sings Gertrude Michael (in a verse from "Marihuana" by Johnston and Coslow) in Paramount's Murder at the Vanities, as topless chorines cover their breasts with their hands. Although the PCA did require extensive cuts for the 1935 reissue of this film, a complete version did escape; hence, the uncut video released by MCA Universal in 1987.

"Oh, you nasty man / Taking your love on the easy plan!" sings Alice Faye (in a verse from "Nasty Man" by Yellen, Caesar, and Henderson) in Fox Film's George White's Scandals, as four tiers of chorines shake bizarre costumes designed by Charles LeMaire. This film was denied a reissue seal, so it survives in its original form.

"A ga-ga girl sits over there / Angelic face and baby stare / Engrossed in her new love affair!" sings Alice Faye (in a verse from "Fooling with the Other Woman's Man" by Yellen and Ager) in Fox Film's Now I'll Tell. *Photograph by Emmett Schoenbaum. (This film may exist in a private collection, but its one-time copyright holder has no preprint material.)*

TOP:
In Universal's The Black Cat, *Hjalmar Poelzig (Boris Karloff) has a beautiful young wife named Karin (Lucille Lund). She does not know that he stole her from her father and murdered her mother, or that they live in the rebuilt fortress where he murdered 10,000 men in World War I. And that's merely the backstory of this unique film. Photograph by Roman Freulich.*

BOTTOM:
"Humanum est errare." ["To err is human."] Latin incantations signal the beginning of a Black Mass. Photograph by Roman Freulich.

OPPOSITE:
A Roman Freulich portrait of Boris Karloff made for The Black Cat. *This most perverse of all horror films was released in 1934—and reissued in 1938— without cuts!*

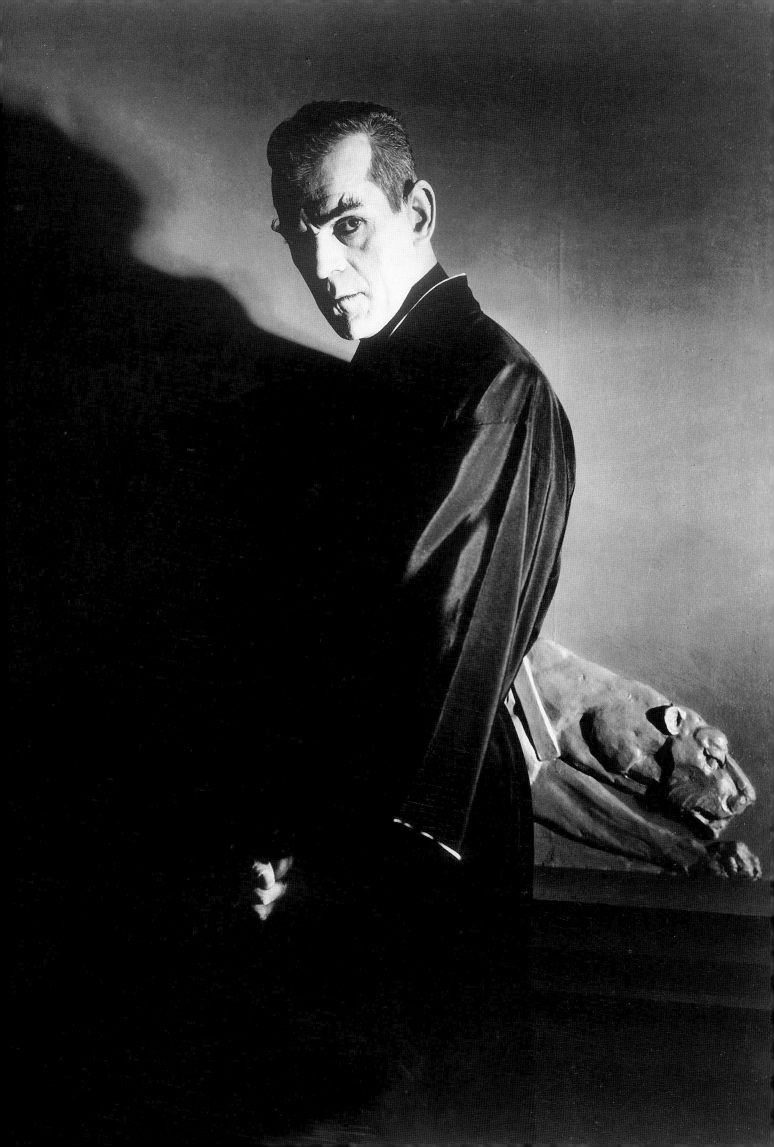

Larry "Buster" Crabbe and a roomful of tawny athletes are seen au naturel in Paramount's irreverently racy Search for Beauty. *Adapted from a play called* Love Your Body, *it ridiculed censorship while flouting the Code.*

OPPOSITE:
Tarzan and His Mate *was the first film to lose an appeal to the AMPP jury. The cut sequences were restored by the Turner Entertainment Corporation for a 1991 release by MGM-UA Home Video.*

This Ted Allan portrait of Tarzan (Johnny Weissmuller) and Jane (Maureen O' Sullivan) from M-G-M's
Tarzan and His Mate *ran in* Modern Screen, *but after the PCA came into power, the master copy in the studio's key set*
of stills was stamped "Rejected"—right on Jane's posterior.

THE PRODUCTION
CODE
ADMINISTRATION

In June of 1934, the Catholic crusade roared on, gathering momentum and force. Will Hays likened it to an "avenging fire, seeking to clean as it burned." Pledges were signed, speeches were delivered, and hundreds of editorials were flung at Hollywood. The Hays Office counted more than two hundred editorials in one week. In the *Los Angeles Times,* film critic Edwin Schallert wrote a three-part article that began: "Hollywood is in the most serious crisis of its history." Its most telling part dealt with the transitory appeal of film. This was the argument that motion pictures were indefensible as art and, therefore, unworthy of protection from censorship: "Making pictures is not like writing literature or composing music or painting masterpieces. The screen story is essentially a thing of today and once it has had its run, that day is finished. So far there has never been a classic film in the sense that there is a classic novel or poem or canvas or sonata. Last year's picture, however strong its appeal at the time, is a book that has gone out of circulation." He was apparently unaware that many "strong" films— *Grand Hotel, Red-Headed Woman, She Done Him Wrong*—had never gone out of circulation. But this was a crisis, and the air was filled with half-truths.

In Chicago, Cardinal George Mundelein claimed credit for the Production Code and charged the film companies with deception: "To them it was just another scrap of paper." Father Daniel Lord used the same metaphor in the *Queen's Work*: "This is the story of a great betrayal. It is the story of signatures written on scraps of paper. It is the record of words given and instantly violated, of men who made solemn pledges that they did not

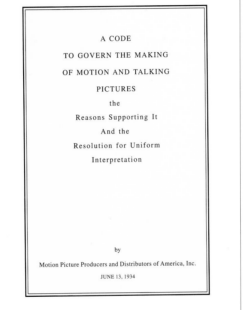

A CODE

TO GOVERN THE MAKING

OF MOTION AND TALKING

PICTURES

the

Reasons Supporting It

And the

Resolution for Uniform

Interpretation

by

Motion Picture Producers and Distributors of America, Inc.

JUNE 13, 1934

The cover of the amended Production Code, which took effect July 1, 1934. The term pre-Code *refers to films made before this strictly enforced document.*

keep beyond the moment when the ink dried on the paper." In St. Louis, the Lord camp continued to foment ill will, gaining coverage in the *Saturday Evening Post* and the *New York Times.* In Chicago, Martin Quigley worked with Joe Breen to formulate a document that would avoid the pitfalls of the 1930 Code. Before they could pitch it to the bishops, though, they had to be sure the film companies would back it.

A meeting of the MPPDA was convened in New York on June 13. At it, Joe Breen unveiled a modest pamphlet entitled "A Code to Govern the Making of Motion and Talking Pictures, the Reasons Supporting It and the Resolution for Uniform Interpretation." The new Code contained an addendum written by Breen, "Compensating Moral Values." It required that evil be identified as such by a major character in the film, and that it be punished, promptly and fully. The Code also addressed political concerns, specifying that films could never question "duly constituted authority" nor could they demonstrate their "cynical contempt for conventions" by showing topics such as racism, labor disputes, unemployment, social conditions, or alien political beliefs. Breen wrote: "Communistic propaganda, for example, is banned from the screen."

The meeting also addressed the problem of salacious and misleading advertising. Humorist Will Rogers had commented: "You can't make a picture as bad as the ads lead you to believe it is." A resolution was passed requiring theaters to conform to the same advertising standards as the producers. The meeting's most important accomplishment was to take the Studio Relations Committee away from the AMPP. It was henceforth answerable only to the MPPDA and could halt a film at the script stage. The AMPP jury was abolished and replaced by the New York board of directors, a more impartial body. Would these changes be enough to make the Catholics call off their attack? Breen and Quigley went to Cincinnati for the June 19 bishops' meeting. They were the only ones there without clerical collars, but Archbishop John McNicholas made them welcome; neither Daniel Lord nor Will Hays had been invited to the conclave.

"The meeting lasted three days," remembered Hays. "None of us in the Association knew what was going on in Cincinnati. There was nothing to do but wait." While they waited, Breen and Quigley worked to convince McNicholas and the Episcopal Committee that their plan was worth backing. In addition to the concessions made at the MPPDA meeting, this plan offered theaters the option of canceling 10 percent of their block-booking if they did not like all the films in the block. It also intended to pull offensive films such as *She Done Him Wrong* and *Convention City* from circulation. Furthermore, Breen now had absolute authority: (1) a film could not be produced if he didn't approve its script; (2) it could not be released if he didn't give it a "seal"; and (3) if a company tried to release it without a seal, no MPPDA theater could play it.

Breen and Quigley told the bishops that the Catholic crusade should continue, but that wildcat

Joe Breen, presiding over the Production Code Administration.

boycotts and blacklists should cease. Father Fitz-George Dinneen disagreed, but was outvoted. He returned to the rival camp, where he prevailed upon Daniel Lord, Cardinal Mundelein, and Cardinal O'Connell to break with the Episcopal Committee. This schism was ill-advised; it caused momentary confusion and long-term bitterness.

On June 22, the MPPDA board of directors assembled in the Hays Office to wait for Breen and Quigley. A late train made them wait four hours. Among the executives waiting with Will Hays was Harry Warner, who had been hit hardest by the Philadelphia boycott. When Breen and Quigley made their entrance, wrote Hays, "I knew everything was all right from the cat-ate-canary expressions on their faces. Everyone crowded around them anxiously, but they, being Irish, could not resist having a little fun with us." Breen later described the scene for Jack Vizzard:

> There was Harry Warner, standing up at the top of the table, shedding tears the size of horse turds, and pleading for someone to get him off the hook. And well he should, for you could fire a cannon down the center aisle of any theater in Philadelphia, without danger of hitting anyone! And there was Barney Balaban [of Paramount Theatres], watching him in terror, wondering if he was going to be next in

Madeleine Carroll in The World Moves On, *the first film to earn a "Certificate of Approval" from the newly empowered Studio Relations Committee.*

Chicago, and Nick Schenck [of Loew's], wondering when he was going to be hit by a bucket of shit in New York.

Breen moved to the back of the room to await his cue. Quigley took the floor and announced that "the war had been called off." Effective July 1, the SRC would become the Production Code Administration (PCA). There was applause. "At last we [have] a police department," said Hays, with conscious irony. There was more applause. But who would run it? "Gentlemen, we have the very man right here in our midst." Breen was brought to the front of the room, and he accepted the post of Production Code Administrator; still more applause. He held up his hands: "But on one condition. And the condition is that you understand that I come from a race of people who have a long history of committing suicide—on the other guy!" To arm his assaults on "the other guy," another provision was added to the Code: a $25,000 fine, levied against any producer who would dare to produce a film without PCA approval or to release a film without the PCA seal.

The Production Code Administration opened for business on July 11, in the same rundown offices at 5504 Hollywood Boulevard. On that day it awarded the first seal, "Certificate of Approval No. 1," to a film made about Irish people by an Irish director, John Ford. *The World Moves On* was the three-generation saga of a family that learns to hate war. Unfortunately for Fox Film, it was not a success. Universal, Warner Bros., M-G-M, and Paramount also submitted films. They featured—respectively—a wife-beater, a kept woman, a fallen woman, and Mae West.

The complete text of Joseph I. Breen's "Compensating Moral Values" may be found in Appendix III, on page 219.

IT AIN'T NO SIN

The first film to run the gauntlet in July was James Whale's *One More River,* which Universal adapted from the John Galsworthy novel. Breen made screenwriter R. C. Sherriff minimize the scenes in which Sir Gerald (Colin Clive) beats Lady Clare (Diana Wynyard): "The changes and deletions made in the film get away definitely from the subject of sadism as well as the frankness of the dialogue." This bowdlerized version was not good enough for the Legion of Decency, which promptly condemned it. Breen apologized to Carl Laemmle, Jr.: "This is the first picture passed under the recently set-up machinery to be so condemned. I suppose it is the divorce angle which brings down condemnation of the Catholics; and I suppose that in the face of their very definite viewpoint on the subject of divorce, we are helpless."

A Warner Bros. production, William Dieterle's *Madame Du Barry,* was Breen's next problem. It had begun in January, when Jack Warner saw M-G-M making money with *Queen Christina* and Paramount making *Catherine the Great.* He also saw Columbia's comedy *It Happened One Night:* "It has eleven reels. In other words, maybe we are cutting our pictures too fast and making them too snappy." A lavish, sexy movie was in order. Warner hired playwright Edward Chodorov to put a kept woman in period costumes. They chose Marie Jeanne Bècu, Comtesse du Barry, the last mistress of France's King Louis XV. Chodorov's script was a combination of *Convention City* and *Female,* but more overtly sexual than either of them, and in place of their charm, it had a smirking nastiness.

Breen read the script on March 13 and flatly refused it. He wrote Warner: "It is our considered judgment that the story, as written, is so filled with vulgarity, obscenity and blatant adultery, that it suggests the kind of picture which, if made, we would be compelled to reject." It began with "the horror and fear of Louis XV, when he discovers that the [forty-five-year-old] Duchess de Grammont has sneaked into his bed . . . Louis forces his valet [Lebel] to take his place in the bed alongside the Duchess and then, himself apparently naked, wakes the lady with 'a tremendous slap on the backside.' The Duchess thereupon displays 'coy shock,' whereafter we have the King's question, 'Are you through with my valet? I want my clothes.'"

The King scoffs at the Duchess: "Come, come. It's very difficult for a woman of forty-five to be compromised. Besides, everyone knows that Lebel is a vegetarian." The next scene introduces a nude Madame du Barry, who has just slept with the Duc de Richelieu so that he will introduce her to the King, who meanwhile has gone, "like Diogenes, in search of a dishonest woman." At the Deer Park, a lodge full of nubile young women, he meets du Barry, who charms him, seduces him, and redecorates his bedroom—with ceiling mirrors. Breen would have none of it.

Warner demanded a meeting, and Breen hastened to Burbank the next day. Breen found producer Hal Wallis "sneering and argumentative," saying that if Breen had his way, Warner Bros. would have to go into the milk business. Breen bellowed at him: "If people like you *would* get out of the way and sell milk, maybe it would free the screen of a lot of its whorehouse crap, and decent people could sit down and enjoy themselves in a theater without blushing!" A revised script was approved on March 22, and the film went into production. Warner went to New York in a huff. On the 28th, Will Hays convened an emergency meeting of the MPPDA to hear Warner's complaint. The board turned him down, and he had no choice but to assure Hays that Wallis would be careful.

When Breen saw the completed film in early May, he angrily rejected it. A bewildered Warner pleaded with Breen to give him a list of cuts. The film lost its ceiling mirrors and a few other Code violations. In the meantime, the SRC became the PCA. Though *Madame Du Barry* was one of the first nine Warner films to receive a PCA certificate from Breen in July, the state board in New York called it "indecent, obscene, and immoral," and rejected it. This was worse than a Legion condemnation, proof that Breen was indeed "not infallible."

He worked with Warner Bros. on another round of cuts and resubmitted it. Not until early October did the New York, Massachusetts, Ohio, and Pennsylvania boards pass the harried *Du Barry*. Nevertheless, the Legion of Decency condemned it. The finished film retained more of its sex than it lost, but it now had a confusing plot and unsympathetic characters, not to mention a miscast Dolores Del Rio, Sol Polito's clinically flat lighting, and such distasteful scenes as the pudgy, puerile dauphin (Maynard Holmes) being shown pornographic etchings to prepare him for his wedding night. *Madame Du Barry* did poorly.

Breen's next test was an M-G-M film, *Eadie Was a Lady*, whose director, Sam Wood, quit when Breen's edicts came too fast and furious. Jack Conway replaced him and transformed Jean Harlow from a fallen woman to a self-consciously decent "lady"— in some scenes. In other scenes, she was the gold digger of the first script. Her motivation was as uncertain as the film's title; in short order, it was *Born to Be Kissed, 100% Pure,* and *The Girl from Missouri.* After numerous rewrites and retakes, Breen took the sheen off the "Platinum Blonde." Harlow's fans were so desperate to see her that they overlooked the film's inconsistencies.

Metro's other stars were lucky, too. In *Chained,* Joan Crawford enjoyed a laughably chaste relationship with a married man (Otto Kruger), and the film got a seal. Irving Thalberg was preparing *Marie Antoinette* for Norma Shearer, but he and Breen could not agree on a way to suggest the dauphin's impotence. He chose a safer project. In Sidney Franklin's *The Barretts of Wimpole Street,* Shearer was discreetly covered in Victorian garb, playing bedridden poet Elizabeth Barrett, whose father (Charles Laughton) forbids her to marry. Is it because he harbors an incestuous desire for her? The film implies it, but not boldly enough to invite censorship. Laughton said it best: "They can't censor the gleam in my eye." Both *Chained* and *Barretts* were very profitable.

Breen's toughest test was *It Ain't No Sin.* For her third starring vehicle, Mae West used her intimate knowledge of the underworld to dream up a racy tale of the 1890s, her favorite period and the one Paramount evoked better than any other studio. The end of her synopsis read: "Tiger and Ruby are in a cabin of the upriver boat. 'Well,' he says, 'where do we go from here?' Ruby smiles. 'Didn't your mother ever tell you anything?'"

Prepared for the worst, Breen received her script in late February. He went over it scrupulously with his entire staff. On March 7, he wrote to producers A. M. Botsford and John Hammell that West's script was a "glorification of prostitution and violent crime without any compensating moral values of any kind," and that it was "certain to throw the sympathy of the audience with sin, crime, wrong-doing and evil." Botsford and Hammell tried to persuade him that the comic tone of West's films softened their seedy aspects. Breen was unyielding: "Ruby Carter displays all the habits and practices of a prostitute, aids in the operation of a dishonest gambling house, drugs a prizefighter, robs her employer, deliberately sets fire to his premises, and, in the end, goes off scot free in the company of her illicit lover who is a self-confessed criminal, a thief, and a murderer." Breen and Paramount went back and forth until the eve of shooting, but Breen didn't budge.

On March 23, the film went into production, with dialogue coach Boris Petroff and studio president William LeBaron hovering protectively. As the Catholic crusade heated up, the sparkle of West's diamonds made her an easy target. Posters began appearing in New York, trumpeting *It Ain't No Sin*. Priests picketed the sign, carrying placards that read: "IT IS!" Breen was now sending periodic bulletins to the studios, informing them of the latest progress in the crusade. Mae West proudly finished *It Ain't No Sin*.

On June 1, Breen rejected the film. In a heated discussion, Emanuel Cohen "damned Breen and the Code to hell!" Breen responded by quoting a Rabbi Goldberg, who had recently "attacked Jewish movie producers who bring disgrace upon the Jewish people." When everyone cooled down, a compromise was reached. Breen agreed not to inform Paramount's New York executives of the offensive film if the Hollywood executive agreed to make extensive cuts, especially of the "violent and lustful kissing" that occurred through most of the film.

When Breen returned to his office, he discovered that what he had promised was in violation of the Code. He promptly carbon-copied New York and let the chips fall. New York made Hollywood comply. The resulting cuts muted Ruby Carter's background, criminal tendencies, and seductive talents. On June 6, Breen approved the film. Most of the sin was gone, but West's troubles were not. On June 25, the New York State censor board rejected the film.

On June 28, Paramount hopefully changed the film's title to *St. Louis Woman,* then learned that this title was held by another film. More important, the Film Without a Name now lacked continuity. According to Harrison Carroll of the *Evening Hollywood Express,* Cohen drove to West's apartment to tell her that the film could not be released as it stood. West resignedly said: "Well, boys, let's get to work." She canceled plans to attend a Marion Davies benefit and spent the evening in a Paramount projection room, notepad in hand. On July 6, the film returned to the soundstage. "If they saw me and thought I was a little too frank, why, I'm trying to do as they suggest," said West. "I have never intentionally written anything or acted in a way that would offend." Years later, she was more candid: "I

resented a type of censorship that quibbled over every line as if a devil were hiding behind each word." The three days of retakes were more for coherence than for decency. A new title was chosen: *The Belle of the Nineties.*

On July 13, Will Hays looked at a rough cut, and according to West, he "leaned on a scene where . . . the impression was conveyed (by lap dissolves) that the Tiger Kid not only spent the night but several days. The lapse of time shown by the dissolves added up to a great laugh. The censor didn't laugh. He cut." West later admitted: "*Belle of the Nineties* was not a good story, because they made me make it three times before I knew what they wanted." Finally, on August 6, Joe Breen gave the film his imprimatur: PCA Certificate No. 136.

By the September 6 preview, the press knew something had happened: Mae West *married* her leading man (Roger Pryor) in the last scene of the movie! *Variety* snickered at this "obvious curtsey to Joe Breen." The *Hollywood Citizen-News* wrote: "This picture proves that Mae can still be funny in the midst of a Church crusade. Call her an artist or not, she's entertaining." *Belle of the Nineties* was a funny, lovingly photographed film, but its scars were visible; it lacked the unity of her previous films.

In one scene, West admonishes her maid: "Don't ever let a man put anything over on you—outside of an umbrella." It was obvious that Breen had put something over on West. In future scripts, she adopted a ploy: "I wrote scenes for them to cut! These scenes were so rough that I'd never have used them. But they worked as a decoy. They cut them and left the stuff I wanted. I had these scenes in there about a man's fly and all that, and the censors would be sittin' in the projection room laughin' themselves silly. Then they'd say 'Cut it' and not notice the rest."

Breen knew he was being watched—by the industry that was paying him $30,000 a year and by the 7 million Catholics who had by now taken the pledge. Father FitzGeorge Dinneen told him: "Watch your step. If the pictures are not cleaned up, you will be the most discredited man in the country." So far, his reputation was a formidable one. In a scathing article in the British trade paper *Film Weekly,* Glyn Roberts called him "the Hitler of Hollywood." In September, Breen bragged that the morality of films would no longer be "fogged." Thanks to his vigilance, there would be no more sin, in soft focus or otherwise.

Breen had promised to pull objectionable films from circulation, so he began to reclassify those already in release. Class I films would be pulled and never rereleased. They included *She Done Him Wrong*, *I'm No Angel*, *George White's Scandals*, *The Story of Temple Drake*, *Baby Face*, and *Convention City*. Class II films would complete their exhibition contracts, never to be rereleased. These included *Riptide*, *Sadie McKee*, and *Queen Christina*. Class III films would be recut and then resubmitted for PCA seals. *Tarzan and His Mate* was a typical Class III film. A 1932 film that was still trying to recoup its cost was Ernst Lubitsch's *Trouble in Paradise*. The Legion of Decency had recently condemned it, so Breen put it in Class I. As Breen ordered Paramount to yank it, Lubitsch was at M-G-M, finishing his first post-Code film, *The Merry Widow*.

Lubitsch took a risk making a film at a studio that did not respect directors, but Irving Thalberg respected Lubitsch, and each man compromised a bit. Thalberg let Lubitsch have the final cut, and Lubitsch let Thalberg have a week's work for free—as long as he did not tell Paramount. *The Merry Widow*, though nominally based on both the 1905 Franz Lehar operetta and the 1925 Erich von Stroheim film, was Lubitsch's own story of a young widow, Sonia (Jeanette MacDonald), who needs to be wooed as much as dashing Count Danilo (Maurice Chevalier) needs to woo her. He wants her for himself, but his country (a mythical kingdom) wants her for her fortune, which represents 52 percent of its wealth. Lubitsch told his story with M-G-M's resources and his own inimitable "touch." The result was airy and sexy, a saucy soufflé that in many ways improved on his Paramount films.

Thalberg was making *The Merry Widow* under the aegis of his new production unit. He was not anxious to have censorship problems reported to the various parties who wanted him to fail. He pre-

Joe Breen made Universal Pictures remove most of the scenes in which Colin Clive beat Diana Wynyard in One More River.

In Warner Bros.' Madame Du Barry, *Louis XV (Reginald Owen), shocked at the impudence of Du Barry (Dolores Del Rio), asks her: "Madame, what are you trying to do to France?" She answers: "Just what it's doing to me!"*

viewed the film for Breen on August 10. Breen found Thalberg, the coauthor of the original Code, extremely cooperative, to the extent of running all angles of a can-can dance that takes place in the famous Maxim's of Paris, so that they could "cut this scene with as little damage as possible." One bit showed a "Maxim's girl" walking out of the night-club on the arm of a policeman, saying: "You know, the trouble is—the policeman on my corner just doesn't understand me."

On September 25, Breen looked at a new version of the film and recommended four cuts. At this point, Thalberg asked his indulgence. The cuts all took place in scenes that involved the mixing of multiple sound tracks. The film was scheduled to open in two weeks. Breen thought it over; the cuts would "entail considerable expense in the musical scoring and rescoring for this film. In the face of this, we waived our suggestions contained in the let-

ter of September 26." The film was innocuous, a "light, gay, frivolous operetta." Breen granted a "Certificate of Approval" and thought no more of it.

The Merry Widow opened October 11 in New York, amid so much fanfare that both Martin Quigley and Will Hays were invited. After seeing the film, they stood in the lobby, where Quigley expressed his disgust at this "industry double-cross" and at Breen's lack of perception. The next day Quigley wrote a letter to Breen, asking how he had let Thalberg introduce a "lot of filth" into a harm-less musical while Hollywood's position was still ten-uous. "If this picture goes out, the jig is up; if M-G-M gets away with this, others will follow." Before Breen could defend himself, the Pharisaic Quigley had informed Archbishop McNicholas and bullied Hays into calling Breen to New York. For once Hays had the upper hand, and he used it, calling Breen on the carpet for failing to recognize how dirty the

M-G-M's The Girl from Missouri *took a drubbing from the Studio Relations Committee, but Jean Harlow's platinum persona survived for a few more films. Portrait by C. S. Bull.*

Warner Bros.' Madame Du Barry *was a nasty movie that not even ruthless cutting could improve; it hastened the end of Dolores Del Rio's stardom. Portrait by Bert Longworth.*

film was. Then Hays had Breen watch the film again with Father Wilfred Parsons; Pat Scanlan, Catholic editor of the *Brooklyn Tablet*; and M-G-M representatives. It was up to them to improve *The Merry Widow*.

In a memo to Hays, Breen focused on the ambience of Maxim's and on Count Danilo's morals: "When he meets up with Sonia, he again proceeds with the tactics of a 'coxsman' and we have the talk about 'going upstairs,' followed by a private dining room, with the emphasis on the couch." Breen proposed thirteen cuts to "make him [Danilo] a more attractive character to the mass audiences" outside the big cities. A chastised Breen finished by echoing Quigley: "I sincerely hope that Mr. Schenck [of M-G-M] will make the eliminations herein suggested. It is going to embarrass us all seriously if the picture gets out as it now is." Quigley hammered at Hays, who then called Thalberg with the bad news. The conversation, predictably, was "a long one." Thalberg had allowed Lubitsch unusual latitude in making the film. He did not appreciate having his judgment—or Lubitsch's—questioned. He was also quite pleased with the quality of *The Merry Widow*. But Quigley demanded action. After Thalberg pondered the cuts, he sent Hays a telegram:

> While I reiterate promises made to you over the telephone I again plead with you to help save this picture from being made jumpy and choppy wherever possible. It was made in the best of faith and $100,000 at least was spent in making retakes. . . . If these men are our friends, I am sure they would not use threats nor turn on us at the first opportunity.
>
> If they are sincere about the whole movement certainly they have been shown that we have made great improvements under a policy of cooperation sufficient to have us enjoy continuance of that policy. In the long run, no one will be served by vicious attacks. The public today will certainly regard as completely unreasonable a war waged on any one picture out of a great group. Certainly the fact that so many agencies completely disassociated have passed the picture without even the usual minor cuts means that while their contentions may be right in certain small particulars such as a line here and there, still we couldn't have erred very far on the picture as a whole. . . .

Mae West posed as the Statue of Liberty in the opening sequence of Paramount's It Ain't No Sin.
By the time of the film's release, it was called Belle of the Nineties *and West's literary liberty was indeed a pose.*

This scene in Paramount's Belle of the Nineties *was amended by the PCA so that Roger Pryor leaves Mae West's apartment two days earlier than her script intended. Photograph by Don English.*

Ruby Carter (Mae West) sings Sam Coslow's "My Old Flame" to the accompaniment of the Duke Ellington Orchestra in The Belle of the Nineties. *The finished film shows only this angle, beautifully lit by Karl Struss. Alternate takes used in the theatrical trailer reveal a wider angle in which West and Ellington were recorded live and improvising. The wider angle was not used because West was manipulating her torso more than the PCA would allow.*

M-G-M's The Merry Widow *became a testing ground for Breen's new power when publisher Martin Quigley saw evils in it that Breen had missed. Irving Thalberg fought to preserve the integrity of Ernst Lubitsch's masterpiece, but Will Hays pressed Breen to order negative cuts. Although* The Merry Widow *was released to video, laser disc, and cable with the thirteen cuts made in 1934, the 35mm theatrical prints, 16mm rental prints, and the Turner Classic Movies version are complete. Portrait of Jeanette MacDonald as Sonia by Ted Allan.*

Paramount's The Scarlet Empress *was a financial disaster in 1934, but the most libidinous film of the entire pre-Code period did not sustain a single cut, either before or after the enforcement of the Production Code. By a quirk of fate, Josef von Sternberg's masterpiece survived Joe Breen's regime to become a universally acknowledged classic. Portrait of Marlene Dietrich by William Walling (designed by Sternberg).*

Thalberg's wire was in vain, and even though the state boards did not agree with Quigley, the PCA had to save face. Three days later, Thalberg had a memo sent to all distribution branches, instructing them to make thirteen cuts in each print of *The Merry Widow*. One cut deleted a garter embroidered with sequins: "Many happy returns." Another cut shortened a telegram read by Una Merkel. "I know what to do but am too old to do it" became "I know what to do but—BUP!" Most of the cuts were abrupt and obvious.

The editing memo concluded: "After the 'A' quota of prints is completed, we will cut the negative." With this simple sentence, the mightiest studio in the world admitted its defeat by a petty politician, a fanatical publisher, and Joe Breen.

THE DEVIL IS A MOVIE

After *The Merry Widow*, Joe Breen took no chances. He pounced on any story element that was even remotely suspicious. He was not about to repeat the error that had driven a wedge between him and Martin Quigley. Breen and his newly augmented staff were coldly effective; little got past them. An item in *Variety* reported: "The millennium has arrived, according to film row. In the past four weeks, the Chicago censor board, admittedly the toughest in the country, did not make one cut on any picture."

There was an occasional throwback. In late November, Breen got resistance from M-G-M over W. S. Van Dyke's *Forsaking All Others*, a big-budget film starring Joan Crawford, Clark Gable, and Robert Montgomery. When Breen previewed the film, he was "very gravely concerned" that Van Dyke had ignored most of his directives. Van Dyke had an unwilling conference with Breen and his "band of seven." After arguing with the director, Breen declared that he was washing his hands of the film: M-G-M could make retakes, appeal to Hays, or shelve the film. He and Van Dyke exchanged words, which may have led to the incident related by Jack Vizzard: "The director, miffed, made an uncautious slur on Joe's honesty. Joe took a roundhouse swing at the man and hit him on the nose."

Breen's version of the story was disputed by Joseph L. Mankiewicz, screenwriter of the film. He told Vizzard that the short, beefy Breen could not have bested the tall, wiry Van Dyke. After the dust cleared, the studio ordered retakes. Van Dyke wrote to Breen: "I am not shooting on 'Naughty Marietta' this morning so I have been asked to do the retakes. I just want to say that I am heartily in accord with the thing and that this present lineup can do the picture nothing but good. Regards, Van. P. S. I still think I'm right!" According to cinematographer George Folsey: "Richard Boleslavsky directed the retakes. We redid a lot of Crawford's close-ups, too. We were always going in there and reshooting things that Van Dyke had rushed through." Breen passed *Forsaking All Others*, and M-G-M had another hit.

In the critical new atmosphere, it was not surprising that a reformer could be overly zealous. A Mrs. James F. Looram of the IFCA breathlessly reported that she had heard Marion Forsythe (Ann Harding) speak a shocking line to Leander Noland (Edward Everett Horton) in E. H. Griffith's *Biography of a Bachelor Girl*: "Of course, you were always interesting, even fornicationally." On closer inspection, the line was found to be: "You used to be quite a nice boy—even fun occasionally." Looram made no mention of the scene in which Orrin Kinnicott (Charles Richman) asks Harding: "Do you eat enough roughage?"

Irving Thalberg had purchased the play for Norma Shearer, but she passed on it because of a pregnancy—and the Code. Because of its restrictions, there would be no more daring roles for her. The First Lady of M-G-M now shopped for more conventional plays, including the ill-advised *Romeo and Juliet*. This sharp right turn and the disappearance of her pre-Code films would dim the memory of her sexy persona. Both she and Harlow lost a great deal to the Code.

Harlow's next film, *China Seas*, managed to tow the line, making it clear that China Doll (Harlow) was not sleeping with "old rough-on-rats" Jamesy (Wallace Beery), although she may have slept with Captain Gaskell (Clark Gable). Thalberg told one writer, John Lee Mahin: "After the trouble we had with Vantine [Harlow's *Red Dust* character], such as protests from women, the China Doll should be less obviously a tramp." In the script by James Kevin McGuinness, Gaskell tells China Doll: "What a vicious little slut you are." Was Thalberg baiting the PCA? Was he using the technique espoused by Donald Ogden Stewart and Mae West in order to

A Ray Jones portrait of Claudette Colbert for Paramount's Cleopatra. *The film had symbolism that eluded the censors, and C. B. DeMille did so well with it that he held a press conference at which he stated that films "must have normal sex." Martin Quigley jumped on this: "[T]he word* normal *seems to have been brought up and for the moment our mind's eye is all a-whirl with that celebrated bit of demillinery known now to tradition of the screen as 'that Lesbian dance.'" Predictably,* The Sign of the Cross *was butchered for reissue a year later.*

The curt Mr. Kurt (Robert Montgomery) confronts promiscuous portraitist Marion Forsythe (Ann Harding) in the Irving Thalberg production of Biography of a Bachelor Girl. *Much of S. N. Behrman's wit was lost to the new Code. Photograph by James Manatt.*

keep the things he really wanted?

If so, he only succeeded in *China Seas* and in *Escapade*, which had Virginia Bruce posing semi-nude for artist William Powell. Director Robert Z. Leonard filmed shots of Bruce naked under a chinchilla wrap, but they did not appear in the film. To make *Escapade*, the studio bought the German film *Maskerade* and copied it shot for shot, even using some wide shots of a music hall from its negative. *Escapade* also pirated some of *Maskerade*'s more

imperiled. As Sidney Kent pondered a merger with Darryl Zanuck's Twentieth Century Pictures, Sol Wurtzel produced the only blockbuster of his career, *Dante's Inferno*. The imaginative film was directed by Harry Lachman and photographed by Rudolph Maté. Its magnificent re-creation of the Gustave Doré engravings was the work of art director Willy Pogany, scenic designer Ben Carré, dance adviser Hubert Stowitts, and special effects director Fred Sersen; they deserved credit for showing the

This Ted Allan photograph of William Powell and Virginia Bruce captured a camera setup that was excluded from the final cut of M-G-M's Escapade.

most naked extras the Code would allow for the next forty years. Breen noted: "There is a suggestion of nudity in certain figures which we saw, but the general context which surrounds the exhibition of these figures is such, as in our judgment, to definitely characterize these scenes as inoffensive and necessary for proper plot motivation, and therefore acceptable under the Code." According to *Variety*, the sequence "brought a burst of applause at the Rivoli, although the audience seemed to issue a sigh of relief when the inferno dissolved back to the story once more." Perhaps it was because they knew that the Legion of Decency had condemned the film for that very scene.

If burning sinners had gotten past Joe Breen, maybe Marlene Dietrich and Josef von Sternberg could, too. In the spring of 1935, they were preparing their seventh film, *Caprice Espagnole*. As Sternberg went to the PCA, he had reason to think that he could outwit Breen. His last film, *Catherine the Great*, had managed, thanks to a quirk of fate. This fanciful biography of Russia's oversexed sovereign had been ready for release in April 1934. At that moment British producer Alexander Korda was releasing his own *Catherine the Great*, starring Elizabeth Bergner. Sternberg retitled his film *The Scarlet Empress*, and Paramount held up its release until the Korda film had played itself out in a few art houses. But Sternberg could not resist the opportunity of opening his film in London. To do this, he had to rush the film

worldly moments. In a music hall, patrons sing the film's theme song, "You're All I Need." A series of shots show William Powell and Luise Rainer singing the refrain, then an old drunk serenading a bottle of champagne, and then a rich older man with two young women, who gaze longingly at one another as they sing "You're All I Need."*

In the spring of 1935, the Fox Film Corporation had only Warner Baxter, Janet Gaynor, and Will Rogers in its stable, and its attempts to launch new stars such as Lilian Harvey had failed. Its theaters were in receivership, and its grand facility was through the SRC. When Breen saw what was the most adult, perverse, sex-obsessed film of the entire pre-Code period, he brought Will Hays in, ran the film again, and called an emergency meeting with Sternberg and Paramount executives. But the Catholic crusade required his attention more than this one movie, and Sternberg was insistent about the opening. When Breen left to consult with Quigley, an intimidated minion passed *The Scarlet Empress*. It premiered at the Carlton Theatre in London on May 9.

In July, when Breen was putting PCA seals on Paramount films, he did not bother to look at *The Scarlet Empress* because it had already been passed. He gave it a seal and sent it out. The Legion of Decency got as far as the first reel, in which an eight-year-old girl's dream shows three beheadings, a naked woman falling out of an "iron maiden," three topless women being burned at the stake, and a "human clapper" swinging inside a huge bell. *The Scarlet Empress* made the condemned list, but it created no problems for Breen. No one went to see it. Everyone, including Mae West, dismissed it as an "arty disaster." What was possibly the best-scripted, best-photographed, and best-directed film of the period was written off as a waste of film. But Breen kept score, and he was waiting for Sternberg.

Caprice Espagnole was the John Dos Passos adaptation of the Pierre Louÿs novel *The Woman and the Puppet*. The script, as reworked by Sternberg, told the unpleasant story of Don Pascual, a Spanish officer who degrades himself for a surpassingly seductive woman, Concha Perez. Pascual pursues Concha, ostensibly without reward, until he spends the last of his wealth and self-respect on her. "At this point, of course," said Sternberg, "the two principals have a brief romantic interlude."

"You mean they fuck," said Breen.

This was not the way to communicate with the coldly opaque Sternberg. But the aloof genius needed the PCA so badly that he joined Breen in the vernacular: "Yes. They fuck."

Breen passed *Caprice Espagnole*. New Paramount head Ernst Lubitsch changed its title to *The Devil Is a Woman* and the strange film went to its press preview. Earl E. Bright, an aide to Will Hays, happened to see it. Bright sent Breen a threatening memo: "Mr. Hays raises the question how the boys figured that adultery was not profitable. This girl does not seem to pay anything. She comes out just fine,

doesn't she? He is afraid it is successful and progressive prostitution. He is a little worried. Just the same as you are."

For the first time in months, Breen had to kick himself for not seeing the obvious. Concha Perez (Marlene Dietrich) and Don Pascual (Lionel Atwill) were involved in a sadomasochistic relationship. Worse than that, the character of Concha was a flagrant violation of the Code. As conceived by Sternberg, she is a loose woman, bestowing her favors on anyone who can afford her. She transcends this status to become a kept woman, which enables her to torture Pascual. She is also a powerful woman, running her family, making men buy up her contracts, influencing politicians, inciting men to kill one another over her, and dismissing the voices of morality with a wave of her black lace handkerchief. Worst of all, she is a thoroughly impenitent woman. Nowhere in the film does she express remorse or sympathy for the men she degrades. Though the film was made six months after the Code, Concha Perez was the last pre-Code woman—powerful, sexual, and self-determining.

Breen had already made Mae West an honest woman, Joan Crawford a virtuous shopgirl, Jean Harlow a "brownette," and Norma Shearer a virgin. He now tried to make an angel out of Marlene Dietrich. He suggested that Pascual strangle Concha to death, and that she repent with her dying breath. Sternberg refused. Breen had to content himself with making Dietrich less devilish. He worked on Concha's lines: "I had intended to give myself to you like a flower—but you wished to buy me like dead beef which is auctioned off after a bullfight." There was also the scene in which Pascual finally loses his temper. Concha taunts him: "What right have you to tell me what to do? Are you my father? No. Are you my husband? No! Are you my *lover?* No! Well, I'm afraid you're content with *very little!*" Breen required that the word "lover" be muffled by a clap of thunder. But Pascual still administered a beating to Concha: "We recommend omitting the action of Pascual kicking Concha as she lies on the floor." Breen also worked on Pascual's most significant speech: "I realized I had only two choices—to leave her or kill her. I chose a third. I submitted." Breen cut the words "I submitted." After the Code, no man could submit to a woman for gratification. Other cuts included the "romantic interlude" referred to by Sternberg and a song, "(If It Isn't

TOP:

Before it merged with Darryl Zanuck's Twentieth Century Pictures, the Fox Film Corporation went out with a bang. Dante's Inferno *featured a loving re-creation of the famous Gustave Doré engravings. The anatomy of hundreds of glistening sinners was obscured by airbrushed steam only in the still photographs.*

BOTTOM:

On May 29, 1935, the Fox Film Corporation became Twentieth Century-Fox, and offbeat films such as Dante's Inferno *were suddenly a thing of the past. Photographs by Frank Powolny.*

OPPOSITE:

In Paramount's The Devil Is a Woman, *Josef von Sternberg transformed Marlene Dietrich into Concha Perez.* Variety *called her a "glorious achievement, the supreme consolidation of the sartorial, make-up and photographic arts." Another character in the film called her "the most dangerous woman you'll ever meet." Both Will Hays and Joe Breen thought she was, and though the film was severely trimmed and released nearly a year after the new Code, Concha Perez survives as the apotheosis of the wicked, willful, unrepentant pre-Code woman.*

Pain) Then It Isn't Love."* *The Devil Is a Woman* lost seventeen minutes.

Even with the cuts, Concha Perez remained a threatening woman, the apotheosis of all those wicked, willful, unrepentant pre-Code women. An angry film critic at the *New York Journal American* wrote: "Every scene fairly shrieks for Jim Cagney and a grapefruit." In rapid succession, the Legion of Decency condemned the film, the public ignored it, and the Spanish government protested its portrayal of the Civil Guard. Paramount went through the motions of burning a print to assure Spain that the film was being withdrawn and its negative destroyed. The stench of burning nitrate was already in the air.

In mid-1935, Joe Breen had begun to inspect the Class III films. In case after case, he found scenes and lines that could no longer be screened, let alone filmed. To reissue these films as they were would negate the progress of the PCA. He also believed that these films were "dangerous" to anyone who might see them. He fully believed that innocent viewers would be harmed by them. But these films represented potential income to the studios; their stars were still popular and their titles still known. Breen acknowledged this problem with a regrettable solution. For the next nineteen years, if the studios wanted to rerelease a film, he made them cut scenes—not from prints, not from fine-grain positives, not from dupe negatives—*from master "camera" negatives.*

His victims included *All Quiet on the Western Front, Animal Crackers, Mata Hari, Monkey Business, Public Enemy, Frankenstein, Dracula, Dr. Jekyll and Mr. Hyde, The Beast of the City, A Farewell to Arms, Blonde Venus, Love Me Tonight, Shanghai Express, The Bowery, State Fair, The Eagle and the Hawk, Counsellor-at-Law, King Kong, 42nd Street, Manhattan Melodrama, Murder at the Vanities, Tarzan and His Mate,* and *Viva Villa!*

To call these films victims is to assert that they, though made only of chemicals and imagination, were works of art with souls. Until the *Miracle* case of 1952, when the Supreme Court declared that films were protected by the First Amendment, no one had proven that films were art.† As film after film came up for reissue, the splicing blade fell. Hundreds of films were cut, and the nitrate "trims" were thrown away.

Joe Breen's tenure ended in 1954. When he retired, the Academy of Motion Picture Arts and Sciences presented him with the coveted Academy Award for Lifetime Achievement. The Oscar™ was inscribed: "To our industry's benevolent conscience." This was a long way from the contentious days of 1934. Joe Breen, who had railed against the immorality of the Hollywood Jews, had learned from them—and they from him. They would not have asked him to run RKO Pictures if he had been truly anti-Semitic. They would not have flown him here and there. They would not have invited him into their homes. And they certainly would not have given him an Academy Award. He had convictions. He was a fighter, but he didn't hate.

According to Jack Vizzard, who worked with Breen from 1944 to 1954: "Towards the end of his career, I asked Joe why he didn't write the story of the Code. He waved off the suggestion with a touch of irritation. 'Jack,' he said, 'I have too many friends in the industry, and I wouldn't want to say anything to embarrass them.' I think the same thing happened to him as happened to me. I came running down out of the theological hills, where I was studying for the priesthood, to save the world from the Jews. They reciprocated by saving me from myself."

But who saved the real objects of Joe Breen's wrath, the "sinful" and "fogged" pre-Code films? Even if his Production Code Administration was not Hitler's fifth column, as some scholars posit, it did damage films of the 1930s, especially those produced before it. Who saved the films that Breen pulled from circulation in 1934, and retired to vaults of ignominy? What happened to the ten films most responsible for the Legion of Decency and the Production Code Administration? Where are *The Cockeyed World, The Divorcee, Possessed, Red-Headed Woman, Scarface, The Sign of the Cross, She Done Him Wrong, The Story of Temple Drake, Baby Face,* and *Convention City?*

EPILOGUE

When Edwin Schallert wrote in the *Los Angeles Times* in 1934 that there never had been a classic film, he was expressing popular opinion, at least that of the film capital. The idea that anyone would want to own an old movie or even look at one was absurd. Time would prove him wrong.

In the 1950s, television's voracious appetite for programming induced the major studios to open their film libraries. Many of their films were Class I or Class II titles, but they were not worried. America had been through two wars, and could stand to see Jean Harlow wiggle on a small screen. By the late 1950s, virtually every pre-Code film had found a home on the "Late, Late Show." The only films missing were those of the Fox Film Corporation. A 1937 warehouse fire had destroyed their negatives, and other than the Shirley Temple and Charlie Chan films, Twentieth Century-Fox did not consider the premerger films commercial enough to justify the cost of preserving them. Each Fox film existed in one decomposing nitrate print. For fans of the other studios' films, there was good news and bad news.

The good news was that most of the problem titles of the pre-Code period, films such as *The Divorcee, She Done Him Wrong,* and *Red Dust,* were intact. Some Class III films that had been cruelly cut were now being printed from fine-grain positives made *before* the cuts. *The Mask of Fu Manchu, Manhattan Melodrama,* and *Viva Villa!* were seen in their original, uncut versions on TV. For some reason, there was also a fine-grain positive of the complete *Merry Widow;* perhaps Thalberg had been so revolted by having to cut the negative that he first made a preservation positive.

The bad news was that some puritanical TV programmers got copies of PCA memos and made permanent physical cuts in the 16mm prints they were leasing. *The Story of Temple Drake* was slated for TV packages, but was pulled at the last minute, as was *Red-Headed Woman. A Farewell to Arms* and *The Sign of the Cross* existed only in truncated reissue versions. *Possessed* and *Scarface* did not make it to TV because of rights problems.

Thirty years later, home entertainment markets brought happy endings to some of these stories. A number of Class I and II titles were found to have complete fine-grain positives, so they were transferred to cable and video in pristine, uncut versions: *Strangers May Kiss, Possessed, Scarface, Red-Headed Woman, Blonde Venus, Baby Face.* The discovery of complete prints, fine-grain positives, and even negatives has allowed for the restoration of a number of Class III titles: *All Quiet on the Western Front, Frankenstein, Dr. Jekyll and Mr. Hyde, King Kong, Tarzan and His Mate,* and *Murder at the Vanities.* Sad to say, a number of other Class III titles went to cable and video in cut versions: *Animal Crackers, Beast of the City, Counsellor-at-Law, Dracula, The Eagle and the Hawk, Love Me Tonight, Mata Hari,* and *Public Enemy.* For these, no restoration is possible.

Almost fifty pre-Code titles produced by the Fox Film Corporation were saved in a last-minute preservation effort by archivist Alex Gordon and the late film historian William K. Everson. Titles now preserved on video masters by Twentieth Century-Fox include *The Cockeyed World, Just Imagine, Quick Millions, Call Her Savage, State Fair, Pilgrimage, Six Hours to Live, The Devil's in Love, Zoo in Budapest,* and *Broadway Bad.* Other Fox Film titles *(Transatlantic, The Spider, The Brat, The Man Who Came Back, While Paris Sleeps, Hoopla, I Loved You Wednesday, The Warrior's Husband, I Am Suzanne!)* exist only in 35mm and/or 16mm prints at the Museum of Modern Art or the University of California, Los Angeles. Perhaps they will become available to the general public; perhaps not.

The most spectacular pre-Code restoration took place in 1993, with MCA-Universal's transfer to video of Cecil B. DeMille's own nitrate print of *The Sign of the Cross.* The consensus was that the cut scenes were still strong stuff. *A Farewell to Arms, Letty Lynton, The Story of Temple Drake, Escapade, Only Yesterday, Search for Beauty,* and many others do exist in complete versions. They will sit in vaults until there is sufficient consumer interest to justify the expense of rights clearance, restoration, transfer, and marketing. "Consumer interest" means letters, e-mail, faxes, and calls. Perhaps there will be a happy ending for these films; there will be no happy ending for the happiest pre-Code film of all.

In 1936, Jack Warner submitted a list of Class I and II titles to the PCA, hoping for permission to rerelease them. One of them was *Convention City.* On September 3, 1936, Breen wrote him that no amount of cutting could make these films suitable for rerelease. Warner was constantly being pestered by conventioneers who wanted, for obvious reasons, to rent *Convention City.* He found himself in an awkward position. He could not rent the film without getting into trouble with Breen, but he could not deny that he had the film. Of course, if he did not have the film, he could not rent it.* His solution was to destroy all prints, the negative, and the fine-grain positive of a film that was, if not a work of art, one of the most enjoyable products ever to roll off the Hollywood assembly line.

So we will never see an amorous Dick Powell suddenly becoming nauseated, or a soused conventioneer cornering "Elmer the Goat," or Mary Astor knocking back a glass of gin, or Guy Kibbee's toupee flying out the window, or Joan Blondell's "bulbs" glowing, all in the sinful soft focus of *Convention City.*

And that, to paraphrase Mae West, *is* a sin.

Joan Blondell invites us to a film we can never see.

APPENDIX I

THE DON'TS AND BE CAREFULS

Resolved, that those things which are included in the following list shall not appear in pictures produced by the members of this Association, irrespective of the manner in which they are treated:

1. Pointed profanity—either by title or lip—this includes words "God," "Lord," "Jesus," "Christ" (unless used reverently in connection with proper religious ceremonies), "hell," "damn," "Gawd," and every other profane and vulgar expression, however it may be spelled.
2. Any licentious or suggestive nudity—in fact or in silhouette; and any lecherous or licentious notice thereof by other characters in the picture.
3. The illegal traffic in drugs.
4. Any inference of sex perversion.
5. White slavery.
6. Miscegenation (sex relationships between the white and black races).
7. Sex hygiene and venereal diseases.
8. Scenes of actual childbirth—in fact or in silhouette.
9. Children's sex organs.
10. Ridicule of the clergy.
11. Willful offense to any nation, race, or creed.

And be it further resolved that special care be exercised in the manner in which the following subjects are treated, to the end that vulgarity and suggestiveness may be eliminated and that good taste may be emphasized:

1. The use of the flag.
2. International relations (avoiding picturization in an unfavorable light another's religion, history, institutions, prominent people, and citizenry).
3. Arson.
4. The use of firearms.
5. Theft, robbery, safecracking, and dynamiting of trains, mines, buildings, etc. (having in mind the effect which a too-detailed description of these may have upon the moron).
6. Brutality and possible gruesomeness.
7. Technique of committing murder by whatever method.
8. Methods of smuggling.
9. Third-degree methods.
10. Actual hangings or electrocutions as legal punishment for crime.
11. Sympathy for criminals.
12. Attitude toward public characters and institutions.
13. Sedition.
14. Apparent cruelty to children and animals.
15. Branding of people or animals.
16. The sale of women, or of a woman selling her virtue.
17. Rape or attempted rape.
18. First-night scenes.
19. Man and woman in bed together.
20. Deliberate seduction of girls.
21. The institution of marriage.
22. Surgical operations.
23. The use of drugs.
24. Titles or scenes having to do with law enforcement or law-enforcing officers.
25. Excessive or lustful kissing, particularly when one character or the other is a "heavy."

Resolved, that the execution of the purpose of this resolution is a fair trade practice.

APPENDIX II

THE 1930 PRODUCTION CODE

CODE
TO GOVERN THE MAKING OF
TALKING, SYNCHRONIZED AND SILENT
MOTION PICTURES

Formulated by
Association of Motion Picture Producers, Inc.
and The Motion Picture Producers and
Distributors of America, Inc.

Motion picture producers recognize the high trust and confidence which have been placed in them by the people of the world and which have made motion pictures a universal form of entertainment.

They recognize their responsibility to the public because of this trust and because entertainment and art are important influences in the life of a nation.

Hence, though regarding motion pictures primarily as entertainment without any explicit purpose of teaching or propaganda, they know that the motion picture within its own field of entertainment may be directly responsible for spiritual or moral progress, for higher types of social life, and for much correct thinking.

During the rapid transition from silent to talking pictures they have realized the necessity and the opportunity of subscribing to a Code to govern the production of talking pictures and of reacknowledging this responsibility.

On their part, they ask from the public and from public leaders a sympathetic understanding of their purposes and problems and a spirit of cooperation that will allow them the freedom and opportunity necessary to bring the motion picture to a still higher level of wholesome entertainment for all the people.

GENERAL PRINCIPLES

1. No picture shall be produced which will lower the moral standards of those who see it. Hence the sympathy of the

audience should never be thrown to the side of crime, wrongdoing, evil, or sin.

2. Correct standards of life, subject only to the requirements of drama and entertainment, shall be presented.

3. Law, natural or human, shall not be ridiculed, nor shall sympathy be created for its violation.

PARTICULAR APPLICATIONS

I. Crimes Against the Law

These shall not be presented in such a way as to throw sympathy with the crime as against law and justice or to inspire others with a desire for imitation.

1. *Murder*
   a. The technique of murder must be presented in a way that will not inspire imitation.
   b. Brutal killings are not to be presented in detail.
   c. Revenge in modern times shall not be justified.

2. *Methods of crime should not be explicitly presented.*
   a. Theft, robbery, safe-cracking, and dynamiting of trains, mines, buildings, etc., should not be detailed in method.
   b. Arson must be subject to the same safeguards.
   c. The use of firearms should be restricted to essentials.
   d. Methods of smuggling should not be presented.

3. *Illegal drug* traffic must never be presented.

4. *The use of liquor* in American life, when not required by the plot or for proper characterization, will not be shown.

II. Sex

The sanctity of the institution of marriage and the home shall be upheld. Pictures shall not infer that low forms of sex relationship are the accepted or common thing.

1. *Adultery*, sometimes necessary plot material, must not be explicitly treated or justified, or presented attractively.

2. *Scenes of Passion*
   a. They should not be introduced when not essential to the plot.
   b. Excessive and lustful kissing, lustful embraces, suggestive postures and gestures are not to be shown.
   c. In general passion should so be treated that these scenes do not stimulate the lower and baser element.

3. *Seduction or Rape*
   a. They should never be more than suggested, and only when essential for the plot, and even then never shown by explicit method.
   b. They are never the proper subject for comedy.

4. *Sex perversion or any inference to it is forbidden.*

5. *White-slavery shall not be treated.*

6. *Miscegenation* (sex relationships between the white and black races) is forbidden.

7. *Sex hygiene* and venereal diseases are not subjects for motion pictures.

8. Scenes of *actual child birth*, in fact or in silhouette, are never to be presented.

III. Vulgarity

The treatment of low, disgusting, unpleasant, though not necessarily evil, subjects should be subject always to the dictates of good taste and a regard for the sensibilities of the audience.

IV. Obscenity

Obscenity in word, gesture, reference, song, joke, or by suggestion (even when likely to be understood only by part of the audience) is forbidden.

V. Profanity

Pointed profanity (this includes the words, God, Lord, Jesus, Christ—unless used reverently—Hell, S.O.B., damn, Gawd), or every other profane or vulgar expression however used, is forbidden.

VI. Costume

1. *Complete nudity* is never permitted. This includes nudity in fact or in silhouette, or any lecherous or licentious notice thereof by other characters in the picture.

2. *Undressing scenes* should be avoided, and never used save where essential to the plot.

3. *Indecent or undue exposure* is forbidden.

4. *Dancing costumes* intended to permit undue exposure or indecent movements in the dance are forbidden.

VII. Dances

1. Dances suggesting or representing sexual actions or indecent passion are forbidden.

2. Dances which emphasize indecent movements are to be regarded as obscene.

VIII. Religion

1. No film or episode may throw *ridicule* on any religious faith.

2. Ministers of religion in their character as ministers of religion should not be used as comic characters or as villains.

3. *Ceremonies* of any definite religion should be carefully and respectfully handled.

IX. Locations

The treatment of bedrooms must be governed by good taste and delicacy.

X. National Feelings

1. *The use of the Flag* shall be consistently respectful.

2. *The history*, institutions, prominent people, and citizenry of other nations shall be represented fairly.

XI. Titles

Salacious, indecent, or obscene titles shall not be used.

XII. Repellent Subjects

The following subjects must be treated within the careful limits of good taste:

1. *Actual hangings* or electrocutions as legal punishments for crime.

2. *Third-degree* methods.

3. *Brutality* and possible gruesomeness.

4. *Branding* of people or animals.

5. *Apparent cruelty* to children or animals.

6. *The sale of women*, or a woman selling her virtue.
7. *Surgical operations*.

REASONS SUPPORTING PREAMBLE OF CODE

I. Theatrical motion pictures, that is, pictures intended for the theater as distinct from pictures intended for churches, schools, lecture halls, educational movements, social reform movements, etc., are primarily to be regarded as ENTERTAINMENT.

Mankind has always recognized the importance of entertainment and its value in rebuilding the bodies and souls of human beings.

But it has always recognized that entertainment can be of a character either HELPFUL or HARMFUL to the human race, and in consequence has clearly distinguished between:

a. Entertainment which tends to improve the race, or at least to re-create and rebuild human beings exhausted with the realities of life; and

b. Entertainment which tends to degrade human beings, or to lower their standards of life and living.

Hence the MORAL IMPORTANCE of entertainment is something which has been universally recognized. It enters intimately into the lives of men and women and affects them closely; it occupies their minds and affections during leisure hours; and ultimately touches the whole of their lives. A man may be judged by his standard of entertainment as easily as by the standard of his work.

So correct entertainment raises the whole standard of a nation.

Wrong entertainment lowers the whole living conditions and moral ideals of a race.

Note, for example, the healthy reactions to healthful sports, like baseball, golf; the unhealthy reactions to sports like cockfighting, bullfighting, bear baiting, etc.

Note, too, the effect on ancient nations of gladiatorial combats, the obscene plays of Roman times, etc.

II. Motion pictures are very important as ART.
Though a new art, possibly a combination art, it has the same object as the other arts, the presentation of human thought, emotion, and experience, in terms of an appeal to the soul through the senses.

Here, as in entertainment,

Art enters intimately into the lives of human beings.

Art can be morally good, lifting men to higher levels. This has been done through good music, great painting, authentic fiction, poetry, drama.

Art can be morally evil in its effects. This is the case clearly enough with unclean art, indecent books, suggestive drama. The effect on the lives of men and women is obvious.

Note: it has often been argued that art in itself is unmoral, neither good nor bad. This is perhaps true of the THING which is music, painting, poetry, etc. But the thing is the PRODUCT of some person's mind, and the intention of that mind was either good or bad morally when it produced the thing. Besides, the thing has its EFFECT upon those who come into contact with it. In both these ways, that is, as a product of a mind and as the cause of definite effects, it has a deep moral significance and an unmistakable moral quality.

Hence: The motion pictures, which are the most popular of modern arts for the masses, have their moral quality from the intention of the minds which produce them and from their effects on the moral lives and reactions of their audiences. This gives them a most important morality.

1. They reproduce the morality of the men who use the pictures as a medium for the expression of their ideas and ideals.

2. They affect the moral standards of those who, through the screen, take in these ideas and ideals.

In the case of the motion pictures, this effect may be particularly emphasized because no art has so quick and so widespread an appeal to the masses. It has become in an incredibly short period the art of the multitudes.

III. The motion picture, because of its importance as entertainment and because of the trust placed in it by the peoples of the world, has special MORAL OBLIGATIONS:

A. Most arts appeal to the mature. This art appeals at once to every class, mature, immature, developed, undeveloped, law abiding, criminal. Music has its grades for different classes; so has literature and drama. This art of the motion picture, combining as it does the two fundamental appeals of looking at a picture and listening to a story, at once reaches every class of society.

B. By reason of the mobility of a film and the ease of picture distribution, and because of the possibility of duplicating positives in large quantities, this art reaches places unpenetrated by other forms of art.

C. Because of these two facts, it is difficult to produce films intended for only certain classes of people. The exhibitors' theatres are built for the masses, for the cultivated and the rude, the mature and the immature, the self-respecting and the criminal. Films, unlike books and music, can only with difficulty be confined to certain selected groups.

D. The latitude given to film material cannot, in consequence, be as wide as the latitude given to book material. In addition:

a. A book describes; a film vividly presents. One presents on a cold page; the other by apparently living people.

b. A book reaches the mind through words merely; a film reaches the eyes and ears through the reproduction of actual events.

c. The reaction of a reader to a book depends on the keenness of the reader's imagination; the reaction to a film depends on the vividness of presentation.

Hence many things which might be described or suggested in a book could not possibly be presented in film.

E. This is also true when comparing the film with the newspaper.

a. Newspapers present by description, film by actual presentation.

b. Newspapers are after the fact and present things as having taken place; the film gives the events in the process of enactment and with apparent reality of life.

F. Everything possible in a play is not possible in film:

a. Because of the larger audience of the film, and its consequential mixed character. Psychologically, the larger the audience, the lower the moral mass resistance to suggestion.

b. Because through light, enlargement of character, presentation, scenic emphasis, etc., the screen story is brought closer to the audience than the play.

c. The enthusiasm for and interest in the film actors and actresses, developed beyond anything of the sort in history, makes the audience largely sympathetic toward the characters they portray and the stories in which they figure. Hence the audience is more ready to confuse actor and actress and the characters they portray, and it is most receptive of the emotions and ideals presented by their favorite stars.

G. Small communities, remote from sophistication and from the hardening process which often takes place in the ethical and moral standards of groups in larger cities, are easily and readily reached by any sort of film.

H. The grandeur of mass settings, large action, spectacular features, etc., affects and arouses more intensely the emotional side of the audience.

In general, the mobility, popularity, accessibility, emotional appeal, vividness, straightforward presentation of fact in the film make for more intimate contact with a larger audience and for greater emotional appeal.

Hence the larger moral responsibilities of the motion pictures.

REASONS UNDERLYING THE GENERAL PRINCIPLES

I. No picture shall be produced which will lower the moral standards of those who see it. Hence the sympathy of the audience should never be thrown to the side of crime, wrongdoing, evil, or sin.

This is done:

1. When evil is made to appear attractive or alluring, and good is made to appear unattractive.

2. When the sympathy of the audience is thrown on the side of crime, wrongdoing, evil, sin. The same thing is true of a film that would throw sympathy against goodness, honor, innocence, purity, or honesty.

Note: Sympathy with a person who sins is not the same as sympathy with the sin or crime of which he is guilty. We may feel sorry for the plight of the murderer or even understand the circumstances which he has done. The presentation of evil is often essential for art or fiction or drama. This in itself is not wrong provided:

a. That evil is not presented alluringly. Even if later in the film the evil is condemned or punished, it must not be allowed to appear so attractive that the audience's emotions are drawn to desire or approve so strongly that later the condemnation is forgotten and only the apparent joy of the sin remembered.

b. That throughout, the audience feels sure that evil is wrong and good is right.

II. Correct standards of life shall, as far as possible, be presented.

A wide knowledge of life and of living is made possible through the film. When right standards are consistently presented, the motion picture exercises the most powerful influences. It builds character, develops right ideals, inculcates correct principles, and all this in attractive story form.

If motion pictures consistently hold up for admiration high types of characters and present stories that will affect lives for the better, they can become the most powerful natural force for the improvement of mankind.

III. Law, natural or human, shall not be ridiculed, nor shall sympathy be created for its violation.

By natural law is understood the law which is written in the hearts of all mankind, the great underlying principles of right and justice dictated by conscience.

By human law is understood the law written by civilized nations.

1. The presentation of crimes against the law is often necessary for the carrying out of the plot. But the presentation must not throw sympathy with the crime as against the law nor with the criminal as against those who punish him.

2. The courts of the land should not be presented as unjust. This does not mean that a single court may not be represented as unjust, much less that a single court official must not be presented this way. But the court system of the country must not suffer as a result of this presentation.

REASONS UNDERLYING PARTICULAR APPLICATIONS

I. Sin and evil enter into the story of human beings and hence in themselves are valid dramatic material.

II. In the use of this material, it must be distinguished between sin which repels by its very nature, and sins which often attract.

a. In the first class come murder, most theft, many legal crimes, lying, hypocrisy, cruelty, etc.

b. In the second class come sex sins, sins and crimes of apparent heroism, such as banditry, daring thefts, leadership in evil, organized crime, revenge, etc.

The first class needs less care in treatment, as sins and crimes of this class are naturally unattractive. The audience instinctively condemns all such and is repelled.

Hence the important objective must be to avoid the hardening of the audience, especially of those who are young and impressionable to the thought and fact of crime. People can become accustomed even to murder, cruelty, brutality, and repellent crimes, if those are too frequently repeated.

The second class needs great care in handling, as the response of human nature to their appeal is obvious. This is treated more fully below.

III. A careful distinction can be made between films intended for general distribution, and films intended for use in theatres restricted to a limited audience. Themes and plots quite appropriate for the latter would be altogether out of place and dangerous in the former.

Note: The practice of using a general theatre and limiting its patronage during the showing of a certain film to "Adults Only" is not completely satisfactory and is only partially effective.

However, maturer minds may easily understand and accept without harm subject matter in plots which do younger people positive harm.

Hence: If there should be created a special type of theatre, catering exclusively to an adult audience, for plays of this character (plays with problem themes, difficult discussions, and maturer treatment) it would seem to afford an outlet, which does not now exist, for pictures unsuitable for general distribution but permissible for exhibitions to a restricted audience.

I.   Crimes Against the Law
The treatment of crimes against the law must not:
1. Teach methods of crime.
2. Inspire potential criminals with a desire for imitation.
3. Make criminals seem heroic and justified.

Revenge in modern times shall not be justified. In lands and ages of less developed civilization and moral principles, revenge may sometimes be presented. This would be the case especially in places where no law exists to cover the crime because of which revenge is committed.

The use of liquor should never be excessively presented. In scenes from American life, the necessities of plot and proper characterization alone justify its use. And in this case, it should be shown with moderation.

II.   Sex
Out of regard for the sanctity of marriage and the home, the triangle, that is, the love of a third party for one already married, needs careful handling. The treatment should not throw sympathy against marriage as an institution.

Scenes of passion must be treated with an honest acknowledgment of human nature and its normal reactions. Many scenes cannot be presented without arousing dangerous emotions on the part of the immature, the young, or the criminal classes.

Even within the limits of pure love, certain facts have been universally regarded by lawmakers as outside the limits of safe presentation.

In the case of impure love, the love which society has always regarded as wrong and which has been banned by divine law, the following are important:
1. Impure love must not be presented as attractive and beautiful.
2. It must not be the subject of comedy or farce, or treated as material for laughter.
3. It must not be presented in such a way as to arouse passion or morbid curiosity on the part of the audience.
4. It must not be made to seem right and permissible.
5. In general, it must not be detailed in method and manner.

III.   Vulgarity; IV. Obscenity; V. Profanity; hardly need further explanation than is contained in the Code.

VI.   Costume
General Principles:
1. The effect of nudity or semi-nudity upon the normal man or woman, and much more upon the young and upon immature persons, has been recognized by all lawmakers and moralists.
2. Hence the fact that the nude or semi-nude body may be beautiful does not make its use in the films moral. For, in addition to its beauty, the effect of the nude or semi-nude body on the normal individual must be taken into consideration.
3. Nudity or semi-nudity used simply to put a "punch" into a picture comes under the head of immoral actions. It is immoral in its effect on the average audience.
4. Nudity can never be permitted as being necessary for the plot. Semi-nudity must not result in undue or indecent exposures.
5. Transparent or translucent materials and silhouette are frequently more suggestive than actual exposure.

VII. Dances
Dancing in general is recognized as an art and as a beautiful form of expression of human emotions.

But dances which suggest or represent sexual actions, whether performed solo or with two or more; dances intended to excite the emotional reaction of an audience; dances with movement of the breasts, excessive body movements while the feet are stationary, violate decency and are wrong.

VIII. Religion
The reason why ministers of religion may not be comic characters or villains is simply because the attitude taken toward them may easily become the attitude taken toward religion in general. Religion is lowered in the minds of the audience because of the lowering of the audience's respect for a minister.

IX.   Locations
Certain places are so closely and thoroughly associated with sexual life or with sexual sin that their use must be carefully limited.

X.   National Feelings
The just rights, history, and feelings of any nation are entitled to most careful consideration and respectful treatment.

XI.   Titles
As the title of a picture is the brand on that particular type of goods, it must conform to the ethical practices of all such honest business.

XII. Repellent Subjects
Such subjects are occasionally necessary for the plot. Their treatment must never offend good taste nor injure the sensibilities of an audience.

APPENDIX III

COMPENSATING MORAL VALUES

Time and again there occur in the decisions of the Production Code Administration the words: "Compensating moral values." The code demands "that in the end the audience feels that evil is wrong and good is right." To satisfy this requirement of the Code, stories must contain at least sufficient good to compensate for any evil they relate. The compensating moral values are: good characters, the voice of morality, a lesson, regeneration of the transgressor, suffering, and punishment.

Respect for Law

On the general subject of respect for law, the Code says:

"Law, natural or divine, must not be belittled or ridiculed, nor must a sentiment be created against it.

"The presentation of crimes against the law, human or divine, is often necessary for the carrying out of the plot. But the presentation must not throw sympathy with the criminal as against the law, nor with the crime as against those who must punish it.

"The courts of the land should not be presented as unjust."

The Production Code Administration has considered this section as conferring a full mandate to enforce respect for all law and all lawful authority, and has invariably given it such interpretation.

Within the meaning of this section, as hitherto construed, the following rules are established:

1. Religion, religious practices, and church authorities must be treated with respect, in the widest sense of the word.
2. Nothing subversive of the fundamental law of the land and of duly constituted authority can be shown. Communistic propaganda, for example, is banned from the screen.
3. High government officials must not be presented as untrue to their trust, without suffering the proper consequences.
4. The judiciary and the machinery of criminal law must not be presented in such a way as to undermine faith in justice. An individual judge, or district attorney, or jail warden may be shown to be corrupt; but there must be no reflection on the law in general, and the offender must be punished.
5. The police must not be presented as incompetent, corrupt, cruel, or ridiculous, in such a way as to belittle law-enforcing officers as a class.
6. Perjury, under any circumstances whatever, is wrong.
7. Riot, and agitation inciting to public violence, can be indicated only to the extent necessary for the purposes of plot development.

Under Working Principles, the concluding caution of the Code, is as follows: "As far as possible, life should not be misrepresented in such a way as to place in the minds of youth false values on life." There is added a note on "the magnificent possibilities of the screen for character development."

It has been remarked in these annotations that it is not the primary purpose, or task, of motion pictures to educate. Yet, will it or not, they have a powerful formative influence, not only upon minds and morals but also upon manners and customs. Therefore, besides avoiding offense against morals, it is incumbent upon them, from the standpoint of social spirit, of patriotism, and of policy, not to delude and confuse youth with regard to the true joys, and the all-too-true sorrows, of life. It is a reprehensible mistake, to say the least, and it is positively wrong when done beyond dramatic requirements, to tantalize youth by flaunting before it flashy clothes, easy money, luxurious living, habitual drinking, gambling, cynical contempt for conventions, and all the realism of problems that do not trouble an average person's existence.

1. "Details of crime" must never be shown and care should be exercised at all times in discussing such details.
2. Action suggestive of wholesale slaughter of human beings, either by criminals, in conflict with police, or as between warring factions of criminals, or in public disorder of any kind, will not be allowed.
3. There must be no suggestion, at any time, of excessive brutality.
4. Because of the alarming increase in the number of films in which murder is frequently committed, action showing the taking of human life, even in the mystery stories, is to be cut to a minimum. These frequent presentations of murder tend to lessen regard for the sacredness of life.
5. There must be no display, at any time, of machine guns, sub-machine guns, or other weapons generally classified as illegal weapons in the hands of gangsters or other criminals, and there are to be no offstage sounds of the repercussions of these guns.
6. The flaunting of weapons by gangsters or other criminals will not be allowed.
7. All discussions and dialogue on the part of gangsters regarding guns should be cut to a minimum.
8. There must be no scenes at any time showing law-enforcing officers dying at the hands of criminals. This includes private detectives and guards for banks, motor trucks, etc.

APPENDIX IV

100 PRE-CODE FILMS: A REFERENCE CHART
by Karl Thiede

This appendix provides a reference chart for a selection of pre-Code films. It is limited to 100 titles because figures are unavailable for many films and incomplete for others. Only titles with complete histories have been included. This book does not treat foreign-language versions or foreign censorship, so the chart does not include foreign negative costs or foreign film rentals. However, foreign film rentals contributed an average of 32 percent to a film's gross, so worldwide film rentals are used as the final measure of a film's gross.

Some of the headings require a brief explanation. "Cost" is short for "negative cost," i.e., the manufacture of the film, including raw film stock, story rights, salaries, publicity stills, and overhead. "Profit/Loss" tells whether the film had made a profit or lost money (indicated by parentheses) when the studio closed the books on it, usually five years after its initial release. "Avail?" tells if a film is available on video and/or laser disc from: MGM-UA Home Video ("MGM"); Turner Classic Movies Home Video ("TCM"); Twentieth Century-Fox Classics ("TWC"); or Universal Home Video ("UNIV"). When "W:" precedes one of these abbreviations, it signifies that preprint material exists on this title and that you should write to that company, urging it to release the film. "NO" means that the title is unavailable because no preprint material exists or because the rights have reverted to the original author's estate. The text identifies such films and provides explanations, either in their captions or in the Notes to the Text.

REFERENCE CHART

Title	Cost	Rentals	Profit/Loss	Avail?
Affairs of Cellini	$549,369.16	$857,869	($88,690)	W:TWC
All Quiet on . . .	$1,448,863.44	$3,000,000	$516,741	UNIV
Ann Vickers	$303,000	$527,000	$65,000	W:TCM
Another Language	$272,297.39	$654,000	$158,703	W:MGM
As You Desire Me	$460,733	$1,363,000	$457,267	MGM
Baby Face	$187,000	$452,000	$93,135	MGM
The Barbarian	$444,398.64	$843,000	$102,601	W: MGM
Beast of the City	$217,923.76	$610,000	$155,076	W: MGM
Blondie of the . . .	$602,620.68	$737,000	($132,680)	W: MGM
Blood Money	$238,591.02	$419,776	($62,301)	W: TWC
Born to be Bad	$252,238.62	$333, 255	($136,513)	W: TWC
Bowery, The	$421,495.65	$1,494,294	$506,957	W: TWC
Brat, The	$243,093	$383,788	($13,045)	W: TWC
Broadway Bad	$239,308	$343,203	($38,609)	W: TWC
Call Her Savage	$489,652	$842,456	$17,407	W: TWC
Cavalcade	$1,180,280	$2,960,782	$664,128	TWC
Chandu the Magician	$349,456	$488,496	$53,441	W: TWC
Christopher Strong	$284,000	$386,000	$15,000	W: TCM
Cockeyed World	$661,315	$2,640,157	$1,083,209	W: TWC
Convention City	$239,000	$522,000	$93,635	NO
Dancing Lady	$920,055.26	$2,406,000	$746,945	MGM
Dante's Inferno	$748,900	$786,200	($269,900)	W: TWC
Dinner at Eight	$391,737.71	$2,156,000	$1,041,262	MGM
Divorcee, The	$340,691.46	$1,218,000	$335,309	MGM
Dr. Monica	$167,000	$443,000	$70,962	W: TCM
Escapade	$490,096.83	$975,000	$149,903	NO
Ex-Lady	$93,000	$283,000	$60,385	MGM
Faithless	$203,420.45	$418,000	$48,580	W: MGM
Female	$286,000	$451,000	($6,615)	MGM
Footlight Parade	$703,000	$2,416,000	$1,050,135	MGM
42nd Street	$439,000	$2,281,000	$1,212,885	MGM
Four Frightened . . .	$509,006.96	$494,426	($305,000)	W: UNIV
Freaks	$310,607.37	$341,000	($158,607)	MGM
Free Soul, A	$520,095.27	$1,422,000	$252,905	MGM
George White's . . .	$510,000	$1,092,900	$63,730	W: TWC
Girl From Missouri	$508,508.21	$1,081,000	$213,492	MGM
Going Hollywood	$761,243.79	$962,000	($116,244)	MGM
Grand Hotel	$695,341.20	$2,594,000	$951,659	MGM
Guardsman, The	$312,654.81	$510,000	($88,655)	W: MGM
Heat Lightning	$169,000	$214,000	($102,788)	W: MGM

REFERENCE CHART

Title	Cost	Rentals	Profit/Loss	Avail?
Hello, Sister!	$367,366	$235,789	($233,220)	W: TWC
Hell's Angels	$2,857,807.07	$2,361,125	($1,339,416)	W: UNIV
Hips, Hips, Hooray!	$336,000	$625,000	$8,000	W: TCM
Hold Your Man	$262,949.30	$1,073,000	$436,051	MGM
Hot Pepper	$381,256	$683,598	$28,706	W: TWC
I Am a Fugitive . . .	$228,000	$1,599,000	$918,984	W: MGM
I Loved You Wed . . .	$372,049	$475,384	($96,345)	W: TWC
Illicit	$249,000	$548,000	$111,530	MGM
Inspiration	$417,683.40	$1,127,000	$306,317	MGM
King Kong	$672,254.75	$1,856,000	$626,945	W: TCM
Kongo	$156,998.25	$406,000	$82,002	W: MGM
Ladies They . . .	$176,000	$375,000	$46,385	MGM
Letty Lynton	$316,192.23	$1,172,000	$420,808	NO
Little Caesar	$281,000	$752,000	$232,530	MGM
Mad Genius, The	$441,000	$400,000	($191,470)	W: MGM
Madam Satan	$965,320.98	$1,015,000	($368,321)	MGM
Madame du Barry	$383,000	$587,000	($37,038)	W: MGM
Mandalay	$294,000	$629,000	$83,462	W: MGM
Mask of Fu Manchu	$327,627.26	$625,000	$72,373	MGM
Mata Hari	$552,475	$2,227,000	$884,525	MGM
Men in White	$206,788.04	$1,455,000	$790,212	W: MGM
Midnight Mary	$161,757.32	$517,000	$158,243	W: MGM
Modern Hero, A	$260,000	$274,000	($148,788)	W: MGM
Most Dangerous . . .	$217,000	$443,000	$75,000	W: TCM
Now I'll Tell	$308,200	$472,300	($45,290)	NO
Of Human Bondage	$403,000	$592,000	($45,000)	W: TCM
One Hour With You	$1,012,000	$1,205,000	($296,000)	W: UNIV
Our Blushing Brides	$337,479.84	$1,211,000	$411,520	W: MGM
Paid	$334,985.38	$1,231,000	$465,015	W: MGM
Possessed	$370,862.08	$1,030,000	$618,138	MGM
Public Enemy	$230,000	$557,000	$137,280	MGM
Queen Christina	$1,130,937	$2,610,000	$645,063	MGM
Rain	$591,532.39	$704,371	($197,786)	W: TCM
Rasputin . . .	$1,019,404.39	$1,379,000	($182,404)	MGM
Red Dust	$405,219.79	$1,223,000	$401,780	MGM
Red-Headed Woman	$394,736.52	$761,000	$75,263	MGM
Riptide	$766,000.73	$1,741,000	$335,999	MGM
Sadie Mckee	$607,450.93	$1,302,000	$230,549	MGM
Sailor's Luck	$240,904	$507,208	$46,691	W: TWC
Scarface	$711,379.92	$905,298	($189,012)	UNIV
Scarlet Dawn	$176,000	$276,000	($21,266)	MGM
Shanghai Express	$851,000	$1,525,000	$33,000	UNIV
Sign of the Cross	$694,064.67	$2,738,993	$627,207	UNIV
Sin of Madelon . . .	$363,014.17	$957,000	$151,986	MGM
Strange Interlude	$641,883.19	$1,237,000	$102,117	MGM
Strangers May Kiss	$394,483.81	$1,272,000	$335,516	W: MGM
Susan Lenox . . .	$572,638.65	$700,000	$371,361	MGM
Tarzan and His Mate	$1,279,142.51	$2,239,000	$167,857	MGM
Tarzan the Ape Man	$652,675.36	$2,540,000	$926,325	MGM
Thin Man, The	$226,402.06	$1,423,000	$733,598	MGM
This Modern Age	$354,162.52	$891,000	$224,837	W: MGM
Three on a Match	$135,000	$444,000	$139,135	MGM
Thunder Below	$535,000	$465,000	($251,000)	W: UNIV
Today We Live	$659,710.94	$1,035,000	($19,711)	W: MGM
Trader Horn	$1,312,636.35	$3,595,000	$946,364	MGM
Viva Villa!	$1,017,400.33	$1,875,000	$91,600	MGM
Warrior's Husband	$393,701	$475,607	($128,693)	W: TWC
Wonder Bar	$675,000	$2,035,000	$756,962	MGM
World Moves On, The	$727,400	$714,200	($371,760)	W: TWC
Zoo in Budapest	$436,649	$697,689	($48,012)	W:TWC

NOTES TO THE TEXT

Preface

6   *During our Norma Shearer* . . .   Elliot Lavine to author, June 21, 1997.

      Scores of . . .   Stack, "Shearer Luck."

      Before the . . .   LaSalle, "The Golden Age of Sex, Violence and Perversity."

7   *"Block-booking" was the practice that compelled a theater owner to book a specified number of films in order to book a particular film, whether he wanted the other films or not.

8   *Never before* . . .   Ernst and Lorentz, *Censored*, p. 24.

      Maybe it's . . .   *The Callahans and the Murphys* script, M-G-M story file collection, Cinema-Television Library, University of Southern California (hereafter MGM-USC).

      Unless . . . *Paramount* . . .   R. H. Cochrane, letter to Will H. Hays, Apr. 5, 1927, on microfilm of selected Hays Papers at the Cinema-Television Library, University of Southern California (hereafter WHH-USC).

Part I: 1930

12   *a big, good-looking* . . .   Jack Vizzard to the author, Dec. 16, 1997.

      disrespect of . . .   Ernst and Lorentz, *Censored*, p. 42.

      I show you . . .   Ibid., p. 29.

      Cut scenes . . .   Ibid., p. 30.

      *Unless otherwise noted, dialogue quotations are transcribed from VHS tapes provided by the respective copyright holders of the films cited.

13   *Anyone employed* . . .   Harry M. Warner, letter to Hays, Sept. 24, 1929.

      Silent smut . . .   Lord, *Played by Ear*, p. 295.

      an institution around . . .   Wall, "Oral Interview with Geoffrey Shurlock," AFI, p. 69.

      a worrier about . . .   Ibid., p. 68.

14   *the public now* . . .   R. H. Cochrane, letter to Hays, Apr. 5, 1927, WHH-USC.

      This industry . . .   Forman, *Our Movie-Made Children*, p. 121.

      A man used . . .   Ernst and Lorentz, *Censored*, p. 135.

      (caption)   *degradation of a* . . .   Ibid.

15   (caption)   *It is just too* . . .   Ibid.

16   *There is a* . . .   James B. M. Fisher, "Résumé," Oct. 19, 1929; *The Love Parade* file, in the Production Code Administration papers, MPAA Collection, Margaret Herrick Library, Center for Motion Picture Study, Academy of Motion Picture Arts and Sciences, Beverly Hills (hereafter PCA).

      'The Love Parade' is . . .   Egerton D. Lakin, letter to Pedro J. Lemos, Mar. 12, 1930, *Love Parade*, PCA.

      [The] dialogue . . .   Colonel Jason S. Joy, letter to Walter Wanger, Sept. 18, 1929, *Applause*, PCA.

      The assumption . . .   Ibid.

      if Anna's past . . .   Joy, letter to Albert Lewin, Apr. 13, 1929, *Anna Christie*, PCA.

      I was in . . .   Ibid.

      something like . . .   Ibid.

      Then in . . .   W. F. Willis, "Censorship Comments," Dec. 26, 1929, *Anna Christie*, PCA.

17   *My eyes* . . .   Hays, *The Memoirs of Will H. Hays*, p. 439.

morality of . . .   Maltby, "The Genesis of the Production Code," p. 19.

We do not . . .   Ibid.

The motion . . .   Ibid., p. 35.

We are really . . .   Ibid., p. 19.

The motion . . .   Ibid., p. 35.

You set . . .   Ibid., p. 20.

sit there . . .   Ibid.

the immoral . . .   Ibid., p. 19.

a special . . .   Ibid., p. 40.

three lively . . .   Hays, *The Memoirs of Will H. Hays*, p. 442.

18   *Hays is* . . .   Black, *Hollywood Censored*, p. 44.

      Sound, which . . .   Press release, Apr. 1, 1930, WHH-USC.

      How can a . . .   Sherwood, "This Is What They're Saying: Will Hays."

      That the code . . .   "Morals for Profit."

      nominal alliance . . .   "Hollywood Promises," p. 668.

      entire office . . .   Leff and Simmons, *The Dame in the Kimono*, p. 13.

      had a sixth sense . . .   Weingarten Interview, USC.

19   *presents divorce* . . .   Maltby, *Harmless Entertainment*, p. 20.

      That's how we built . . .   Weingarten Interview, USC.

      She had to . . .   "The Norma Shearer Irving Thalberg Loves," p. 71.

      It is a great . . .   Willis, "Review," Mar. 6, 1930, *Divorcee*, PCA.

      Where men . . .   Joy, report on Ohio cuts, May 24, 1930, *All Quiet on the Western Front*, PCA.

20   (caption)   *expose her body* . . .   Joy, letter to Schulberg, Apr. 3, 1930, *Monte Carlo*, PCA.

22   *The line* . . .   James B. M. Fisher, "Résumé," Apr. 29, 1930, ibid.

      I'll never . . .   Joy, report on Ohio cuts, May 24, 1930, ibid.

      audience reaction . . .   Fisher, "Résumé," Apr. 29, 1930, ibid.

      The difficulty . . .   Lamar Trotti, letter to Hays, Sept. 13, 1930, *Hell's Angels*, PCA.

23   (caption)   *Who wouldn't take* . . .   Joy, letter to Thalberg, Apr. 4, 1930, *Our Blushing Brides*, PCA

25   *When the couples* . . .   Ibid.

      I didn't relish . . .   James E. West, letter to Hays, Sept. 9, 1930, *Hell's Angels*, PCA.

      (caption)   *Say, sister, howdja* . . .   Script, *Within the Law [Paid]*, Sept. 5, 1930, MGM-USC.

26   *Some of the* . . .   John V. Wilson, letter to Robert M. Yost, Oct. 16, 1930, *Just Imagine*, PCA.

      Not the usual . . .   Vasey, *The World According to Hollywood*, p. 256.

      After reading . . .   Arthur Debra, assistant secretary, MPPDA, letter to Joy, Feb. 6, 1930, *Madam Satan*, PCA.

      a terrific . . .   Unsigned "Memo," Dec. 13, 1930, *The Blue Angel*, PCA.

      We are struggling . . .   Joy, letter to Trotti, June 21, 1930, *The Divorcee*, PCA.

      By the way . . .   Editorial, *The New York Telegraph*.

27 (caption) *Hurrah for...* C. B. DeMille, telegram to Joy, Oct. 1, 1930, *Madam Satan,* PCA.

Part II: 1931

30 *a man of...* Silke, *Here's Looking at You, Kid,* p. 65.

children applaud... Trotti, letter to Hays, Apr. 14, 1931, WHH-USC.

[LaGuardia] is... Maurice McKenzie, letter to Joy, Jan. 27, 1931, *Little Caesar,* PCA.

Children ... see... Trotti, letter to Hays, Apr. 14, 1931, WHH-USC.

I saw 'Little Caesar'... Joy, letter to McKenzie, Jan. 30, 1931, *Little Caesar,* PCA.

Everything else... Ibid.

the more... Joy, letter to Dr. James Wingate, New York Education Department, Motion Picture Division, Feb. 5, 1931, *Little Caesar,* PCA.

Always drama... Ibid.

33 *Our character...* Silke, *Here's Looking at You, Kid,* p. 65.

In PUBLIC... Zanuck, letter to Joy, *Public Enemy,* PCA.

People are... Mosley, *Zanuck,* p. 115.

That's not... Gussow, *Don't Say Yes Until I Finish Talking,* p. 46.

The greatest... AMPP Press Release, Apr. 6, 1931, WHH-USC.

a story... Trotti, letter to Hays, Apr. 14, 1931, WHH-USC.

it is another... Ibid.

the picture... Ibid.

showing Tommy... Trotti, "Résumé," Apr. 24, 1931, *Public Enemy,* PCA.

At the end... Undated memo, ibid.

Reel 8... Jason Joy, "Report," May 20, 1931, ibid.

Do you mean... Ibid.

long trained... "*Public Enemy.*"

every effort... Ben Koenig, Milwaukee Film Board of Trade, letter to C. C. Pettijohn, MPPDA, June 4, 1931, *Public Enemy,* PCA.

33; 38 *Well, these gang...* "Dealing with Capone."

36 (caption) *It was my...* Gussow, *Don't Say Yes Until I Finish Talking,* p. 45.

(caption) *When I made...* Ibid.

(caption) *At least you...* Breen, "Report," Aug. 18, 1953, *Public Enemy,* PCA.

38 *involved everything...* Shorris and Bundy, *Talking Pictures,* p. 76.

there is a... Trotti, letter to Hays, Apr. 14, 1931, WHH-USC.

absolutely necessary... Fisher, "Résumé," Mar. 13, 1930, *Divorcee,* PCA.

a sordid... Winter, letter to Hays, "5–31," WHH-USC.

excessive drinking... Ibid.

unnecessary drinking... Ibid.

an ex-flier... Dieterle interview, *Last Flight* press book, USC-Warner Bros. Collection, University of Southern California (hereafter *Last Flight* press book, WB-USC).

The replies... Joy, letter to Warner, Apr. 1, 1931, *Last Flight,* PCA.

40 (caption) *Louis B. Mayer told...* Chester W. Schaeffer to

author, Oct. 9, 1971.

42 *The taste for...* *Last Flight* press book, WB-USC.

seek a... Riley, *Dracula,* p. 30.

Absolutely... Ibid.

It will be... Ibid.

Dracula should... Ibid., p. 56.

As a producer... Gatiss, *James Whale,* p. 62.

Everything that... Savada and Skal, *Dark Carnival,* p. 150.

parading... Mank, *Karloff and Lugosi,* p. 14.

quite satisfactory... Joy, letter to Carl Laemmle, Jr., Jan. 9, 1931, *Dracula,* PCA.

*In 1938, Universal asked the PCA for permission to reissue *Dracula.* On March 17, 1938, Joseph I. Breen specified a number of cuts: Helen Chandler's screams, Dwight Frye's groans, Bela Lugosi's grunts, and Edward Van Sloan's "curtain speech," in which he tells the audience, "After all, there *are* such things." The most substantial cut was from the scene on board the schooner *Vesta.* The restoration done by MCA-Universal Home Video could not find this or the speech.

Dracula is... Fisher, "Résumé," Jan. 14, 1931, ibid.

Is this the... Joy, letter to Hays, Dec. 5, 1931, ibid.

I was a... Gatiss, *James Whale,* p. 70.

I chose... Ibid., p. 71.

This was... Mank, *Karloff and Lugosi,* p. 21.

43 **Frankenstein* production files do not include call sheets, so there are two schools of thought about the location of this scene. In *James Whale: A New World of Gods and Monsters,* James Curtis sets it at Lake Sherwood, "an irregular, privately owned body of water nestled in an area of the Santa Monica Mountains known as Sherwood Forest." Others set it at man-made Malibou Lake, a private recreation area maintained by the Malibou Lake Mountain Club. The author visited Lake Sherwood in September 1998 and was able to match topography and angle of sunlight.

Here is... Mank, *It's Alive!,* p. 31.

He had... Mank, *Karloff and Lugosi,* p. 24.

Well, Jimmy... Mank, *It's Alive!,* p. 32.

This was... Ibid.

The death... Ibid.

fumbled for... Ibid.

Throw her... Riley, *Frankenstein,* p. 39.

As it... Curtis, *James Whale,* p. 86.

Jesus, God... Ibid.

You're insane... Ibid., p. 87.

I don't know... *Motion Picture Herald,* Nov. 14, 1931, quoted in Curtis, *James Whale,* p. 155.

Junior urgently... "J. P. H.," letter to Joy, Dec. 10, 1931, *Frankenstein,* PCA.

I didn't want... Greenberg, *The Celluloid Muse,* p. 152.

The change... Higham, *Hollywood Cameramen,* p. 123.

Hyde is the... Greenberg, *The Celluloid Muse,* p. 152.

dragged in... Joy, letter to Schulberg, Dec. 1, 1931, *Dr. Jekyll and Mr. Hyde,* PCA.

43; 50 *Frankenstein is...* Joy, letter to Hays, Jan. 11, 1932, ibid.

45 (caption) *Ah, what letters...* Mank, *Karloff and Lugosi,* p. 15.

50   *We were rather . . .* Joy, letter to Thalberg, Dec. 18, 1930, *The Easiest Way,* PCA.

While the kept . . . Joy, telegram to Wingate, Jan. 21, 1931, ibid.

Have you . . . Trotti, letter to Joy, Jan. 22, 1931, ibid.

Yvonne: I like . . . *Inspiration* script, Oct. 11, 1930, MGM-USC.

"The Easiest . . . Lord, letter to Joy, Feb. 14, 1931, *The Easiest Way,* PCA.

Moral values . . . Winter, letter to Hays, "5–31," WHH-USC.

alluring evils . . . Wingate, letter to Joy, Feb. 11, 1931, *The Easiest Way,* PCA.

too explicit . . . Trotti, letter to Joy, Feb. 21, 1931, ibid.

Yesterday we . . . Captain Robert Pearson, letter to Joy, Mar. 10, 1931, ibid.

We have . . . Trotti, letter to Joy, Jan. 22, 1931, ibid.

52   *Her clothes . . .* Quirk, *Norma,* p. 130.

at the moment . . . Joy, letter to Louis B. Mayer, Apr. 30, 1931, *A Free Soul,* PCA.

ELIMINATIONS . . . Bernard Hyman, telegram to Joy, May 27, 1931, ibid.

Mr. Irving . . . Joy, "Memo," *Strangers May Kiss,* PCA.

This world . . . *Strangers May Kiss* script, Dec. 30, 1930, MGM-USC.

vigorously oppose . . . Joy, letter to Thalberg, May 6, 1931, *Strangers May Kiss,* PCA.

I saw STRANGERS . . . "L. A. W.," letter to "McKinnon," undated, ibid.

derogatory to . . . Mexican consulate, letter to AMPP, Nov. 23, 1931, ibid.

54   *She is seducing . . .* Higham, *Hollywood Cameramen,* p. 57.

*This is an excerpt from the December 16, 1931, "Cutting Continuity" of the scene Daniels recalled, but which was cut from the negative in 1939:

CS—Lighted cigarettes of Mata Hari and Rosanoff—the lights move about—Mata's hand is seen as it reaches toward light—and as she puts cigarettes on ash tray at right—their voices are heard . . .

ROSANOFF: I wish I could look into your eyes.

MATA HARI: Shall I turn on the light?

ROSANOFF: No, please don't.

MATA HARI: Why not?

ROSANOFF: Well—besides, I could never see into your eyes. You have such ridiculously long lashes.

Your advice . . . William Randolph Hearst, letter to Hays, Jan. 2, 1931, WHH-USC.

the three . . . Winter, letter to Hays, "5–31," ibid.

My dear . . . Joseph I. Breen, letter to Monsignor Joseph M. Corrigan, Oct. 17, 1930, WHH-USC.

I respectfully . . . Ibid.

The responsible . . . Breen, letter to Hays, Aug. 29, 1931, WHH-USC.

We ought to . . . Ibid.

Who that . . . Ibid.

With crime . . . Joy, letter to Breen, Dec. 15, 1931, *Possessed,* PCA.

My fear . . . Trotti, telegram to Joy, Oct. 21, 1931, ibid.

We didn't . . . Trotti, letter to Joy, Oct. 22, 1931, ibid.

I haven't . . . Fred W. Beetson (executive vice president, MPPDA), letter to Thalberg, Oct. 22, 1931, ibid.

55   *You will be . . .* Mrs. Alonzo Richardson, secretary, Atlanta Board of Review, letter to Carl W. Milliken, Dec. 3, 1931, ibid.

What are the . . . Mrs. Patrick Bray, "Audience Reaction Card," Dec. 7, 1931, ibid.

all modern . . . Peet, "Possessed," p. 439.

school girls . . . Ibid.

Norma Shearer . . . Walsh, *Sin and Censorship,* p. 97.

Norma Shearer's . . . Forman, *Our Movie-Made Children,* p. 51.

Economic independence . . . Hall, "Norma Shearer Tells What a 'Free Soul' Really Means," p. 96.

Your authors . . . Daniel Lord, "The Code—One Year Later," Apr. 23, 1931, WHH-USC.

60   (caption) *Rosanoff turns . . .* "Dialogue Cutting Continuity," Dec. 16, 1931, *Mata Hari,* MGM-CMPS.

Part III: 1932

63   *It will really . . .* Berg, *Goldwyn,* p. 216.

[If] the girls . . . Wilson, letter to Joseph Schenck, June 14, 1931, *The Greeks Had a Word for Them,* PCA.

small boy . . . Joy, "Résumé," no date, *The Bird of Paradise,* PCA.

64   *I remember . . .* Greenberg, *The Celluloid Muse,* p. 178.

Because the victim . . . Joy, letter to Laemmle, Jan. 8, 1932, *Murders in the Rue Morgue,* PCA.

69   *Without a 'hello' . . .* Riley, *The Mummy,* p. 19.

the pace . . . Ibid., p. 31.

There rose . . . Lord, *Played by Ear,* p. 307.

conveyed visions . . . Keats, *Howard Hughes,* p. 51.

the most harsh . . . McCarthy, *Howard Hawks,* p. 140.

Under no . . . McCarthy, Ibid., p. 144.

Screw the . . . Lawrence, *Actor,* p. 160.

inferences of . . . McCarthy, *Howard Hawks,* p. 144.

70   *As you . . .* Lincoln Quarberg to Howard Hughes, Jan. 30, 1932, p. 1, Lincoln Quarberg Collection, CMPS.

masterpiece . . . Ibid.

hysterical . . . Ibid.

I am convinced . . . Keats, *Howard Hughes,* p. 54.

grim determination . . . "Movie Censors Hear Their Master's Voice."

discerning New . . . McCarthy, *Howard Hawks,* p. 153.

an absolutely . . . Gussow, *Don't Say Yes Until I Finish Talking,* p. 59.

a good . . . Ibid.

a lowbrow . . . Koszarski, *The Man You Loved to Hate,* p. 253.

Reynard the . . . Temple, *Child Star,* p. 70.

71   *To hell . . .* Schulberg, *Moving Pictures,* p. 376.

Fox in . . . Everson, "Film Treasure Trove," p. 595.

Fox had . . . Gussow, *Don't Say Yes Until I Finish Talking,* p. 60.

OPEN WITH . . . *Hat Check Girl* script, June 8, 1932, Twentieth Century-Fox Script Collection, Doheny Library, University of Southern California (hereafter 20th-USC).

It is becoming . . . Joy, letter to Winfield Sheehan, Sept. 28, 1932, *Hat Check Girl*, PCA.

Fox [is] strongly . . . Milliken, letter to Joy, July 11, 1932, *Red-Headed Woman*, PCA.

The book . . . Joy, letter to Hays, June 24, 1932, *Call Her Savage*, PCA.

the background . . . *The American Film Institute Catalog, 1931–1940*, p. 269.

took most . . . Joy, letter to Hays, June 24, 1932, *Call Her Savage*, PCA.

76 *Because it . . .* Joy, letter to Beverly O. Skinner, Nov. 10, 1932, ibid.

Call Her . . . *The American Film Institute Catalog, 1931–1940*, p. 269.

must have . . . Behlmer, *Inside Warner Bros.*, p. 9.

Don't bore . . . Silke, *Here's Looking at You, Kid,* p. 63.

Lilyan Tashman . . . *Scarlet Dawn* pressbook, WB-USC.

I want . . . Zanuck, letter to Joy, Aug. 17, 1932, *Red-Headed Woman*, PCA.

box-office . . . Zanuck, letter to Joy, Sept. 21, 1932, *Three on a Match*, PCA.

kidnapping is . . . Ibid.

79 *While it . . .* Joy, letter to Hays, Feb. 26, 1932, *I Am a Fugitive From a Chain Gang*, PCA.

these lousy . . . Black, *Hollywood Censored*, p. 70.

These Jews . . . Ibid.

One very prominent . . . Breen, letter to Hays, Aug. 29, 1931, WHH-USC.

Ninety-five . . . Black, *Hollywood Censored*, p. 70.

Mr. Thalberg . . . Amory and Bradlee, *Cavalcade of the 1920s and 1930s*, p. 129.

80 *Flaemmchen looks . . .* "Script from Mr. Goulding," Oct. 24, 1931, *Grand Hotel*, MGM-USC.

When he's . . . "Story Conference," Dec. 26, 1931, *Grand Hotel*, MGM-USC.

I know . . . Joy, letter to Thalberg, Jan. 5, 1932, *Grand Hotel*, PCA.

By the way . . . Ibid.

full of life . . . "Story Conference," Dec. 26, 1931, *Grand Hotel*, MGM-USC.

80 (caption) *I'm determined . . .* "Emma" of the Chicago Film Board of Trade, letter to Joy, Sept. 17, 1932, *Public Enemy*, PCA.

81 *It was a man . . .* Maureen O'Sullivan, interview, "M-G-M: When the Lion Roars."

lubricious . . . Walker, *Joan Crawford: The Ultimate Star*, p. 183.

*Edward Sheldon later sued M-G-M for plagiarism and won. The film exists but cannot be exhibited.

The woman in . . . Unsigned and undated memo, *Letty Lynton*, PCA.

underlying philosophy . . . Ibid.

justified homicide . . . Walker, *Joan Crawford: The Ultimate Star*, p. 183.

The wicked . . . Parry, "I Dare Say."

82 *most of the . . .* Trotti, letter to Hays, Aug. 1, 1931, *Cock of the Air*, PCA.

I want to . . . "Story Conference—'Good Time Girl,' " May

6, 1932, *Blondie of the Follies*, MGM-USC.

We have . . . Ibid.

84 *like a circus . . .* Barrymore, *We Three*, p. 72.

The Romanovs . . . Thomas, *Thalberg*, p. 228.

I'm not interested . . . "Cutting continuity," Dec. 21, 1932, *Rasputin and the Empress*, MGM-USC.

Die, you . . . "Rewrite," Nov. 1, 1932, ibid.

85 *even more . . .* Thomas, *Thalberg*, p. 187.

He looked . . . Savada and Skal, *Dark Carnival*, p. 164.

People run . . . Marx, *Mayer and Thalberg*, p. 180.

If it's a . . . Ibid.

Halfway through . . . Savada and Skal, *Dark Carnival*, p. 174.

loathsome . . . Ibid., p. 178.

90 *She hasn't . . .* Greenberg, *The Celluloid Muse*, p. 177.

made out . . . Loos, *Kiss Hollywood Good-by*, p. 40.

Do you . . . Ibid.

make fun . . . Ibid., p. 34.

This is in . . . Trotti, letter to McKenzie, Apr. 27, 1932, *Red-Headed Woman*, PCA.

He and I . . . Trotti, letter to Hays, Apr. 30, 1932, ibid.

His contention . . . Ibid.

Well, you . . . Thomas, *Thalberg*, p. 210.

That did it . . . Loos, *Kiss Hollywood Good-by*, p. 43.

My feeling . . . Joy, letter to Hays, June 17, 1932, *Red-Headed Woman*, PCA.

When we . . . Joy, letter to Vincent Hart, June 15, 1932, ibid.

We have . . . Richardson, letter to Milliken, June 22, 1932, ibid.

In the cold . . . Joy, letter to Milliken, July 7, 1932, ibid.

Somehow M-G-M . . . Fragmentary clipping, *Hollywood Citizen-News*, July 11, 1932, *Red-Headed Woman*, PCA.

Pictures of . . . *The American Film Institute Catalog, 1931–1940*, p. 1758.

Red-Headed . . . Parry, "I Dare Say."

91 *I insist . . .* Zanuck, letter to Joy, Aug. 17, 1932, *Red-Headed Woman*, PCA.

I am in . . . Joy, letter to Milliken, July 7, 1932, ibid.

It is my . . . Martin Quigley, letter to Hays, Aug. 4, 1932, WHH-USC.

the extremely . . . Joy, letter to Thalberg, Oct. 10, 1932, *Red Dust*, PCA.

The sex . . . Ibid.

derogatory . . . Ibid.

Harlow's line . . . Ibid.

saw the Code . . . Wall, "Oral Interview with Geoffrey Shurlock," AFI, p. 68.

Given Red . . . Parish and Mank, *The Best of M-G-M*, p. 179.

I say the . . . Marx, *Mayer and Thalberg*, p. 201.

bacchanalia . . . Ibid.

95 *Successful production . . .* Baxter, *Just Watch!*, p. 67.

The story is . . . "Story Report," Aug. 8, 1932, *No Man of Her Own*, Paramount Script Collection, Margaret Herrick Library, Center for Motion Picture Study, Academy of Motion Picture Arts and Sciences, Beverly Hills (hereafter Para-CMPS).

burned up . . . Lord, *Played by Ear,* p. 307.

seemed to . . . Black, *Hollywood Censored,* p. 64.

was a sin . . . Ibid.

thousands of . . . Ibid.

There seems . . . Baxter, *Just Watch!,* p. 62.

95–96 *When Claire's . . .* Joy, letter to Schulberg, Jan. 7, 1932, *This Is the Night,* PCA.

96 *The risqué . . .* Joy, letter to Schulberg, Mar. 26, 1932, ibid.

It has . . . Trotti, letter to Joy, Nov. 17, 1931, *One Hour with You,* PCA.

There is . . . Eyman, *Ernst Lubitsch: Laughter in Paradise,* p. 197.

the delicate . . . Joy, letter to Schulberg, Feb. 11, 1932, *One Hour with You,* PCA.

Lubitsch touch . . . Eyman, *Ernst Lubitsch: Laughter in Paradise,* p. 189.

The first pictures . . . Unpublished Jeanette MacDonald interview, c. 1961, author's collection.

the most sparkling . . . Geoffrey Shurlock, "Review," Dec. 10, 1932, *Trouble in Paradise,* PCA.

As for pure . . . Eyman, *Ernst Lubitsch: Laughter in Paradise,* p. 200.

They had no . . . Greenberg, *Celluloid Muse,* p. 153.

May I add . . . Trotti, letter to Schulberg, Apr. 20, 1932, *Love Me Tonight,* PCA.

97 *discharged for . . .* "Cutting Continuity," *Shanghai Express,* Para-MHL.

The argument . . . Joy, "Memo" to Hays, May 21, 1932, *Blonde Venus,* PCA.

Never are . . . Joy, letter to John Hammell, Sept. 16, 1932, ibid.

live or . . . Trotti, "Memo," July 19, 1932, *A Farewell to Arms,* PCA

because of the . . . "Jury Report," Dec. 6, 1932, ibid.

99 (caption) *A peach must . . .* Breen, letter to Hammell, June 7, 1949, *Love Me Tonight,* PCA.

106 *Remember, Cecil . . .* DeMille, *The Autobiography of Cecil B. DeMille,* p. 321.

nightclubbish . . . Walsh, *Sin and Censorship,* p. 78.

Do you . . . Higham, *Cecil B. DeMille,* p. 216.

How would . . . DeMille, *The Autobiography of Cecil B. DeMille,* p. 322.

Making the . . . Chierichetti, *Mitchell Leisen,* p. 43.

I play him . . . Higham, *Cecil B. DeMille,* p. 216.

DeMille wanted . . . Chierichetti, *Mitchell Leisen,* p. 43.

Oh, boy . . . Higham, *Hollywood Cameramen,* p. 128.

great challenge . . . Ibid.

107 *We've just . . .* Chierichetti, *Mitchell Leisen,* p. 43.

Ordinarily we . . . Joy, letter to Harold Hurley, Nov. 16, 1932, *Sign of the Cross,* PCA.

sensibilities survive . . . *The American Film Institute Catalog, 1931–1940,* p. 1935.

vicious excursion . . . Hamann, *Mae West in the 30s,* p. 11

the most unpleasant . . . Black, *Hollywood Censored,* p. 68.

sex perversion . . . Walsh, *Sin and Censorship,* p. 79.

that lesbian . . . Quigley, "Mr. DeMille on Sex."

The scene is . . . Quigley, *Decency in Motion Pictures,* p. 39.

Are there many . . . Black, *Hollywood Censored,* p. 69.

I am with . . . DeMille, *The Autobiography of Cecil B. DeMille,* p. 324.

Part IV: 1933

112 *Nearly every . . .* Ibid., p. 325.

It was a . . . West, *Goodness Had Nothing to Do With It,* p. 152.

My part . . . Ibid., p. 150.

There is no . . . John Wilson, "Memo," Nov. 11, 1932, *She Done Him Wrong,* PCA.

there is no danger . . . Hays, telegram to Harry Warner, Oct. 19, 1932, ibid.

By all means . . . Hays, letter to Zukor, Nov. 23, 1932, ibid.

In order to . . . Wingate, letter to Hurley, Nov. 29, 1932, ibid.

develop the . . . Ibid.

114 (caption) *She rubbed them . . .* Wall, "Oral Interview with Geoffrey Shurlock Oral History, AFI, p. 123.

(caption) *Sorry, baby . . .* Leider, *Becoming Mae West,* p. 252.

116 *The drama . . .* Thomas, *Thalberg,* p. 308.

She was the . . . Zukor, *The Public Is Always Right,* p. 267.

We are not . . . Wingate, letter to Hays, Jan. 13, 1933, *She Done Him Wrong,* PCA.

I believe . . . Sidney R. Kent, undated letter to Hays, ibid.

the most flagrant . . . Hamann, *Mae West in the 30s,* p. 11.

just as naughty . . . Ibid., p. 12.

She is humorously . . . "Daily Report," Feb. 21, 1933, p. 1, WHH-USC.

She Done . . . Hamann, *Mae West in the 30s,* p. 15.

That night I . . . Eels, *Ginger, Loretta, and Irene Who?,* p. 205.

There is no . . . Vasey, *The World According to Hollywood,* p. 129.

117 *Middle-aged . . .* Ernst and Lorentz, *Censored,* p. 76.

Your reports are . . . Zanuck, letter to Wingate, Mar. 29, 1933, *Mary Stevens, M.D.,* PCA.

He couldn't explain . . . Wall, "Oral Interview with Geoffrey Shurlock," AFI, p. 89.

narrower . . . Jacobs, *The Wages of Sin,* p. 181.

the general . . . Ibid.

Love stories . . . Behlmer, *Inside Warner Bros.,* p. 10.

Oh, Christ . . . Gussow, *Don't Say Yes Until I Finish Talking,* p. 52.

Jack went . . . Ibid.

The reference . . . Wingate, letter to Zanuck, Dec. 27, 1932, *42nd Street,* PCA.

Department Store . . . *Employees' Entrance* press book, WB-USC.

118 *women's pictures . . .* Zanuck, letter to Wingate, Feb. 28, 1933, *Baby Face,* PCA.

It is made . . . Wingate, letter to Warner, July 17, 1933, *Female,* PCA.

Well, what . . . *Ex-Lady* press book, WB-USC.

Just because the . . . Joy, letter to Harry Cohn, July 11, 1932, *The Bitter Tea of General Yen,* PCA.

The nature of . . . Walker, *The Light on Her Face,* p. 186.

127   *The story was . . .* Madsen, *Stanwyck,* p. 95.

         **The Bitter Tea of General Yen* premiered at Radio City Music Hall on January 11, 1933.

         both the sex . . . The American Film Institute Catalog, *1931–1940,* p. 960.

         a little dirtier . . . Ibid.

127–28   *These lines . . .* Winfield Sheehan, letter to Wingate, May 24, 1933, *I Loved You Wednesday,* PCA.

128   *scene in which . . .* Wingate, letter to Joy [at Fox Film Corp.], May 18, 1933, ibid.

         From the lives . . . "Treatment," December 3, 1932, p. 1, *Broadway Bad,* 20th-USC.

         (caption) *I can't imagine . . .* Chester W. Schaeffer to author, Oct. 9, 1971.

128; 130   *A vehicle . . .* Quigley, *Decency in Motion Pictures,* p. 35.

130   *The church people . . .* Black, "Hollywood Censored," p. 178.

         You would learn . . . Eyles, "Donald Ogden Stewart," p. 53.

         Don't watch . . . Bob Board to author, July 7, 1974.

         It's a smash . . . Marx, *Mayer and Thalberg,* p. 243.

         A few more . . . Ibid.

         I didn't know . . . Kobal, *People Will Talk,* p. 393.

131   *We recommend . . .* Wingate, letter to Al Rockett, Oct. 14, 1933, *Hoopla,* PCA.

         I know you . . . Hays, letter to Kent, Nov. 2, 1933, ibid.

         No exposure . . . Wingate, night letter to McKenzie, Nov. 17, 1933, ibid.

         I don't wanna . . . Stenn, *Clara Bow: Runnin' Wild,* p. 245.

         chiefly interested . . . Koszarski and Everson, "Stroheim's Last 'Lost' Film," p. 7.

         turned the . . . Ibid.

         An Inconsequential . . . "Screenplay," July 14, 1932, *Hello, Sister,* 20th-USC.

         Well—if it ain't . . . Ibid.

         Von Stroheim . . . Joy, letter to Hays, July 25, 1932, ibid.

         was supposed . . . Koszarski, *The Man You Loved to Hate,* pp. 252–53.

132   *Luckily, we . . .* Higham, *Hollywood Cameramen,* p. 129.

         pansy craze . . . Chauncey, *Gay New York,* p. 301.

         Pangborn is . . . Russo, *The Celluloid Closet,* p. 34.

133   *You should be . . .* Wingate, letter to Warner, June 6, 1933, *Footlight Parade,* WB-USC.

         It may . . . Quigley, letter to Hays, Feb. 25, 1933, WHH-USC.

         If there is . . . Kent, letter to Sheehan, Mar. 7, 1933, *The Power and the Glory,* PCA.

148   *nobody out . . .* Black, "Hollywood Censored," p. 175.

         a foul bunch . . . Walsh, *Sin and Censorship,* p. 84.

         abject fear . . . Ibid., p. 83.

         quick money . . . Black, *Hollywood Censored,* p. 151.

         complete washout . . . Ibid., p. 150.

         I never saw . . . Maltby, "Baby Face," p. 39.

         merrily to . . . Black, *Hollywood Censored,* p. 151.

         Following up . . . Behlmer, *Inside Warner Bros.,* p. 8.

         The theme . . . Wingate, letter to Hays, Dec. 20, 1932, *Baby Face,* PCA.

         We go as . . . Ibid., p. 17.

         the element . . . Wingate, letter to Zanuck, Jan. 3, 1933, *Baby Face,* PCA.

         That is . . . Ibid.

149   *I deleted . . .* Zanuck, letter to Wingate, Mar. 29, 1933, *Baby Face,* PCA.

         For many . . . Zanuck, letter to Warner, Apr. 14, 1933, Darryl F. Zanuck File, WB-USC.

         Breen normally . . . Leff, *The Dame in the Kimono,* p. 299.

         Nowhere is . . . Wingate, letter to Hal Wallis, May 11, 1933, *Baby Face,* PCA.

         A woman . . . "Revised Final," *Baby Face,* WB-USC.

         Three cheers . . . Miller, *Censored Hollywood,* p. 68.

         been out to . . . Hays, *The Memoirs of Will H. Hays,* p. 449.

         Everyone else . . . Smith, *Starring Miss Barbara Stanwyck,* p. 55.

         This is a . . . Trotti, "Résumé," Sept. 4, 1931, *The Story of Temple Drake,* PCA.

         utterly unthinkable . . . Ibid.

         We simply . . . Black, *Hollywood Censored,* p. 95.

149–50   *As a parting . . .* Wingate, letter to McKenzie, Mar. 1, 1933, *The Story of Temple Drake,* PCA.

150   *the greatest . . .* Ibid.

         technical adviser . . . Negulesco, *The Things I Did and the Things I Think I Did,* p. 92.

         Jean, are my legs . . . Ibid. (This comes under the heading of things he did, because the finished scene matches the sketches in his book—except for a few conspicuously missing frames.)

         sordid, base . . . Breen, letter to Wingate, Mar. 17, 1933, *The Story of Temple Drake,* PCA.

         wrathful condemnation . . . Ibid.

         This script . . . Breen, letter to Wingate, May 5, 1933, *Ann Vickers,* PCA.

         pander to . . . Merian C. Cooper, letter to Wingate, May 11, 1933, ibid.

         spokesman for . . . B. B. Kahane, letter to Hays, June 27, 1933, ibid.

         We cannot . . . Ibid.

         frankly doubtful . . . Ibid.

         voice for . . . Ibid.

150–51   *to establish . . .* Hays, letter to Kahane, July 5, 1933, ibid.

151   *affirmatively establish . . .* Kahane, letter to Hays, July 10, 1933, ibid.

         illicit sex . . . Hays, letter to Kahane [et al.], July 31, 1933, ibid.

         The mainspring . . . Vizzard, *See No Evil,* p. 75.

         Me. I was . . . Vizzard, ibid., p. 40.

         it seemed to . . . Wingate, letter to Warner, Sept. 14, 1933, *Convention City,* PCA.

         Page 27 . . . Ibid.

         Ted, she's only . . . "First Draft," *Convention City,* p. 128, WB-USC.

151–52   *Mr. Wingate . . .* "Revised Final," Sept. 15, 1933, *Convention City,* p. 141, WB-USC.

152   *I'm stinkin' . . .* Ibid.

         We must put . . . Warner, memo to Wallis, Oct. 5, 1933, *Con-*

vention City, WB-USC.

That is the raunchiest . . . Kobal, *People Will Talk,* p. 193.

Let's place our . . . "Revised Final," Sept. 15, 1933, *Convention City,* p. 45, WB-USC.

While not as . . . Wingate, letter to Hays, Nov. 25, 1933.

prostituting the . . . Black, *Hollywood Censored,* p. 159.

serving to build . . . Ibid.

dirt and filth . . . Walsh, *Sin and Censorship,* p. 85.

narrow-minded . . . Black, *Hollywood Censored,* p. 160.

*Population figure based on census conducted by the *Catholic Directory,* quoted in Facey, *The Legion of Decency,* p. 58.

Catholics are . . . Ibid., p. 87.

What a massacre . . . Hays, *The Memoirs of Will H. Hays,* p. 450.

152–53   *apparently every* . . . Forman, *Our Movie-Made Children,* p. 44.

153   *Buddy Rogers* . . . Ibid., p. 154.

When I see a . . . Ibid., p. 222.

After I have . . . Ibid.

When I see these . . . Ibid., p. 225.

I imagined . . . Durgnat and Kobal, *Greta Garbo,* p. 59.

Does not . . . Viertel, *The Kindness of Strangers,* p. 175.

He wanted . . . Ibid.

We assume . . . Wingate, letter to Mannix, Aug. 7, 1933, *Queen Christina,* PCA.

Garbo strokes . . . Greenberg, *The Celluloid Muse,* p. 155.

All the light . . . Higham, *Hollywood Cameramen,* p. 72.

Wingate took . . . Vizzard, *See No Evil,* p. 40.

vile and nauseating . . . Black, *Hollywood Censored,* p. 163.

The pest hole . . . Ibid., p. 164.

154   *I always divide* . . . Greenberg, *The Celluloid Muse,* p. 155.

Do you think . . . Wingate, letter to Mannix, Sept. 5, 1933, *Queen Christina,* PCA.

which registers . . . Quigley, *Decency in Motion Pictures,* p. 37.

I know that the . . . Breen, letter to Mayer, Jan. 8, 1934, *Queen Christina,* PCA.

155   *I think Miss Garbo* . . . Ibid.

This jury . . . Jury, letter to Mannix, Jan. 11, 1934, ibid.

perverted creature . . . Walsh, *Sin and Censorship,* p. 97.

Part V: 1934–35

162   *I was only one* . . . Lord, *Played by Ear,* p. 307.

We can settle . . . Walsh, *Sin and Censorship,* p. 92.

faking observance . . . Lord, *Played by Ear,* p. 308.

cheap, low-tone . . . Walsh, *Sin and Censorship,* p. 88.

163   *should be shot* . . . Wallis, memo to Robert Presnell, Oct. 21, 1933, *Mandalay,* WB-USC.

When you show . . . Wallis, memo to Michael Curtiz, Oct. 21, 1933, ibid.

irregular sex . . . Wingate, letter to Warner, Oct. 30, 1933, *Wonder Bar,* WB-USC.

the changes . . . Lord, memo to Wallis, Nov. 1, 1933, ibid.

Granted, no . . . Lord, memo to Wallis, Jan. 2, 1934, ibid.

there was nothing . . . Breen, letter to Warner, Mar. 5, 1934, *Wonder Bar,* PCA.

one item which . . . McKenzie, letter to Breen, Mar. 1, 1934, ibid.

the ballroom scene . . . Breen, letter to Warner, Mar. 5, 1934, ibid.

The man and the . . . "Revised Final," p. 25, *Wonder Bar,* WB-USC.

163–64   *Neither can I* . . . Breen, letter to McKenzie, Mar. 13, 1934, *Wonder Bar,* PCA.

When I spoke . . . Vizzard, *See No Evil,* p. 64.

He was not a . . . Jack Vizzard to author, Apr. 12, 1998.

Mr. Breen knew . . . "Breen Gives Voice," p. 21.

What's all this . . . Vizzard, *See No Evil,* p. 51.

169   (caption) *[A] man and a* . . . Breen, letter to Warner, Mar. 5, 1934, *Wonder Bar,* PCA.

172   *I wish* . . . Leff and Simmons, *The Dame in the Kimono,* p. 47.

We Demand . . . Moley, *The Hays Office,* p. 81.

It is unfit . . . Lord, "Code Violators," p. 1.

172; 174   *libidinous persons* . . . Breen, "Memo," Jan. 18, 1934, *The Affairs of Cellini,* PCA.

174   *did a great* . . . *The American Film Institute Catalog, 1931–1940,* p. 211.

shot of Letty . . . Ibid.

We realize . . . Ibid.

We are not . . . Ibid.

I hated it . . . Kobal, *People Will Talk,* p. 393.

It is difficult . . . Lord, "Code Violators," p. 1.

I have learned . . . Breen, "Memo," Mar. 16, 1934, *George White's Scandals,* PCA.

We still believe . . . *The American Film Institute Catalog, 1931–1940,* p. 2280.

175   *I am* . . . Ibid.

something of a . . . Breen, "Memo," Feb. 10, 1934, ibid.

The picture . . . Breen, "Memorandum for the Files," Feb. 10, 1934, *Of Human Bondage,* PCA.

filthy Frenchman . . . Black, *Hollywood Censored,* p. 204.

Sequence F-3: This . . . Breen, letter to Harry Zehner, Feb. 26, 1934, *The Black Cat,* PCA.

176   *Motion pictures* . . . Quigley, "Mr. DeMille on Sex," p. 5.

He surely can . . . Ibid.

All she wants . . . Wingate, letter to A. M. Botsford, Oct. 23, 1933, *Bolero,* PCA.

Throughout the stage . . . Breen, letter to Botsford, Jan. 12, 1934, *Murder at the Vanities,* PCA.

177   *The shot of Crabbe* . . . Breen, letter to Botsford, Jan. 8, 1934, *Search for Beauty,* PCA.

MARY: This is . . . "Revised Final," Feb. 9, 1934, *Dr. Monica,* WB-USC.

In the first . . . Breen, letter to Wallis, Apr. 24, 1934, ibid.

where he said . . . Hays, letter to Breen, (no date), *Manhattan Melodrama,* PCA.

178   *Myrna Loy fell* . . . Ted Allan to the author, Mar. 2, 1986.

dog gag . . . Wingate, "Résumé," Apr. 19, 1934, *The Thin Man,* PCA.

New Tarzan . . . Behlmer, "Tarzan, Hollywood's Greatest Jungle Hero," p. 47.

180   *They tried different* . . . Maureen O'Sullivan, interview,

"M-G-M: When the Lion Roars."

After a rather . . . Breen, letter to Hays, Apr. 10, 1934, *Tarzan and His Mate*, PCA.

From all evidence . . . Behlmer, "Tarzan, Hollywood's Greatest Jungle Hero," p. 47.

181 *Riptide is unfortunately . . .* Lord, "Code Violators," p. 1.

His unwise . . . Black, *Hollywood Censored*, p. 181.

our ideas of . . . Ibid., p. 180.

I have no real . . . Ibid., p. 179.

positive command . . . Walsh, *Sin and Censorship*, p. 102.

181–82 *Harry Warner, who . . .* Wall, "Oral Interview with Geoffrey Shurlock," AFI, p. 98.

182 *How would you . . .* Lord, *Played by Ear*, p. 309.

Hollywood knew . . . Ibid., p. 311.

Will, you've got . . . Wall, "Oral Interview with Geoffrey Shurlock," AFI, p. 98.

Joe, look! . . . Ibid., p. 99.

The Catholic authorities . . . Black, *Hollywood Censored*, p. 181.

You have a Code . . . Wall, "Oral Interview with Geoffrey Shurlock," AFI, p. 99.

Purify Hollywood . . . Black, "Hollywood Censored," p. 177.

191 *avenging fire . . .* Hays, *The Memoirs of Will H. Hays*, p. 453.

Hollywood is . . . Schallert, "Film Producers Shaken by Clean-up Campaign," p. 1.

Making pictures . . . Ibid.

To them it was . . . "Production Code Scrap of Paper Says Mundelein."

This is the story . . . Lord, "Hollywood Treats Own Code as 'Scrap of Paper' in Great Public Betrayal," p. 1.

You can't make . . . Hays, *The Memoirs of Will H. Hays*, p. 452.

192 *The meeting lasted . . .* Ibid., p. 453.

I knew everything . . . Ibid.

There was Harry . . . Vizzard, *See No Evil*, p. 50.

193 *the war had . . .* Hays, *The Memoirs of Will H. Hays*, p. 453.

At last we . . . Ibid.

Gentlemen, we . . . Vizzard, *See No Evil*, p. 50.

But on one . . . Ibid., p. 51.

The changes and . . . Breen, memo to files, July 27, 1934, *One More River*, PCA.

This is the first . . . Breen, letter to Laemmle, Jr., Aug. 17, 1934, ibid.

It has eleven . . . Warner, letter to Wallis, Mar. 8, 1934, *Madame du Barry*, WB-USC.

It is our considered . . . Breen, letter to Warner, Mar. 15, 1934, ibid.

the horror and . . . "Final Script," ibid.

Come, come . . . Ibid.

like Diogenes . . . Ibid.

194 *sneering and . . .* Breen, "Memo," Mar. 14, 1934, *Madame du Barry*, PCA.

If people like . . . Vizzard, *See No Evil*, p. 52.

indecent, obscene . . . Black, *Hollywood Censored*, p. 178.

They can't censor . . . Thomas, *Thalberg*, p. 260.

Tiger and Ruby . . . Miller, *Censored Hollywood*, p. 95.

glorification of . . . Breen, letter to Botsford, Feb. 23, 1934, *Belle of the Nineties*, PCA.

certain to throw . . . Ibid.

Ruby Carter displays . . . Breen, letter to Botsford, Mar. 7, 1934, ibid.

195 *IT IS . . .* Black, *Hollywood Censored*, p. 175.

damned Breen . . . Leff and Simmons, *The Dame in the Kimono*, p. 49.

attacked Jewish . . . Ibid.

violent and lustful . . . Breen, "Memo," June 6, 1934, *Belle of the Nineties*, PCA.

Well, boys . . . Hamann, *Mae West in the 30s*, p. 82.

If they saw . . . Ibid., p. 83.

I have never . . . Ibid.

I resented . . . West, *Goodness Had Nothing to Do With It*, p. 175.

leaned on a . . . Ibid., p. 176.

"Belle of the . . . "Miss West Talks Shop," p. 5.

obvious curtsey . . . The American Film Institute Catalog, *1931–1940*, p. 138.

This picture . . . Hamann, *Mae West in the 30s*, p. 87.

I wrote scenes . . . Kobal, *People Will Talk*, p. 159.

Watch your . . . Walsh, *Sin and Censorship*, p. 106.

the Hitler . . . Leff and Simmons, *The Dame in the Kimono*, p. 57.

fogged . . . Ibid.

197 *cut this scene . . .* Thalberg, letter to Breen, Aug. 23, 1934, *The Merry Widow*, PCA.

You know, the . . . Breen, "Memo," Aug. 13, 1934, ibid.

entail considerable . . . Breen, "Memo," Sept. 27, 1934, ibid.

light, gay, frivolous . . . Walsh, *Sin and Censorship*, p. 109.

industry double-cross . . . Black, *Hollywood Censored*, p. 201.

lot of filth . . . Ibid.

If this picture . . . Walsh, *Sin and Censorship*, p. 109.

198 *When he meets . . .* Breen, memo to Hays, Oct. 22, 1934, *The Merry Widow*, PCA.

make him a more . . . Black, *Hollywood Censored*, p. 202.

I sincerely hope . . . Breen, memo to Hays, Oct. 22, 1934, *The Merry Widow*, PCA.

a long one . . . Black, *Hollywood Censored*, p. 202.

While I reiterate . . . Thalberg, telegram to Hays, Oct. 26, 1934, *The Merry Widow*, PCA.

203 *After the 'A' . . .* W. D. Kelly, "Memo to All Branches," Oct. 29, 1934, ibid.

The millennium . . . "Not 1 Chicago Censor Cut in 4 Weeks."

very gravely . . . Breen, memo to files, Nov. 27, 1934, *Forsaking All Others*, PCA.

band of seven . . . Daily Variety, Dec. 3, 1934, quoted in *The American Film Institute Catalog, 1931–1940*, p. 688.

The director, miffed . . . Vizzard, *See No Evil*, p. 52.

I am not . . . W. S. Van Dyke II, letter to Breen, Dec. 6, 1934, *Forsaking All Others*, PCA.

Richard Boleslavsky . . . George Folsey to author, Aug. 19, 1975.

Of course, you . . . Mrs. James F. Looram, letter to Milliken,

Jan. 3, 1935, *Biography of a Bachelor Girl,* PCA.

You used to be . . . Breen, letter to Milliken, Jan. 5, 1935, ibid.

After the trouble . . . "Story Conference," Jan. 18, 1935, *China Seas,* MGM-USC.

What a vicious . . . "Revised Final," Mar. 10, 1935, ibid.

204   (caption) *must have normal* . . . Quigley, "Mr. DeMille on Sex," p. 5.

206   **You're All I Need* . . . According to Richard P. May, vice president, Film Preservation at Warner Bros., which owns the vault print of *Escapade,* it cannot be exhibited or released on video because the rights have reverted to *Maskerade*'s author's estate.

There is a . . . Breen, letter to Joy, Nov. 20, 1934, *Dante's Inferno,* PCA.

brought a burst . . . *Daily Variety,* Aug. 7, 1935.

207   *an arty disaster* . . . West, *Goodness Had Nothing to Do With It,* p. 196.

At this point . . . Vizzard, *See No Evil,* p. 63.

Mr. Hays raises . . . Earl E. Bright, memo to Breen, Feb. 16, 1935, *The Devil Is a Woman,* PCA.

I had intended . . . Breen, memo to files, Apr. 29, 1935, ibid.

We recommend . . . Ibid.

208   (caption) *glorious achievement* . . . Cecelia Ager, *Variety,* May 8, 1935, quoted in Sarris, *The Films of Josef von Sternberg,* p. 42.

210   **"(If It Isn't Pain) Then It Isn't Love"* was written by Leo Robin and Ralph Rainger and ultimately appeared in Mitchell Leisen's *Swing High, Swing Low.*

Every scene fairly . . . Dickens, *The Films of Marlene Dietrich,* p. 120.

†In May 1952, the Supreme Court overturned a lower court decision banning Roberto Rossellini's film *The Miracle,* and in the process threw out *Mutual Film vs Ohio.* As quoted in the May 31, 1952, issue of *Boxoffice,* Justice Tom Clark wrote: "The importance of motion pictures as an organ of public opinion is not lessened by the fact that they are designed to entertain as well as to inform. Nor should film be subject to censorship because it is an industry conducted for profit, as such a category would also include the press. Finally, the medium's supposed capacity for evil, if it existed at all, was not sufficient justification for substantially unbridled censorship such as we have seen here."

Towards the end . . . Jack Vizzard to the author, Apr. 29, 1998.

212   *This hypothetical account is based on interviews with Richard P. May, Noelle Carter of the USC-Warner Bros. Archive, and Rudy Behlmer, author of *Inside Warner Bros.*

BIBLIOGRAPHY

BOOKS

The American Film Institute Catalog of Motion Pictures Produced in the United States, 1931–1940. Berkeley: University of California Press, 1993.

Amory, Cleveland, and Frederick Bradlee. *Cavalcade of the 1920s and 1930s.* New York: Viking Press, 1960.

Barrymore, John. *We Three.* New York: Saalfield Publishing Company, 1935.

Barsacq, Léon. *Caligari's Cabinet and Other Grand Illusions: A History of Film Design.* Boston: New York Graphic Society, 1976.

Baxter, Peter. *Just Watch! Sternberg, Paramount, and America.* London: British Film Institute Publishing, 1993.

Behlmer, Rudy. *Inside Warner Bros. (1935–1951).* New York: Viking Penguin, Inc., 1985.

Behrman, S. N. *People in a Diary.* Boston: Little, Brown and Company, 1972.

Berg, A. Scott. *Goldwyn: A Biography.* New York: Alfred A. Knopf, 1989.

Bernstein, Matthew. *Walter Wanger, Hollywood Independent.* Berkeley: University of California Press, 1994.

Black, Gregory D. *Hollywood Censored: Morality Codes, Catholics, and the Movies.* Cambridge: Cambridge University Press, 1994.

Chauncey, George. *Gay New York: Gender, Urban Culture, and the Making of the Gay Male World, 1890–1940.* New York: BasicBooks, 1994.

Chierichetti, David. *Mitchell Leisen: Hollywood Director.* Los Angeles: Photoventures Press, 1995.

Crowther, Bosley. *The Lion's Share.* New York: E. P. Dutton and Company, 1957.

Curtis, James. *James Whale.* Metuchen, N.J.: Scarecrow Press, 1982.

————. *James Whale: A New World of Gods and Monsters.* Boston: Faber and Faber, 1998.

Davis, Ronald L. *The Glamour Factory.* Dallas: Southern Methodist University Press, 1993.

DeMille, Cecil Blount. *The Autobiography of Cecil B. DeMille.* Englewood Cliffs, N.J.: Prentice-Hall, Inc., 1959.

Dickens, Homer. *The Films of Marlene Dietrich.* New York: Citadel Press, 1968.

Durgnat, Raymond, and John Kobal. *Greta Garbo.* New York: E. P. Dutton, 1965.

Eels, George. *Ginger, Loretta, and Irene Who?* New York: G. P. Putnam's Sons, 1976.

Ernst, Morris L., and Pare Lorentz. *Censored: The Private Life of the Movie.* New York: Jonathan Cape and Harrison Smith, 1930.

Eyman, Scott. *Ernst Lubitsch: Laughter in Paradise.* New York: Simon and Schuster, 1993.

Facey, Paul W. *The Legion of Decency: A Sociological Analysis of the Emergence and Development of a Social Pressure Group.* New York: Arno Press, 1974.

Film Daily Yearbook. New York: Film Daily Publishers, 1934.

Finler, Joel. *The Hollywood Story.* New York: Crown Publishers, 1988.

Forman, Henry James. *Our Movie-Made Children.* New York: MacMillan, 1933.

Gardner, Gerald. *The Censorship Papers: Movie Censorship Letters from the Hays Office, 1934 to 1968.* New York: Dodd, Mead and Company, 1987.

Gatiss, Mark. *James Whale.* London: Cassell, 1995.

Greenberg, Joel, and Charles Higham. *The Celluloid Muse.* New York: Signet, 1972.

Gussow, Mel. *Don't Say Yes Until I Finish Talking.* New York: Doubleday and Company, 1971.

Hamann, G. D. *Mae West in the 30s.* Los Angeles: Filming Today Press, 1997.

Haver, Ronald. *David O. Selznick's Hollywood.* New York: Alfred A. Knopf, 1980.

Hays, Will H. *The Memoirs of Will H. Hays.* Garden City, N.Y.: Doubleday and Company, 1955.

Higham, Charles. *Cecil B. DeMille.* New York: Charles Scribner's Sons, 1973.

_____. *Hollywood Cameramen.* Bloomington: Indiana University Press, 1970.

Jacobs, Lea. *The Wages of Sin: Censorship and the Fallen Woman Film, 1928–1942.* Madison: University of Wisconsin Press, 1991.

Keats, John. *Howard Hughes.* New York: Random House, 1966.

Kobal, John. *People Will Talk.* New York: Alfred A. Knopf, 1985.

Koszarski, Richard. *The Man You Loved to Hate: Eric von Stroheim and Hollywood.* New York: Oxford University Press, 1983.

Kotsilibas-Davis, James. *The Barrymores: The Royal Family in Hollywood.* New York: Crown Publishers, 1981.

_____, and Myrna Loy. *Being and Becoming.* New York: Alfred A. Knopf, 1987.

Lambert, Gavin. *On Cukor.* New York: G. P. Putnam's Sons, 1972.

Lawrence, Jerome. *Actor: The Life and Times of Paul Muni.* New York: G. P. Putnam's Sons, 1974.

Leff, Leonard J., and Jerold L. Simmons. *The Dame in the Kimono: Hollywood, Censorship, and the Production Code from the 1920s to the 1960s.* London: Weidenfeld and Nicolson, 1990.

Leider, Emily Wortis. *Becoming Mae West.* New York: Farrar Straus Giroux, 1997.

Loos, Anita. *Kiss Hollywood Good-by.* New York: Viking Press, 1974.

Lord, Daniel A., S. J. *Played by Ear.* Chicago: Loyola University Press, 1956.

MacAdams, William. *Ben Hecht: The Man Behind the Legend.* New York: Charles Scribner's Sons, 1990.

Madsen, Axel. *Stanwyck.* New York: HarperCollins, 1994.

Maltby, Richard. *Harmless Entertainment: Hollywood and the Ideology of Consensus.* Metuchen, N.J.: Scarecrow Press, 1983.

_____. *Hollywood Cinema: An Introduction.* Cambridge, Mass.: Blackwell Publishers, 1995.

Mank, Gregory William. *It's Alive! The Classic Cinema Saga of Frankenstein.* New York: A. S. Barnes and Company, 1981.

_____. *Karloff and Lugosi: The Story of a Haunting Collaboration.* Jefferson, N.C.: McFarland and Company, 1990.

Marx, Samuel. *Mayer and Thalberg, the Make-Believe Saints.* New York: Random House, 1975.

McBride, Joseph. *Hawks on Hawks.* Berkeley: University of California Press, 1982.

McCarthy, Todd. *Howard Hawks.* New York: Grove Press, 1997.

McGilligan, Pat. *Backstory: Interviews with Screenwriters of Hollywood's Golden Age.* Berkeley: University of California Press, 1986.

Miller, Frank. *Censored Hollywood: Sex, Sin, and Violence on Screen.* Atlanta: Turner Publishing, 1994.

Moley, Raymond. *The Hays Office.* New York: Bobbs-Merrill, 1945.

Mosley, Leonard. *Zanuck: The Rise and Fall of Hollywood's Last Tycoon.* Boston: Little, Brown, 1984.

Nash, Jay Robert, and Stanley Ralph Ross. *The Motion Picture Guide, 1927–1983.* Chicago: Cinebooks, Inc., 1987.

Negulesco, Jean. *The Things I Did and the Things I Think I Did.* New York: Linden Press/Simon and Schuster, 1984.

Parish, James Robert, and Gregory William Mank. *The Best of M-G-M.* Westport, Conn.: Arlington House Publishers, 1981.

Quigley, Martin. *Decency in Motion Pictures.* New York: MacMillan, 1937.

Quirk, Lawrence J. *Norma.* New York: St. Martin's Press, 1988.

Riley, Philip J. *Dracula.* Absecon, N.J.: MagicImage Filmbooks, 1990.

_____. *Frankenstein.* Absecon, N.J.: MagicImage Filmbooks, 1989.

_____. *The Mummy.* Absecon, N.J.: MagicImage Filmbooks, 1989.

Russo, Vito. *The Celluloid Closet.* New York: Harper and Row, 1987.

Sarris, Andrew. *The Films of Josef von Sternberg.* Garden City, N.Y.: Doubleday and Company, 1966.

Savada, Elias, and David Skal. *Dark Carnival: The Secret World of Tod Browning.* New York: Anchor Books, 1995.

Schulberg, Budd. *Moving Pictures: Memoirs of a Hollywood Prince.* London: Alison and Busby, 1993.

Shorris, Sylvia, and Marion Abbott Bundy. *Talking Pictures.* New York: The New Press, 1994.

Silke, James R. *Here's Looking at You, Kid.* Boston: Little, Brown, and Company, 1976.

Smith, Ella. *Starring Miss Barbara Stanwyck.* New York: Crown Publishers, 1974.

Stenn, David. *Clara Bow: Runnin' Wild.* New York: Doubleday, 1988.

Temple, Shirley. *Child Star.* New York: Warner Books, 1989.

Thomas, Bob. *Thalberg: Life and Legend.* Garden City, N.Y.: Doubleday and Company, 1969.

Turk, Edward Baron. *Hollywood Diva: A Biography of Jeanette MacDonald.* Berkeley: University of California Press, 1998.

Vasey, Ruth. *The World According to Hollywood, 1918–1939.* Madison: University of Wisconsin Press, 1997.

Viertel, Salka. *The Kindness of Strangers.* New York: Holt, Rinehart and Winston, 1969.

Vizzard, Jack. *See No Evil: Life Inside a Hollywood Censor.* New York: Simon and Schuster, 1970.

Walker, Alexander. *Joan Crawford: The Ultimate Star.* New York: Harper and Row, 1983.

Walker, Joseph, B., ASC, and Juanita Walker. *The Light on Her Face.* Hollywood: The ASC Press, 1984.

Walsh, Frank. *Sin and Censorship: The Catholic Church and the Motion Picture Industry.* New Haven: Yale University Press, 1996.

West, Mae. *Goodness Had Nothing to Do With It.* Englewood Cliffs, N.J.: Prentice-Hall, Inc., 1959.

Zukor, Adolph. *The Public Is Never Wrong.* New York: G. P. Putnam's Sons, 1953.

SIGNED ARTICLES

Behlmer, Rudy. "Tarzan, Hollywood's Greatest Jungle Hero." *American Cinematographer* 68, no. 11 (Jan. 1987), pp. 38–48.

Black, Gregory D. "Hollywood Censored: The Production Code Administration and the Hollywood Film Industry, 1930–1940." *Film History* 3, no. 3 (1989), pp. 167–89.

Everson, William K. "Film Treasure Trove." *Films in Review* 25, no. 10 (Dec. 1974), pp. 595–610.

Eyles, Allen. "Donald Ogden Stewart." *Focus on Film* no. 5 (Nov./Dec. 1970), pp. 49–57.

Hall, Gladys. "Norma Shearer Tells What a 'Free Soul' Really Means." *Motion Picture* 12, no. 11 (Nov. 1931), pp. 48–49, 96.

Hullinger, Edwin W. "Free Speech for the Talkies?" *North American Review* 8, no. 6 (June 1929), n.p.

Jacobs, Lea. "Industry Self-Regulation and the Problem of Textual Determination." *The Velvet Light Trap* 23 (Spring 1989), pp. 6–15.

Koszarski, Richard, and William K. Everson. "Stroheim's Last 'Lost' Film: The Making and Remaking of 'Walking Down Broadway.'" *Film Comment* 11, no. 3 (May/June 1975), pp. 6–19.

La Salle, Mick. "The Golden Age of Sex, Violence, and Perversity." *San Francisco Chronicle,* May 11, 1997.

Leff, Leonard J. "*A Farewell to Arms:* Unmaking the 1932 Version." *Film Comment* 31, no. 1 (Jan./Feb. 1995), pp. 70–73.

Lord, Daniel, A., S. J. "Code Violators." *The Queen's Work* 26, no. 9 (June 1934), p. 1.

————. "Hollywood Treats Own Code as 'Scrap of Paper' in Great Public Betrayal." *The Queen's Work* 26, no. 9 (June 1934), pp. 1, 10–11.

Maltby, Richard. "*Baby Face,* or How Joe Breen Made Barbara Stanwyck Atone for Causing the Wall Street Crash." *Screen* 27, no. 2 (Mar./Apr. 1986), pp. 22–45.

————. "The Genesis of the Production Code." *Quarterly Review of Film and Video* 15, no. 4 (Mar. 1995), pp. 5–57.

Mitchell, Charles P. "Marilyn and the Monster." *Films of the Golden Age* (winter 1997–98), pp. 44–48.

Parry, Florence Fisher. "I Dare Say." *Pittsburgh Press,* July 17, 1932.

Pedelty, Donovan. "Over Hollywood." *Silver Screen,* May 1932, pp. 14, 60–62.

Peet, Creighton. "Possessed." *Outlook and Independent* 159 (Dec. 2, 1931), p. 439.

Quigley, Martin. "Mr. DeMille on Sex." *Motion Picture Herald* 116, no. 7 (Aug. 11, 1934), p. 5.

Schallert, Edwin. "Film Producers Shaken by Clean-Up Campaign." *Los Angeles Times,* June 10, 1934.

Sherwood, Robert. "This Is What They're Saying: Will Hays, Unhappy Czar of Much Buffeted Film." *Kalamazoo Gazette,* Oct. 6, 1929.

Stack, Peter. "Shearer Luck." *San Francisco Chronicle,* Sept. 15, 1994.

ANONYMOUS ARTICLES

"Breen Gives Voice." *Motion Picture Herald,* Apr. 21, 1934, p. 21.

"Dealing with Capone." *Time* 18, no. 6 (Aug. 10, 1931), p. 15.

"Editorial." *The New York Telegraph,* Sept. 22, 1930.

"Hollywood Promises." *Commonweal* 16 (Apr. 1930), p. 668.

"Miss West Talks Shop." *The New York Times,* Feb. 3, 1935, p. 5.

"Morals for Profit." *The New York World,* Apr. 1, 1930.

"Movie Censors Hear Their Master's Voice." *Christian Century,* July 13, 1932.

"The Norma Shearer Irving Thalberg Loves." *New Movie* 9, no. 5 (May 1934), pp. 32–33, 70–72.

"Not 1 Chicago Censor Cut in 4 Weeks." *Variety,* Sept. 24, 1934, p. 5.

"Production Code Scrap of Paper Says Mundelein." *Motion Picture Herald,* June 9, 1934, p. 40.

"*Public Enemy.*" *Time* 17, no. 18 (May 4, 1931), p. 44.

Untitled item, *Hollywood Spectator* 12, no. 7 (Sept. 12, 1931), p. 14.

UNPUBLISHED DOCUMENT

Wall, James M. "Oral Interview with Geoffrey Shurlock." Louis B. Mayer/American Film Institute Film History Program.

AUDIOTAPE

Knight, Arthur. "Oral Interview with Lawrence Weingarten." Recorded Mar. 5, 1974, in Knight's Cinema 305 Class, History of the American Sound Film, University of Southern California.

DOCUMENTARY FILM

M-G-M: When the Lion Roars. Turner Broadcasting, Mar. 1992.

DISSERTATION

Gustafson, Robert. "The Buying of Ideas: Source Acquisitions at Warner Bros., 1930–1949." Ph.D. diss., University of Michigan, 1983.

INDEX

Page numbers in *italics* refer to illustrations.

234

ACKNOWLEDGMENTS

The files of the Production Code Administration were not available to researchers until 1983. Since then, a number of books have used them to rewrite Hollywood history. I owe a debt to their authors. Without their trailblazing scholarship, I could not have told this story. These books include *The World According to Hollywood* by Ruth Vasey, *Censored Hollywood* by Frank Miller, *The Dame in the Kimono* by Leonard Leff and Jerold L. Simmons, *Hollywood Censored* by Gregory Black, and *Sin and Censorship* by the late Frank Walsh.

All of us owe a debt to *See No Evil* by Jack Vizzard, which was the first book to tell the inside story of Hollywood censorship. Mr. Vizzard's ten years with censor Joseph Breen did not fall within the period described in this book, but his generous recounting of Breen's stories have made it possible to describe the personal styles of the three main censors. I thank Mr. Vizzard for his willingness to check the manuscript for accuracy and fairness.

Since this book is about movies, I wish to thank their present copyright owners: Michael Schlesinger at Columbia Classics Home Video; Steve Wegner at MGM-UA Home Video; Jennifer Sebree at Twentieth Century-Fox; and Christine Hupalo, Ron Roloff, and Diane Gloor at Universal Studios Home Video. I also wish to thank Chris Horak, Dick Costello, and Randy Arnold at Universal Studios. I especially want to thank Mike Polis and Wendy Winks. I want to acknowledge Richard P. May, vice president, Film Preservation at Warner Bros. for preserving, restoring, and upgrading so many of the pre-Code films made by RKO, M-G-M, and Warner Bros. These individuals and corporations are working to ensure that these cinematic treasures not only exist but are also available.

For rights and permissions, I wish to thank: Rex Bell, Jr., and the Clara Bow Estate; Sidney Herman of Famous Music Publishing, Inc.; Judy Noack, Marlene Evans, Judy Singer, and Roger Mayer at Warner Bros.; Cindy Chang and Johnnie Luevanos at Universal Publishing Rights; and David Pearson, Jesse Rodriguez, and Rebecca A. Herrera at Twentieth Century-Fox.

I wish to acknowledge these institutions, archives, and archivists: the library at California State University, Hayward; the Oakland Public Library; the Midwest Jesuit Archives; Edith Kramer of the Pacific Film Archive in Berkeley; Ian Birnie, film curator at the Los Angeles County Museum of Art; Tony Impavido and Kent Jones at Lincoln Center for the Performing Arts; Ron Magliozzi and Charles Silver at the Museum of Modern Art; Terry Geesken and Mary Corliss at the MOMA Film Stills Archive; Caroline Cisneros of the Louis B. Mayer Library at the American Film Institute; Alison Pinsler at the Frances C. Richardson Research Center at Twentieth Century-Fox; Melissa Totten at the Twentieth Century-Fox Stills Archive; Stuart Galbraith and Noelle Carter at the USC-Warner Bros. Archive; and Steve Hanson and Ned Comstock at the Cinema-Television Library of the University of Southern California.

I thank Doug Johnson, Scott Curtis, and Faye Thompson of the Margaret Herrick Library at the Center for Motion Picture Study for helping me maneuver through the files of the Studio Relations Committee and the Production Code Administration. I owe special thanks to Robert Cushman and Linda Mehr of the Academy of Motion Picture Arts and Sciences.

I wish to thank the following scholars for their insights and critiques: Rudy Behlmer, Antonio Bombal, Lisa Burks, David Chierichetti, James Curtis, Alex Gordon, G. D. Hamann, Mick La Salle, Leonard Leff, Emily Wortis Leider, Darrell Rooney, David J. Skal, David Stenn, and Karen Swenson. I thank the following interview subjects for their time and reminiscences: Bob Board, Noelle Carter, Bruce Goldstein, Elliot Lavine, Richard P. May, Carol Morgan, and Jack Vizzard. I acknowledge those interview subjects who are no longer living: Ted Allan, Lee Garmes, Chester W. Schaeffer, John Kobal, and George Folsey.

I did not want to write about any film without having seen it. I thank the following for bringing rarities within reach: Richard Bann, Luke Ellis, Larry Dominguez, Eric Grayson, Lisa Burks, Jim Lindsay, and Sandy Tanaka. Special thanks go to Mimi Christensen, Scott Hartford, and Kevin Burns at FoxStar Productions, who made it possible for me to study the work of the most intriguing entity of the period, the Fox Film Corporation. In addition, I would like to thank three gentlemen who went out of their way to show me some truly eye-opening Paramount films: Paul Meienberg, Gunhard Oravas, and John McElwee. I am happy to say that with the exception of *Convention City*, I have been able to view every pre-Code film discussed in this book.

The following memorabilia dealers helped me find photographs: Joel Reyes at Collectors Bookstore, David Chierichetti, Clare Cameron, Al Morley, Mike Hawks at Larry Edmunds Bookstore, Carole York at Cinema Memories in Key West, and Roy Windham at Baby Jane of Hollywood. The following deserve thanks for impossibly rare finds: David Del Valle and the Del Valle Archive; Melissa Totten and the Twentieth Century-Fox Stills Archive; Marc Wanamaker and the Bison Archive; Ben Carbonetto, Bob Cosenza, Martin Dives, and Simon Crocker at the Kobal Collection; and the staff of Photofest, especially Ed Maguire. I thank the following individuals for lending me photographs: Phil Dockter, Garrett Mahoney, Lou Valentino, Rex Bell, Jr., and John McElwee.

I thank two artists: Carol Ryan, and my brother, Guy Vieira.

Many individuals helped me with research leads: Eric Bernhoft, Tom Bertino, David Chierichetti, Randy Haberkamp, Denis Hulett, Ed Hulse, Peter Mintun, Jon Mirsalis, Robert Nudelman, Charlene Perlmann, and David Stenn. Of especial help was Limelight Bookstore in San Francisco; I thank Derek Mutch and his staff: Ryan Khavari, Meredith Eldred, and Cassandre Fiering. I wish to thank Maimone Attia for his skilled and diligent research. I am deeply grateful to Ned Comstock for his feats of archival prestidigitation.

For my newly acquired computer skills (and computer), I thank the following people: Patrick Morris; Gary Morris; Dianne Cole; Matthew Griffiths; Garrett Mahoney; my brother, John Vieira; and especially my sister, Janine Faelz. Thanks also to Laurie Funnell and the staff of Castro Valley Super Print.

I thank the following for advice, assistance, and just plain thoughtfulness: Matias Bombal; Deborah Thalberg; P. R. Tooke; Garrett Mahoney; Gary Meyer; Ken Richards; Robert E. Shepard; Jo Leggett of *Photo Metro* magazine; Robert Montgomery, Jr.; Margaret Walter and David Gilman;

Judi Randall; Fran Herman and Peter Lebovitz of the Agfa Corporation; Ernie, Alex, Jim, and Robert of Adolph Gasser, Inc.; Keith Altomare of the Bijou Theatre, Lincoln City, Oregon; Tom Luddy of the Telluride Film Festival; Sarah Feldman of WNET; Bernie Birnbaum of CBS News; Ramzi Malouki of IO Productions; Dave Cowan, Anne Fernandes, and Jay Christensen of Wrap Up Productions; and Karin Berger, director of library advancement at USC. Thanks also to the following consultants: Pauli Moss, J. Davis Mannino, and Frank Tingley.

I thank the good people who kept me on the path to Sin: Frann Gordon of AVIS in Burbank, Joel Blackman and Castro Valley AutoHaus, and Joe Delgadillo and Bob Ricardo of Outbound Travel. No author can work without hospitality. For that I thank: Robert M. Cline, Jack Vizzard, and Rex Bell, Jr. I especially thank Chummie Chico for her graciousness and advice. I will always be grateful to Andy Montealegre for letting me turn Glassell Park into Convention City. For helping me find Soft Focus, I thank Brian at Club Tempo and Manuel at Circus Disco.

I offer gratitude to friends of twenty years' duration: Rob McKay, for knowing movies; Robert L. Hillmann, for teaching movies; Ben Carbonetto, for endless generosity; Max, Ana, and Val Savic, for listening; and special thanks to Gary Morris, for guiding a very blue pencil. I thank Howard Mandelbaum for making this ambitious vision possible with his taste and with his friendship.

I thank Alan Nevins of the Renaissance Literary Talent Agency for working on my behalf. I thank my former editor, James Leggio, for suggesting the topic of this book. I thank Ray Hooper for a beautiful design job. I thank my editor, Elisa Urbanelli, for enthusiastically adopting this book.

Finally, I thank my parents for teaching me the meaning of the word "classic."

—M. A. V.

CREDITS